It's Not Necessarily So

A Senior Priest Separates
Faith from Fiction
and
Makes Sense of Belief

Father Richard G. Rento, STL

Rento, Richard G.

It's Not Necessarily So…
A Senior Priest Separates
Faith from Fiction and Makes Sense of Belief

ISBN- 1533091935

ISBN- 9781533091932

Cover Photo by Patricia Doles Photography

The entire profits from the sale of this book will go to charitable organizations stipulated by the author.

Caritas Communications
216 North Green Bay Road, Suite 208
Thiensville, Wisconsin 53092
414.531.0503
dgawlik70@gmail.com

DEDICATION

In memory of my brother, Dr. Robert D. Rento,
beloved pediatrician, loving husband and father.

EDITOR'S NOTE

Having a journalistic background, I approached Fr. Rento's book with the six basic questions stressed in every lecture on good reporting. "Who, What, When, Where, How and Why" could be applied to the present state in which the Catholic Church finds itself. They seemed fitting chapter heads for defining the situation, addressing it and, most importantly, offering solutions.

The word "crisis" in the Chinese logogram, as we have heard many times, translates to "danger plus opportunity." The Catholic Church is indeed in a crisis which includes a shortage of priests, diminishing vocations and empty pews. Disillusioned younger generations are exiting and discouraged older generations are bewildered. The clergy abuse scandals may have been the catalyst, but the crisis has its roots in greater depths of hierarchical and dogmatic dysfunction and failure.

Father Rento's book offers the opportunity Catholics need to weather the storm and glimpse the silver lining. His gentle admonitions and prescriptions provide an antidote to the despair many Catholics experience when they read the headlines or hear the dictates of the Magisterium. He may never receive a *nihil obstat* and *imprimatur* for his labors, as I am sure there will be some hierarchical objections. But his words ring clear and reflect the teachings of the person on whom the Catholic faith is based. It would be a danger not to read his book!

Mary Aktay

TABLE OF CONTENTS

ADDENDA:

FOREWORD

I looked forward to meeting Fr Richard Rento for the first time.

In 1998 my book, *Tomorrow's Catholic: Understanding God and Jesus in a New Millennium* was banned by Archbishop Pell in Melbourne, Australia. Early in 1999 the publisher of the USA edition mentioned that a priest in New Jersey was buying multiple copies and distributing them to friends. I was intrigued and wanted to meet this priest!

It is not easy for a priest to move publicly beyond the boundaries set for "correct thinking," which is perceived by many to be the ultimate measure of loyalty to the church. However, compassion, personal integrity, relationship with Jesus, and the unique demands of our times move many pastorally-minded priests in that direction. Their deep commitment to ministry challenges them to balance competing, and arguably, equally important realities: their love for and allegiance to the church to which they have dedicated their lives; their desire to make faith relevant in rapidly changing times when everything is open to question; their own questioning of what they had been taught was beyond questioning; being truly present to people who have a love of Jesus but are disillusioned with institutional aspects of their religion; and genuine respect for the many parishioners unquestioningly faithful to the church's teaching and tradition.

Dick Rento is such a pastorally-minded priest and *It's Not Necessarily So* is the distillation of his 60 years of teaching and preaching experience. He is a reluctant author and had never considered writing a book. He had to be urged, cajoled and finally prevailed upon to share his wisdom and experience with a wider audience.

Readers will be impressed by the refined and skillful way he shines light on doctrine and scripture. As a consummate story-teller, he effortlessly embeds important ideas into ordinary, everyday situations and human interactions. There is no pretense here, but rather the authenticity of someone rubbing shoulders everyday with people interested in exploring their faith.

Make no mistake, though. In his desire to make faith real, Fr Rento is walking a tightrope. Those who prefer to separate faith from life may likely object and criticize his approach. However, those who long to integrate their faith with life will appreciate the balanced treatment in these pages.

It's Not Necessarily So highlights Fr Rento's respect, his honesty, his openness, his questioning, his insights, and his wonderful way with words! The writing is simple and clear; doctrine is translated into comprehensible terms, questions are dealt with respectfully, scholarship is acknowledged, and clarity is brought to faith issues that perplex many people. Readers will appreciate how this man of deeply committed faith suggests what is no longer believable, what can replace what is not believable anymore, and ways to adjust thinking about some puzzling aspects of faith. Anyone who has been led in any way to inquire, to search, to learn anew, to articulate faith based on Jesus and what he was ready to die for will treasure these pages. These pages will inspire, bring hope, and above all, renew faith in the person of Jesus.

Michael Morwood, Perth. Australia.

PREFACE

Stop, please, before you read a word of this book, and allow me to tell you that I am not a professional theologian, despite the modest degree I received at the Catholic University of America in 1958, the Licentiate in Sacred Theology.

I am an ordinary, diocesan priest of the Diocese of Paterson, New Jersey – "diocesan" meaning that I don't belong to a religious community of priests such as the Franciscans or Jesuits or Dominicans or any other. I practice my ministry in association with the bishop of my home diocese and the bishop of the diocese in which I reside.

I get a salary (now a pension in my official retirement). I live in my own home, where I provide for myself in every way. I am close to my family, especially my siblings and their children, my cousins and theirs. I am blessed with more friends than I find it possible to keep up with.

My ministries have included 5 years of full-time hospital chaplaincy, 20 years as pastor of a large church, 20 years as diocesan director of religious education and the continuing education of priests, 48 years of radio broadcasting (WPAT), 18 years of chaplaincy at a senior citizens retirement community, and dozens of other works responding to the needs of the people I have served. (Need I mention that the foregoing did not all run consecutively?) Nothing dull or boring about my life thus far!

At my present advanced age, enjoying good health and abundant energy, I am eager to express to all who would want to hear them my innermost thoughts concerning our beloved Roman Catholic Church – thus the subtitle of this book referring to the separation of faith from fiction.

But again, I do not speak or write with the earned authority of a trained theologian. I speak and write as one who has spent his life and done his work in the trenches, desiring now to be a voice for those with whom I've been sharing that space and time as a brother.

For assistance in the production of this book, in addition to that from my incomparable editor, Mary Aktay, I thank Jane Lambert and Sheila Lomdardi, Michael and Maria Morwood, Thomas and Mary Heyman, as well as my brother and sister-in-law, David and Roberta, and their daughters, Peggy Anderson and Jacqueline Rento. Their contributions and observations made big and important differences for the better in the book's evolution.

I hope you find yourself very often in these pages.

Father Richard G. Rento

CHAPTER ONE

Who Do You Say I Am?

Ultimately...God will no longer be understood as a supernatural being, who invades the world miraculously from somewhere outside it. God will rather be perceived as the Source of Life calling us to live fully, the Source of Love freeing us to love wastefully and as the Ground of Being empowering us to be all that each of us can be. That is the God presence that I find in Jesus and that is why he calls me to step beyond even the boundaries of religion. Increasingly, God is for me a verb to be lived and not a noun to be defined.

~ Bishop John Shelby Spong 5.22.2014[1]

OUR CONCEPT OF GOD

Among the usual trivia that comes to my desk by way of email, I recall an elaborately adorned message telling me that God is watching me always and that, if I really cared about others, I should pass on this cautionary bulletin to as many people as I could reach. As part of the stunning artistry that accompanied the text, there was an image of God the Father, old and bearded and peering down at the earth from above the billowy clouds. It reminded me of one of the mass-produced pictures that hung in a bedroom in my boyhood home and how I used to wonder how Jesus was able to stand on that flimsy cloud and not fall through when I couldn't stand even on muddy water!

These images, verbal or pictorial, are present everywhere and are very powerful, for they fix in our minds concepts of a God who looks essentially like us but who, like Superman, possesses power over all the forces of nature. Loving and kind, no doubt, but also stern in judgment and as certain to punish as to reward.

It appears to be certain that fear of a God thus portrayed has made generation after generation of conscientious persons obedient to the "law of God" and has kept them from many a serious moral difficulty; but we can be just as sure that such imaginary notions, ultimately pagan in origin, have doomed many of them at the same time to live in a state of fear, frustration and depression as they judged their own spiritual condition to be virtually hopeless and beyond redemption.

My own dear mother was one of those persons who lived in fear of ultimate punishment by God. This affliction, which we, her sons and daughter, were never able to take from her, was produced, we believe, by early childhood massive doses of teachings about a God who has little tolerance for human weakness and who "gets even" in the end. Ideas of a God who is watching, and all that they imply, are very much alive today, causing untold misery for decent human beings.

In the course of the liturgical year, we hear in the appointed Scripture readings more than mere overtones of that harshness. Like a *New Yorker* magazine cartoon, we imagine a long-haired, unshaven, barefoot prophet wearing a sandwich board reading, "Repent! The end is near!" And that is precisely what even certain words attributed to Jesus in the Gospel seem to be saying. What is the meaning, for example, of his emphatic references to a snuffed-out sun and moon, stars cascading from the skies, nature gone out of control, and a majestic, celestial, awe-inspiring happening visible to all who will look up? What are we to make of this? We have a sense that it can't mean what the words signify at their face value, but neither can we write it off as flights of poetic fancy inconsequential in the final analysis.

A picture hangs in my present home, given to me by one of my brothers years ago, a souvenir from a trip he and his wife had recently made to the north of Italy. It is a very small pencil sketch of the head of St. Paul, measuring three inches by two inches. However, the beautifully ornate, hand-carved frame is more than a foot long and proportionately wide. I have calculated that the frame has 35 times the surface of the picture. The function of the frame is to call attention to the picture; the frame attempts to keep away everything in the room that surrounds the picture and threatens to distract the viewer. The frame points to the picture the way the wrappings and the ribbon and the bow point to the item within a Christmas gift package.

3

That is what we are experiencing as we encounter the dramatic, histrionic, ornate descriptions that frame the Scripture message in question. They are not in themselves the message any more than the frame is the picture or the wrappings are the gift. They are attention-getters; they are buffers between the message and all that can compete with it; they honor the message the way a beautiful frame honors a worthy picture.

So again, what is the message? As I understand and interpret it in its colorful presentation, it is that God is not only near, but here! We live in God always and everywhere, and God lives in us. The Christmas that Advent prepares us for each year marks the birth of that one among all human beings who was most aware of, most sensitive to, the divine presence everywhere – so much so, that he was able to say that to know him is to know God: a statement that every human being ought to be able to make about him or herself.

> *God is not watching from above. God is experiencing, with understanding and compassion and from within, our every thought, word, and action.*

God is not watching from above. God is experiencing, with understanding and compassion and from within, our every thought, word, and action. And the task of our lives is to live in such a way that to know and love each other is to know and to love God.

I was pleased to read in the *New York Times* a while back that an official spokesperson of the Archdiocese of New York did not attack the sponsors of a project that was destined to be seen by thousands of persons in a dozen New York subway stations promoting atheism. Instead, the spokesman wisely and fairly made reference to the First Amendment, which honors our right to express publicly our religious beliefs, and added his hope that religious groups will also be respected when they advertise their beliefs. Good response, I thought.

4

The subway posters read, "A million New Yorkers are good without God. Are you?" Another such campaign was conducted in England, you may remember having read, via signs on the sides of buses. Its slogan proclaimed, "There's probably no God. Now stop worrying and enjoy your life."

Pretty mild words, I would say. But they certainly make a highly controversial and inflammatory point that believers in God would instantly grasp and that many of whom would consider offensive. It's obvious that these messages are intended to get people to stop believing in God.

Will I shock you by saying that I applaud them? Not for their attempt to make atheists out of believers, but for their making us think. They make me think about my present image of God and all the images of God that have been given to me over the years of my long life, especially in those early, formative days when I was not capable of discerning what could be true and what could not possibly be true. What I was told, I imbibed lock, stock and barrel and accepted as truth; it has taken a lifetime to purge my mind and heart and soul of the notions I now recognize as false.

So, in response to the appeal that asks me if I am good without God, I would say yes — and then quickly explain that the God I am *without* is the God of threat and punishment, the God who thinks and broods and judges and speaks and acts and maybe even looks like me, the God who takes sides and causes victories and defeats, the God who responds to appeasement and sacrificial offerings.

Instead, the God I have come to know is the God that Jesus knew, whose love is unconditional.

A nun friend of mine told me that she had met a Franciscan priest who, in a retreat he was giving to nuns, asked them, "Why did God make us?" Predictably, they answered with the catechism, "God made us to know Him, love Him, and serve Him in this world and to be happy with Him forever in the next." (Notice all those "Hims"!) The good priest responded, "Wrong! God made us to be happy – period!" She went on to say that she has ever since cherished his simple words, because they encourage her to do those things that bring peace and happiness into her life so that they can overflow into the lives of others.

Good theology, good psychology, I'd say.

WHO DO WE SAY JESUS IS?

"You can't see the forest for the trees."

Too close up, too immersed in something, we develop a distorted perspective. We see details near at hand but not the totality.

I think of that in a window seat on an airplane: rivers, highways, clustered cities, organized mountain ranges, viewed as if through a bird's eye. If I were down below, I'd see none of that massive architectural beauty; I'd see only the trunks and hanging branches of the few trees that surround me.

So it is with the Gospels and with Jesus' life, death and resurrection, and how we fit into it all. We deal with a passage, a law, a fact, a ritual, an event, etc., one at a time. Just as it is easy to mistakenly identify the whole forest with the visible clump of trees in front of us, so is it easy to view the meaning of the whole Jesus-event only in terms of what is immediately before us.

Such myopic vision is what enabled us to believe that we could go to eternal punishment for missing Mass on a single Sunday or eating meat on a day of abstinence, or (worst of all!) committing a *sexual* sin, as if the infinite God and the compassionate Jesus could be reduced to such human legalism. Embarrassing, to say the least.

What if a spiritual helicopter of sorts were to pluck us from where we are right now, away from the particularities, the specifics, of our Catholic faith life and practice, and allow us to look down at it all from a distant new perspective? From that vantage point, what would we discover Jesus and the church to be? I feel strongly that they would be shown to be a lot simpler than we have assumed or have been conditioned to believe they are.

For one thing, we might be surprised to find that, despite his cultural references to heaven and hell, Jesus taught that God is *in* and *among* us, that God does not watch or manage from afar, keeping records and meting out both punishment and reward, partly in this world and completely in the next. No, Jesus tried to tell us – and so many still have not gotten the message – that God lives *within* us, experiencing life with us always, uninterruptedly, non-judgmentally, supportively, lovingly, compassionately.

Actually, we could stop there, for surely that is enough for us to know. How simple, how beautiful, how encouraging! What an incomparable help to a truly human life! Yet, there will continue to be those who spend their lives asking God to become interested in them, to help them, to be with them in their need. Why — when God is already there?

A cousin of mine phoned me two days before he was to undergo surgery for cancer. "Dick," he said, "please pray that God will be with me and the surgical team on Thursday." I answered, not having to think much at all about how to respond, "Bob, I'll do no such thing. The Spirit of God is in us even as we speak. The Spirit will be with you and the surgical team on the day of your operation. Bob, get the point: you can't shake God! Try to remain aware of that divine presence." He told me later that he did understand and that he achieved a deep and enduring peace.

But there's more to the bird's-eye view of Jesus in our lives, also simple and beautiful. It's this: that our relationship with God is one and the same as our relationship with all of creation, in particular with our fellow human beings. That's an important mouthful. It means that the way I treat any person in my life is precisely the way I am treating God. I have a dear friend, a nun, who for years has been saying to me, "God in one person meets God in another." "Namaste" is the word used by our Hindu brothers and sisters to express this universal truth. The way I treat any person in my life is precisely the way I am treating God.

> *The way I treat any person in my life is precisely the way I am treating God.*

My relationship or my conduct with you is in no way distinct from my relationship or conduct with God; the truth is that they are one and the same thing. That is why Jesus said that what we do for each other we do for him.

For many years I've had uncomfortable feelings with regard to our traditional celebration of Jesus' birth. We know full well that he was passionate about the elimination of oppression against the poor and the disadvantaged. His heart ached at the sight of persons who were the victims of their fellow human beings' abuse of power. He identified with them above all and occasioned his own painful death by standing with them and speaking out courageously on their behalf. Yet, at Christmas, very little, if anything, is said about that Jesus. We seem to prefer suggestions of magic and awesome miracles and singing angels and the white purity of improbable snow.

A wise Christian minister, the Reverend Doctor Giles Fraser, in the British publication, *The Guardian*, has pointed out that our religion seems to be composed mainly of the very beginning of Jesus' life, when, in Dr. Fraser's terms, he was a gurgling baby, and the end of his life, when he was a screaming victim. The baby and the cross. And so, he goes on to say, we are left with "a gagged and glorified savior who has nothing to say about how we spend our money or whether or not we go to war."[2]

How does anyone say or think such things without sounding like a Scrooge? Maybe it's not possible to avoid the indictment. When we celebrate Jesus' birth, it must be with the full consciousness that this is only the start of a most challenging life – challenging for him and for us. He knew nothing of how his life would unfold in the 30 years beyond the manger, but there was something in his heritage and in his family upbringing that prepared him to sense the presence of the Divine Spirit and to follow its path of wisdom and love wherever it would take him.

There's an ancient bit of pious folklore that sees the manger in which Jesus was placed after his birth as related to the cross on which he would ultimately be killed. Both were made of rough-hewn wood; both were given him by others without his willing or requesting them. Both crib and cross turned out to be signs of his destiny: the crib proclaimed him as human like the rest of us, though poorer than most; the cross showed the depths of his love, that he would accept it rather than abandon us and the one he called Father.

But between the two – the birth and the death – is the most real and most important story, namely his teachings and his example. We are his true friends only to the extent that we absorb his mind and take on his ways and try to implement them in our lives as best we can. If that is not our actual priority as Christians, then we have reduced ourselves to shallowness and hypocrisy as we celebrate his birthday and his death while bearing little resemblance to him whom we have pledged to follow and imitate.

Don't misunderstand me, please. I am not even remotely suggesting that we tone down our Christmas festivities and customs. By all means, let there be carols and cards and trees and gifts galore! We need them, and they are appropriate. But we've got to realize at the same time that the celebration becomes genuine only to the extent that we more and more commit ourselves to caring about what he said and understanding his prescription for a truly good and human life, and trying our best to be what he urges us to be.

Via a forwarded email a few years ago, a colorful presentation of Christmas came to my desk; I have savored it ever since. With gratitude to the anonymous author,[3] I share that piece with you here:

> *You honor me on this sacred night when you bathe the world in forgiving light in remembrance of one whose holy birth has instilled the prayers for peace on earth.*
>
> *So be pure in heart in all you do and know that I am ever mindful, too, of what rewards your journey may bring when a merciful hand relieves suffering.*
>
> *For I am with you in the air that you breathe, in the spring's first rain, in the autumn leaves, in the sunrise and the sunset and evening's demise; in the loss of a loved one or a newborn's sighs.*
>
> *Know too that my love endures without end as the binding warmth of a constant friend, for I am the keeper of inextinguishable stars and indisputable master of all that you are.*
>
> *So spread your love and Christmas pleasures so that all might share in this evening's treasures, and know that my guidance and love will be with you tonight as my emissary.*

There were many miracle stories created some 2000 years ago about Jesus of Nazareth. How much in them we are to understand or interpret literally is hard for us to determine. What we can be sure of is that they are part of the collection of ancient writings that depicted Jesus as invariably compassionate, a healer whose capacity to empathize with the afflicted was virtually unlimited and whose labors to reach and comfort them were totally generous and unselfish. The possibility of an instant, apparently magical cure on behalf of a blind man in one of those stories, for example, must not distract us from the essential truth it contains: Jesus cared deeply, passionately, for those who suffered in any way and did whatever he could to relieve or banish their pain. He cared not what others thought or said or did about what he was doing.

If, as we are seeing daily in corrupted forms of some world religions, Jesus thought that suffering in this world is a blessing because it merits a glorious life after death, then why didn't he refuse to relieve the afflicted and instead tell them to endure the misery and to treasure it as their ticket to eternal happiness?

No, Jesus placed great value on *this* life, this one earthly existence we are given, and he urged us by word and example to serve one another, making this one earthly journey as good as it can be for all.

That's what the religion named after him, Christianity, is essentially about. Could he have said that any more plainly? "My commandment to you is this: that you love one another as I have loved you."

I once heard a misguided priest say that we are permitted to be only as charitable as the law allows. My earliest ideas about God, now abandoned, would have endorsed that false teaching. But I have learned by watching and listening to Jesus that actually the reverse is true: we must permit ourselves to be ruled only as much as charity will allow.

GOD IN THE WORLD

A beloved seminary priest-professor years ago gave us students a definition that I've never forgotten, so encouraging did I find it to be. He said that the true intellectual is not necessarily a person who knows a lot about many things or about one thing; not necessarily a person who is steeped in scholarly pursuit or esoteric reading; but rather one who is open to all that is true, whether it be old and familiar or new and hitherto unknown. He defined the genuine intellectual as marked by that unprejudiced receptivity, unhindered by the limitations that former knowledge or experience might attempt to impose. The genuine intellectual, he insisted, always uses the available evidence to judge what is right and true and is not held back from assent by any former perception.

In a brilliant conversation on National Public Radio just a few months after the destruction of the World Trade Center and the death of thousands of its occupants, a British scholar expressed his contempt for all three Abrahamic religions (Judaism, Islam, and Christianity) because, he said, they demand unquestioning belief based on what each claims to be divine revelation, not on objective evidence. And, since one religion's claimed divine revelation often conflicts with another's, they are drawn into constant fighting over who is right. It seems hard to deny that he made a good point worthy of consideration.

We believers firmly hold that divine revelation is real – that the unseen God makes God's presence in our world known to us. The way can be as simple as the glorious sunset that causes the beholder to thank and praise its creator, or it can be as complex as some of the Scriptures

13

from which we derive lessons for living – and a virtually infinite range in between. No matter, in today's world people of good will are trying to achieve a mutual understanding with religions other than their own. In part, that's what the ecumenical movement is about: the unprecedented effort to find areas of agreement among us rather than to dwell on the differences and conflicts that have so long divided us.

The prophet Isaiah has God advising the people not to dwell on the past because if they do they'll miss what's happening now: God doing something brand new. Isaiah envisions life springing forth in the most desolate of places, in the most barren lands, on the driest deserts – a good road here, a lush spring or a flowing river there. Sins are forgiven and forgotten – amnesty for all! As Isaiah sees it, those who had burdened God with their crimes are unburdened of their guilt and shame and told to walk on in peace and new hope with carefree hearts.

St. Paul, in his second letter to the Corinthians (an especially difficult writing to unpack, I think), seems to be referring to his having been accused of double-talk by some of his hearers: mixed messages in his preaching, talking out of both sides of his mouth. Paul insists that, regardless of what they thought they heard him say, the message was simply *Jesus Christ* and that Jesus is God's eternal yes – in other words, Jesus is the perfect fulfillment of all the promises ever uttered by God's authentic prophets.

We live in frightening times, but only too similar to what the world has experienced over and over again in times past, distant and recent. But once again we have the chance to say yes to what is new and unprecedented – we can choose negotiation over military aggression; we can opt to forgive rather than retaliate; we can feed instead of kill;

14

heal and not further wound. We Americans can remain the strongest nation in the world and be at the same time gentle and compassionate. We can lead the way to peace instead of to war.

God still "speaks" to the nations of the world. Will we or will we not hear that word and respond with a courageous, confident "Yes!"?

GOD IN CREATION

Violent hurricanes associated with climate change and their lingering, stubborn, wanton attacks perpetuate the age-old controversy over what part the Creator of the universe plays in them.

Fundamentalist Christians, both Catholic and non-Catholic, are quick to interpret the events as signs of God's anger, which also portend even greater calamities yet to come, perhaps the destruction of the world, as they believe is foretold in the Bible. I thought it was amusing that in all of New Orleans the area that was the most spared from the ravages of hurricane Katrina was the very symbol of the city's immorality – Bourbon Street! My saying that gives you a clue as to my understanding of God's role in these horrific acts of nature: God's role is zero, nothing, non-existent. God has no role in the acts of nature.

It is a longstanding figment of human imagination that there is a God who, from some distant perch, manages and directs the forces of the universe. Such a view must have been conceived in the developing brains of primitive humans who reasoned that earthquakes, floods, thunder, lightning and all-consuming fires were the intentional products of some supernatural being who was expressing his disapproval of human conduct or simply flexing his muscles in order to intimidate earth-dwellers and retain control. It is quite natural that our earliest ancestors should have thought that way, and undoubtedly such ideas are still very much implanted in our genes. My reading is that the faith of most religious people today tends in that direction.

The reaction of our first human ancestors to these destructive forces was appeasement: offer the gods gifts, altar sacrifices (including human), and maybe they will be satisfied and leave us alone. One has to wonder how much of that mentality enters into our understand the purported meaning of Jesus' death, namely that it was a sacrifice offered to ransom us sinful people from the punishment that an offended God was ready to inflict, One also has to wonder why we are not more openly reexamining that old theology in search of a truer interpretation, which well might be that Jesus' death was not payment for anyone's sins but rather the expression of his love for us, his fellow human beings, and the God he called Father.

In other words, he knew that if he stopped his preaching and teaching about a loving and merciful God, and if he stopped confronting the powers of oppression and violence, as he was constantly doing, he could have lived serenely into a comfortable old age and died a natural death. But he chose instead to continue the risky business of truth-telling, aware that it would lead to an inevitable and cruel execution. The cross, to me, is the measure of how much he has loved us and the God from whom we all ultimately come.

If hurricanes are instruments of divinely inflicted punishment, we are left with a capricious God who toys with the universe like a cat playing with a doomed mouse. And where would we draw the line of distinction: when a plane falls out of the sky, for example, and many are killed and a few survive, are we to understand that God destroyed the many and spared the few? Nonsense! The universe is filled with the random forces of nature in addition to the intended and the accidental forces of human beings both good and evil. When these forces collide, harm is likely to occur – destruction of all kinds, injury and death. God does not orchestrate the process; it simply happens. But God is present in it all, experiencing it with us, and from that presence of the Creative Spirit we draw the strength to wait in patience and hope and to do what must be done.

We live in a universe full of random forces that are governed, not by reason or will, but by the laws of physics and chemistry and astronomy. These are irrational forces that are incapable of concern for the wellbeing of life — any life, including human. They collide, they attack, they intersect, they conflict, or they blend with awesome power that can destroy life. If we happen to be in or near the action of such forces, we get hurt or we are killed. There is no plan at work, no design, no control by a "supreme being." It all just happens by chance, because that's the way nature is.

Since Hurricane Sandy I have almost never turned on an electric light or adjusted a thermostat or opened a faucet without being more conscious than ever before of how blessed so many of us are to have not only all of life's necessities but also so many of its luxuries.

This is not to suggest that a God-in-Charge has chosen us to be the fortunate ones or has favored us because we are virtuous and deserving; it is simply to say that we are just plain lucky. The circumstances of our lives, however they fell together, beginning with where and to whom we were born, just happened to be such that we — certainly not all, but so many of us — have lived in freedom and plenty.

The only acceptable, reasonable, truly human response to our good fortune is gratitude to the Creative Spirit from whom all good things ultimately come, and the willingness, the eagerness to share our bounty with those who are deprived, for whatever reason, of what is necessary for a safe and happy human life.

But what shall we do with the assurance of Jesus that if we join our voices on earth to pray for something, it shall be granted us by the God he called Father? Whenever nature's destructive forces threaten, can you imagine how many people pray fervently for divine intercession? In the cases of Hurricanes Katrina and Sandy, in how many churches of all denominations were there prayers of petition for this favor of deliverance? And what happened? Only disaster. Storms set their course mindlessly, lethally, and there is no one, including an imaginary God above the clouds, who would or could stop them.

What *is* granted to us in prayer is not miracles of power over nature – subduing of storms, curing of disease, restoration of sight, awakening of the dead, etc. No, what is affirmed is the unfailing gift of the Spirit of God, a divine presence within and among us, the power of which cannot be overcome by any calamity. It is that Spirit that enables us to endure whatever comes and to see a bright future ahead in this world or in the next.

If we listen to some of the misguided TV preachers, we will be tempted to accept their definition of faith, which I believe is wrong and totally misleading. They would have us be convinced that faith is belief in God so strong that we can ultimately control everything that threatens us: we can overcome that cancer, get rid of that addiction, prevent the death of our loved one, exchange poverty for wealth, etc. Don't be deceived; that's not what true faith is. Faith is a belief in God, for us Christians through Jesus, that is so firm and so trusting that even when terrible things happen that are beyond our control we are not dehumanized, we are not denied our human destiny. We still perceive the light that calls us forward.

That's the great gift of Jesus to all who will accept it! The Spirit doesn't change life or make everything in it a source of happiness. Rather, the Spirit enables us to see beyond the present sorrow or pain or distur-

19

bance and to anticipate the peace and the joy that await us beyond.

Are we expressing that faith when we say so often, "The Lord be with you"?

GOD IN SCRIPTURE

We do not have to suspend our intellectual faculties to read the Bible. It is not filled with supernatural tales that defy human rationality. The Bible is a Jewish book composed in the Jewish story-telling style that invites us to step into its meaning. Matthew's original audience would have understood that. We will too when we begin to read this book with Jewish eyes.

~Bishop John Shelby Spong 9.18.2014[4]

I learned a while back that it's not true that in the Hebrew Bible – the Old Testament, as we call it – we find only a God of strict justice and that in the Christian Bible – the New Testament – we are finally introduced to the God of love. That's what we've said for too long. My uncritical acceptance of that false belief was severely challenged by something a rabbi wrote several years ago, demonstrating conclusively that the Old Testament contains many descriptions of God as compassionate and merciful and whose love is like the deep, romantic affection between a man and a woman or like the love a mother has for her child.

But what the scriptures show also is that the ancient Jews and our Christian ancestors had something in common with regard to their ideas about God and how those ideas influenced the way they thought and acted. We show signs of the same today: we live, many of us, with the nagging suspicion that all is not right between us and God and that something we have done is causing God to be angry and upset with us. It would seem that most of us imagine God to be a Super Human Being with pretty much the range of emotions that we earthlings exhibit. When some tragedy befalls us, we are inclined to interpret it as God's judgment and we react by admitting that we had it coming to us all along.

Catholics around my age remember how we children were taught to "go to confession" every week. One principal reason given was that we certainly wouldn't want to be caught off guard by dying unexpectedly, possibly being killed by a truck (somehow my childhood imagination has preserved the image of a *red* truck – what color was yours?) even on our way to church, with unabsolved sins still darkening our little souls. Given that kind of horrific teaching, no matter how innocent and well-intended it was, what could have been our resultant notion of God? Anticipating such a situation — sudden death — we were not being conditioned to think of God as compassionate and forgiving and kind. No, we were trained to think of God as mindful of our unconfessed sins and as threatening to condemn us unless they were by whatever means — an act of "perfect contrition" would do in a pinch — wiped away by direct or mediated divine absolution.

Such habits have endured for most of us right to this very day. There isn't a single time that I am sitting in the reconciliation room, the confessional, hearing grownups recite their sins that I am not reminded of how many of us there are who live with the idea that God is first of all the Supreme Judge who demands that everything in our lives be in good order. With that in mind then, we see the church as the divinely appointed agent that can make things right between us and God. And so we have rituals and prayers and sacramental things to do the cleaning and the purifying and the spiffing up! We make sacrifices, just as our ancestors in the faith did, to appease a displeased God.

Of course it is proper that we be humble about our imperfect humanness. And it doesn't hurt that we include that admission in our public and private prayers; but to live every day with the image of a God who demands perfection from us, and who will not welcome us into complete union unless we have achieved it, is a brand of religious poppycock that has its roots in paganism, not in the Gospel, the Good News, of Jesus.

In the Book of the Prophet Isaiah the notion of a vengeful God is challenged, inspiring Isaiah to exclaim that "something new" is being done. When that good news from Isaiah is proclaimed at Sunday Mass, the responsorial psalm articulates what it is: "Lord, heal my soul, for I have sinned against you." It doesn't have us say, "Punish me, O God, for I deserve your wrath." No, the supposedly offended one, God, is regarded not as punisher, but as healer. For too many of us Christians today that remains undiscovered good news.

> *God's presence with us here on earth is the same as God's love for us, which is the same as God's forgiveness of our sinfulness.*

Perhaps it will be helpful to them to dwell on this simple truth: God's presence with us here on earth is the same as God's love for us, which is the same as God's forgiveness of our sinfulness. We live in an ambience, an atmosphere, of God's compassion, and all we have to do is want it, accept it — breathe it in, as it were — and pass it on generously.

23

GOD IN OUR LIVES

Our Jewish brothers and sisters have an interesting concept of the human search for truth: it appears to begin with the underlying awareness that life and all of reality are complex and don't readily yield their secrets. The rabbi, for example, who gives his students a lengthy, closely-reasoned response to a difficult theological question and then adds, "However, on the other hand..." offers them another possible interpretation, even diametrically opposed to his first one. He is actually reassuring them by showing that he has examined the issue thoroughly and sees that there are various possibilities regarding the truth being sought.

It's quite different, in general, for us who have been raised in an essentially Greek way of thinking; we look for the one, absolute truth. We Catholics are still feeling the painful effects of the absolutism that produced the papal encyclical on birth control (*Humanae Vitae*) in the late 1960s, which proclaimed that there is only one answer to the question of artificial contraception, an unqualified NO. This was decided and promulgated despite the opposite findings and recommendation of the distinguished committee that Pope Paul VI appointed to look into the matter. Catholics were required "under pain of mortal sin" to observe this newly articulated teaching, no matter what the growing majority of Catholics were saying and doing at the time in regard to birth control. It turned out that the ultimate reason for restating the prohibition against contraception was that the church simply could not allow itself to be seen as having reversed so important a teaching that it had promulgated for so long a time. But that's how the perception of truth has been understood for centuries by the Catholic Church: absolute truth attainable through human intelligence and divine assistance.

Here's another debatable question: what does it mean to be "called by God"? We often hear people say this— that they are responding to what they are convinced is a call from God to do or to say a certain thing. We Catholics place heavy emphasis on "vocation," a word that unfortunately gets narrowed down to signify a summons only to priesthood or religious life. (The mother of a priest whom I knew many years ago, when asked about her family, always replied that she has four children: three who are married and one "who has a vocation.") People confidently speak of their state in life or their profession or a particular service or mission that they have undertaken as having been chosen for them by God. It's very common and familiar: the conviction that one has been literally called by God to a way of life or to a project of some sort.

But just how literally are we to take such talk, and what does it reveal about how we think about God? If it need *not* mean that God is directly managing our lives, does it perhaps at least imply that God is offering us a plan that we are free to accept or reject? We do speak, after all, of doing the "will of God" or of discerning and following "God's plan." Are these just pious words, not to be taken at face value, or do they represent factual reality?

The universe of which you and I are a tiny but significant part is the handiwork of wisdom and love beyond our comprehension. We are living as we ought to be when we are trying to remain conscious of that divine presence and to open ourselves to its influence and direction. That wisdom and love are always accessible to and through human beings. We have the power and the "calling" to harmonize with the Creative Spirit that originates and sustains all being, all life. We are at our best when we are deliberately in sync with the Spirit in that way.

If we actually hear voices, as some claim they do, we can be quite sure it is our imagination trying to help us by making things more concrete, more understandable. The basic fact of those Scripture passages that tell of conversation with God is that persons of faith simply open themselves to the subtle, ineffable influence that comes from the invisible, ever-present God. In that sense, we are all meant to be contemplatives – not all of us residing in monasteries, but all of us turning an ear, as it were, to God in the course of our everyday lives, getting helpful signals in an endless variety of very ordinary happenings.

Morality and theology have radically changed over the centuries. The notion, for example, of a "tit-for-tat" God is foreign to most people's thinking today. I would hope that fewer and fewer people believe in a God who kills in retribution for the sins of those who hurt others, a God who doesn't stop even there but extends the punishment to the innocent children of a wrong-doer. But all throughout religious history, including Jewish and Christian, that has been a common characteristic: attributing to God, not only merely human standards of justice, but also human behavior at its worst.

It seems so obvious to me that the ancient prophets were sometimes angry at their people for being unfaithful to God and threatened them with divine punishment as a way of inducing more appropriate behavior. It's what we are inclined to do when we exercise authority over others: we bellow in loud tones and in hyperbole and when cajoling doesn't work, we threaten.

But take a look at the Book of Exodus, chapter 22, verses 24-27, and you might be surprised to discover that it calls immoral and sinful a practice that we regard as perfectly honorable: taking interest on a loan. The sacred author calls that extortion. Notice also how the passage softens as it ends: we are told that if we accept a pledge (I guess we'd call that a deposit today) from someone to whom we are lending something, that deposit has to be returned before sunset – whether or not the borrowed item has been returned. Why? Because the pledge, which in this instance happened to be an outer garment, was the borrower's only cloak, not only useful and comfortable during the day, but essential at night for protection against the cold and for assurance of a restful sleep. The ancient teaching was that, even though the loaned item had not yet been restored to its owner, the borrower's urgent need for it outranked the lender's claim to it as property that belonged to him. Imagine how much sociologists and missionaries, in particular, could make of that one part of the passage, applying it to the unpaid debts, enormous as they are, of third world countries.

So, once we resolve the no-longer-acceptable aspects of this ancient writing, what we have left is a document whose dominant and most enduring meaning is the very same as Jesus regularly emphasizes. It is simply concern for others, especially those who are most likely to be rejected, ignored or despised; those whose economic and social status make them the most vulnerable of all. While I cannot accept the idea of a God who kills those who do wrong, I certainly can imagine a God who is passionately concerned for those who cannot manage on their own and are in desperate need of the kindness and generosity of others. Jesus says that the primary commandment is to love God: that is, to live in harmony with the ever-present Creative Spirit. He implies that another commandment derives from it: to love others as we love ourselves. When you think of the time and attention and energy that we have given to the observance of church law in all of its varied intricacies, you realize how poorly we have understood and absorbed this cardinal teaching of Jesus: Love is the heart and the essence of all valid law.

> *Love is the heart and the essence of all valid law.*

I participated once in a memorial service for a beloved medical doctor who had died only days before. In a jam-packed auditorium, tribute after tribute was paid to this colorful, popular, very human man. While each speaker highlighted various aspects of his character, his personality, and his life, both personal and professional, there was one thing common to all those tributes, and that was his totally unprejudiced, unconditional love and respect for everyone. Those who knew him well said that in his mind there were not great and important persons on the one hand, and on the other the unimportant, the no-accounts. He saw every person he ever met as a child of God and an equal brother or sister. As beautiful and as moving as their words were, the man's very life outshone them all.

Surely you and I, each in our own unique way, are giving others reason to say something similar about us. It is those "shining" aspects of our life that we must constantly cultivate and multiply.

GOD IN INTERVENTION

An old friend of mine was visiting me one day after we'd not seen each other for a long, long time. We went to the beach, engaged in non-stop conversation about the church, its problems and its promises, about our own lives and about our mutual friends. A gust of wind suddenly came up and blew a neighbor's umbrella down, hurling it right toward us. Its sharply tapered pole missed us by inches, and my friend cried out, "Thanks be to God!"

I couldn't resist the urge to call her out on that, and I said, "Why are you thanking God? Do you really think that an accident was prevented by God's intervention?"

She didn't answer; maybe she couldn't. She just laughed.

Maybe you, dear reader, don't feel as strongly about this as I do, but I am, as the expression goes, fed up with this habit of ours that has us attribute everything that happens in our lives to the direct action of God. Three teenagers are killed in a car accident on prom night, one is unhurt, and you can be sure that the press will quote someone as saying that it was a miracle that the one survived. I say that's absurd, another Christian form of paganism. All sorts of terrible things occur in this world of random forces that often cause damage and death. There's nothing to be gained, but there's truth to be lost when we foolishly maintain that God makes terrible things happen or prevents them from happening. As the kids say, let's get real!

Our religious ancestors hardly had a choice in the matter; they were programmed by centuries of tradition to believe that indeed God does manage the universe, including their own personal and social lives. Good things happened, and they gave the credit to God, who was rewarding them. Bad things happened, and they assumed that this was punishment for their sins. God gave victory in war, release from sickness, avoidance of death, abundance to their farms, futures to their children, etc.

If, indeed, at one point in the long journey of the faithful, fleeing Jews an extraordinary happening rescued them from impending starvation, and if perhaps finding something edible like hoarfrost on the ground, it is perfectly understandable that they would have interpreted the event as miraculous and as a direct gift from God. A few millennia later, we still cherish the story under the title, The Manna in the Desert. (By the way, the word manna is thought to come from the ancient Hebrew word "Manhu," which means, "What is this?") This sugar-rich excretion from the cypress tree would provide energy for their undernourished bodies the way a candy bar peps us up in an afternoon slump. But what if the whole celebrated narrative of the "manna in the desert" is really symbolic and not to be taken literally?

In that case, we would see it as an expression of faith and trust in the providence of a loving God, even though our Jewish ancestors more and more interpreted perfectly natural, chance happenings as the direct actions of God on their behalf.

More than 2000 years later, the Christian Church teaches us to use such biased bits of history as symbols of God's unfailing care of us through simple, unfailing, loving presence.

And so we tie these symbols into our understanding of Eucharist. Eucharist is not literally "bread from heaven," no matter what the hymns proclaim. It is an action, replete with rich symbolism, all of which graphically reminds us that we are called to be Jesus in our world. If we accept that bread with our "Amen" and consume it in the presence of others, we are pledging to live and to act more faithfully according to his values, his teachings, his example. It is a small banquet that foreshadows the incomparable banquet of eternity in union with the Creator. It is a powerful source of life for the present, even as it whets our appetites and inspires our confidence in the unimaginably full life that awaits us beyond death.

The glucose that may have fallen quite naturally from the trees that early morning way back then was as nothing when compared with the gift that Jesus offered us the night before his death – a kind of anchor, a connector, between us and him. "Celebrate this meal, and I am with you more closely than you can possibly comprehend."

THE HOLY SPIRIT: GOD IN US!

D espite the fact that there are many among us who could not accept everything that Pope St. John Paul II himself believed and taught, I very much doubt that there is anyone who would dispute his profound reverence for God and his firm conviction that he was an instrument of divine power commissioned to work for the good of all people. We learned from his own words as revealed just before his funeral that he believed he should take no initiative in determining the course of his last days on earth. He said, simply and directly, that God would decide when the time for his life to end had arrived.

Certainly not all Christians understand God as taking such a direct role in our lives; I don't. Many of us believe, on the contrary, that we have sole responsibility for the progress of our lives, using the instruments of intelligence and wisdom and prudence with which we are equipped.

This difference notwithstanding, both sides of the issue believe that we can and are meant to deliver God's power and love to a world that is filled with so much suffering and fear. Maybe the difference between the two schools of thought has to do mostly with our conception of *how* God is a part of our lives. The former imagines God, I would suspect, as a larger-than-life, superhuman being, who watches from afar and intervenes as necessary in particular circumstances and especially in answer to prayer. The latter, on the other hand, perceives God as *experiencing* life with us, not merely looking on from some distant place, but sharing with us the Spirit of wisdom and love, which we are free to welcome or ignore, or even reject. This is the one God who is never absent from the human situation and whose unfailing love makes possible our living always in hope.

THE TRINITY

Had you lived in Jesus' day and asked him if he was the second person of the Trinity, he would not have had the foggiest idea of what you were talking about. The concept of the Trinity – three persons in one God – took shape some 400 years after Jesus' time.

But what are we to say then about the rather clear reference to Trinity that Jesus himself seems to be making in these words that are attributed to him, "…baptize in the name of the Father and of the Son and of the Holy Spirit"? Father Joseph Nolan, liturgical scholar from Boston College in Massachusetts, writes:

"…this is not a transcript of Jesus' words and acts, but a reflection of the early church, baptizing and teaching in his name."[5] What appears to have happened is that the early Christians were gradually coming to terms with the elements that would eventually develop into our familiar doctrine of the Trinity. What does it mean?

One way to look at it is this: God is not simply *one* in the sense of being alone and without relationship or conversation or sharing or love. Virtually all cultures have imagined the Creator to be powerful, distant, jealous, unpredictable, competitive, etc. Jesus, on the contrary, speaks of God as compassionate, loving, forgiving, gentle, and as best characterized by the term "Abba," which is commonly translated as "Daddy." The conclusion his followers came to was that the very nature and essence of God are loving relationship.

In those first four centuries of Christian theological development, the church began to teach that the love between the Father and the Son is so intense that it overflows into yet another person, a third person, the Holy Spirit, and continues to overflow into the creation of the vast universe of which we are a part. The reasoning was that this is the nature of all love, human and divine: it yearns to share, to give and receive, to create beyond itself. And thus came about the notion of the Trinity.

Consider this pregnant statement from a man who is both a priest and a scientist. His name is Father Denis Edwards, an Australian, who wrote in his book, *The God of Evolution: A Trinitarian Theology*:

> *The God of Trinitarian theology is a God of mutual and equal relations. When such a God creates a universe, it is not surprising that it turns out to be a radically relational and interdependent one. When life unfolds through the process of evolution, it emerges in patterns of interconnectedness and interdependence that 'fit' with the way God is.*[6]

Scientists are increasingly heard these days celebrating the fact that the entire universe is relational in nature at its core, each tiniest part and particle connected interdependently with all other parts, down to and beyond even microscopic bacteria.

> *We are the expression of God's overflowing, eternal, intense love.*

To be responsible creatures of our Trinitarian God, we must put the relationships in our lives above all else. "Trinity" is a fundamental statement about the Creator and about us. We are the expression of God's overflowing, eternal, intense love.

We mustn't allow Trinity to be a ho-hum, theological proposition or to be trivialized with demonstrations involving three-leaf clovers or three candle flames blended into one. It must be allowed, instead, to challenge and direct us to be what we are created to be: persons who relate in a life-giving, mutually supportive way to the planet, to the entire universe, to all other persons without discrimination of any kind, and to our very own selves, because we are among the fantastic results of God's outpouring love.

OUR RELATIONSHIP WITH GOD

H*ail, Holy Queen, Mother of Mercy, our life, our sweetness, and our hope! To thee do we cry, poor banished children of Eve; to thee do we send up our sighs, mourning and weeping in this valley of tears... (from the ancient prayer/hymn, Salve Regina)*

At precisely what point in my development as a Catholic I began to bristle at those words "banished children of Eve" I do not know; however, I do know that I will not say them today. To anyone who holds that God's love is constant, infinite, unconditional, the very notion of banishment from that love is inconceivable. There never have been "exiled children of Eve;" and no one, including the mother of Jesus, has ever had to gain access to God for us. Nor are we priests and religious charged with the same service to humanity – to be bridges between the unwashed masses and the unapproachable deity.

I'm hoping that you, my respected reader, and I are united in wanting these perceptions to be put to eternal rest, because they are not factual. It is not true that God is inaccessible to anyone, or that God resides in some distant place that requires intermediaries for those who desire communion with God. Mary is no such link, and neither is Jesus. Jesus urged us always to pay attention to the presence of God in our midst and within us. The Kingdom of God, he said, is *in* us. As theologian/author Michael Morwood puts it, Jesus did not bring God to the people; rather, he named the reality of God's universal presence.[7] To hone our own sensitivity to that divine presence, to affirm it and to communicate it to others, is our task in the world.

News articles have noted what little, if any, immediate satisfaction there can be for missionaries who spend their lives serving others in the hope that they will be attracted to the Christian life. One Anglican minister was quoted as saying that after many years of apostolic labor among Muslims in their native lands, he was hardly "plowing the soil." Another minister of the early 1900s admitted that in 50 years of missionary work in the Arabian Peninsula he could count only five converts.

It's so natural for us human beings to want to share with others what we value ourselves. We see a good movie and we recommend it to family and friends – "You've gotta see this film!" We find an excellent restaurant and urge them to try it. We read a page-turner of a book and buy copies for others. This is part of our inter-relatedness, our need to be united with each other, our sharing of life in a variety of ways, our enjoying life vicariously through each other's experience.

When it comes to religion, we can be downright passionate about getting others to join us. Some men and women, often whole families, dedicate their lives to preaching the Good News of Jesus to people who do not know him, or even know *of* him. They do this, of course, in response to Jesus' mandate that we, his followers, go to all nations, preaching and baptizing, and they are inflamed with zeal as they proclaim the Gospel and its promises. We can only praise and honor them for their zeal and their charity.

St. Francis of Assisi sent his band of brothers on their mission trails with the admonition, "Preach the Gospel – and use words if you have to." He was implying, obviously, that their charitable works would be the heart of their missionary efforts, far more significant and productive than anything they might say.

It's too bad that the history of Christian missionary activity, mostly wonderful and heroic, is also marred by some shameful blemishes. Over the centuries they have included gross examples of duress, violation of human rights, disregard and disrespect for other religions, threats of violence and death for those who reject the preached message, and so forth. We can be absolutely sure that Jesus would never endorse such methods or such attitudes.

To begin with, the missionary must embark upon the task of evangelizing with the expectation of finding evidence, often abundant and beautiful, of the presence of God in the people to whom the Gospel of Jesus is about to be preached. The missionary deceives himself/herself by thinking that he/she is bringing God to a place where God has never been, to a people who have never had experience of the presence of God. Not true. On the contrary, missionary work must honor that venerable divine presence and gently lead the people to an awareness of Jesus in their midst, thus liberating them, if need be, from the superstitions that have held them captive and taken from them the freedom of the children of God.

Missionary work in his name must be further characterized by two chief marks:

* Pure, unconditional charity: learning people's needs and responding to them unselfishly in the most effective ways possible – and this for *their* sake, not for any ulterior motive, even conversion to the Way of Jesus; and

* Respect for the dignity of people to whom the Good News is presented as an option that they are left free to accept or reject according to their consciences. No coercion, no pressure, no intimidation or cautions about eternal damnation or any other such thing.

38

*Our first task in approaching another people, another cul-
ture, another religion is to take off our shoes, for the place
we are approaching is holy. Else we may find ourselves
treading on men's dreams. More serious still, we may forget that God was here before our arrival. We have, then, to
ask what is the authentic religious content in the experience of the Muslim, the Hindu, the Buddhist or whoever
he may be. We may, if we have asked humbly and respectfully, still reach the conclusion that our brothers have
started from a false premise and reached a faulty conclusion. But we must not arrive at our judgment from outside
their religious situation. We have to try to sit where they
sit, to enter sympathetically into the pains and griefs and
joys of their history and see how those pains and griefs and
joys have determined the premises of their argument. We
have, in a word, to be 'present' with them.*

~Max Warren[8]

Peter's words from the Acts of the Apostles (10:34,35) merit special
emphasis these days: "I now realize how true it is that God does not
show favoritism but accepts from every nation the one who fears him
and does what is right." We are told that the Jewish converts to nascent
Christianity in those earliest days of its movement were surprised to discover that the very same Spirit of God that was in them was also in the
non-Jewish converts. Signs of the Spirit's active presence in them
became obvious to all.

St. John adds to the theme his comforting insistence that "whoever
loves is begotten by God and knows God." Imagine: The rock-bottom

criterion of right relationship with God has nothing to do with any religion, but is simply *love* – sincere, generous, unselfish, human love! How can we accept that as a teaching from God and at the same time harbor any prejudice or hatred or aversion toward a religion other than our own? Impossible!

> *We shall know that, if they live in love, they are of God. Period!*

Then how shall we, from this time onward, regard others who are not of our faith? We shall know that, if they live in love, they are of God. Period!

A GROWING, CHANGING FAITH:
A FAITH IN A GOD FOR TODAY

Eighty-five years a Catholic Christian, 58 years a priest, I find the content of my faith undergoing unprecedented development. Why should that not be, I ask myself, when, in the words of Cardinal Newman, "To live is to change, and to change often is to become perfect?" The church has committed itself to change in the Second Vatican Council, and its documents provide us with an initial blueprint, a starting thrust from our long-cultivated inertia, the momentum of which we must maintain.

No one will ever have the last word about the incomprehensible God. Everything we say about God (theology = "talk about God") is by way of analogy. The church speaks the truth when it calls itself "semper reformanda," i.e., always in need of reform. That need applies to its understanding of God as well as to its organizational life and practice.

Christian theology is based on a cosmology, an understanding of the world, that is no longer held and that we know to be totally unscientific – a three-level universe in which heaven is above, hell is below, and earth is in between. Primitive, imaginary, false. But in that context are rooted the very dynamics of Judeo/Christian faith: God is up there, God sends a savior down to us, God is a super being of human, male characteristics who manages the world from above and who scrutinizes and judges human behavior, etc.

There is no God up there, or out there, or wherever, who entertains our petitions and answers sometimes positively, sometimes negatively, sometimes not at all. Such an image is the product of the collective human imagination, taking shape over the ages. Anthropomorphic imagery

41

("measuring" God according to human standards) is a contrivance, a concession, that makes a certain kind of prayer possible on our terms. It is not to be taken literally. God is pure spirit, the Creative Spirit, the ultimate source of life and love and all that is. Through that Creative Spirit this vast universe, you and I included, has come into being and is sustained. We trivialize the Great Spirit when we reduce it to a humanoid creation of our own, no matter what the Scriptures have to say.

The purported "words of God" down the ages are human words that seek to give expression to some aspect of the divine presence. There is no supernatural being that observes, much as we do, the situation of human beings. But there is everywhere and always the divine spirit, the Creative Spirit, living and loving in all things animate and inanimate. To be consciously, deliberately united with that indwelling spirit is in itself a source of abiding strength and hope. It is our assurance that ultimately justice and peace and love and goodness will prevail.

Add to that outmoded, unreal scenario the Adam and Eve story as an understandable human attempt to explain the enigma of evil in the world of a good God, and the drama of redemption, the buying back of errant and banished humanity, finds a congenial and logical setting.

Do not we, who have been fortunate enough to have lived into a new millennium, have the obligation, the responsibility, of examining critically that belief system, built, as it is, on foundations that can no longer be defended? Past generations have done their very best to interpret and articulate the mystery of God's presence in their lives; do we have the moral right to do less?

Non-scholar that I am, I rely on the ordinary reading and learning and praying and practical experiences that have filled my life in order to discern the evolution of truth, encouraged by the wise insistence of the church on the primacy of individual conscience. I depend heavily also on the insights of contemporary theologians and scholars in the resolution of those doubts and instincts that are inevitably an integral part of any sincere faith journey. I also look to the consensus of a rapidly increasing number of Catholics in whose faith I find resonance of my own.

Jesus was scorned for attempting to redefine God. He rebuked his detractors by telling them that they were like the old garment that could not accept a new patch, or like an old wine sack that could not hold the new yield. I reveal God to you in a new way, he said to them equivalently, but you are so wedded to your old mindset that you cannot hear and receive what I am saying.

I am convinced that the situation is much the same today: The Spirit of Truth is speaking to us through the insights of a broad range of human sciences, and many are paralyzed by fear of letting go of the familiar, the traditional. Who is the sage who commented, "Tradition is the living faith of the dead; traditionalism is the dead faith of the living"? Amen!

From the whole of Jesus' life and teachings, at least as far as I know and understand them, I deduce the following as belonging to the basis of a faith for today:

- God and we are never apart: God is not "up there" while we are "down here." God is *in* us, the way two persons are in each other in a union of love – only infinitely more so.

- We and God struggle together; God does not exist in some far-off place, watching, engineering, directing, responding. God is the empowering energy of everything we are and everything we do. God's "kingdom" is within us. God is in everything as the ground of its being; were God not there, it would not be.

* We can't control or manipulate God. We never did, never will, no matter what prayers we say or sacred actions we perform. Nor does God control us; we are always free.

* God is the deepest foundation of our being. (Centering prayer seeks the God within.)

* God is love, and when we love in any way we are actively living in God.

* Our one, common, universal calling is to be good human beings, to live up to our creaturely mandate by caring for others as we care for ourselves, by struggling to overcome our selfishness, by forgiving generously, by moving on in hope even in the worst of times, etc.

* Our prayers and sacred rituals don't save; they don't protect us or win special favors or anything like that. They celebrate the relationship between us and God, between us and all other creatures. They remind us of God's loving presence to us and encourage us to look forward to that life of perfect union with the Creator that we are destined to enjoy after our biological death.

So much for a starter, if only to suggest that our old, inherited, false images of God result in needless pain and confusion, causing people of good will and generous love to live in fear of an offended, punishing God, whose requirements for their entrance into eternal life are onerous and all but unachievable. Crippled by such fear of a God who is the product of human imagination, no one can be life-giving to anyone else. "I have come," he said, "that you may have life and have it in abundance."

CHAPTER TWO

What's It All About?

THE REASON AND RESPONSIBILITY OF FAITH

Our traditional belief is that the sacred authors, each and all of them in both the Old and the New Testament, were guided by the Holy Spirit to write exactly what was the mind, the truth of God, even while they acted in a completely natural, personal way – using their own language, their memories, their imagination, their understanding, etc. The end result, we have traditionally maintained, is not merely a human product, but primarily a divine one – really the word of God.

But reason tells us that some of what we read in Scripture simply cannot, in and of itself, be God's word. Consider some glaring examples:

- Exodus 35:2 unequivocally states that anyone who works on the Sabbath day should be put to death.

* Leviticus 25:44 clearly endorses the purchasing of slaves, both male and female, from surrounding heathen nations.

* Leviticus 11:10 forbids the eating of shellfish (like the shrimp I so enjoy!) on the grounds that it is an abomination.

* In the Gospels we are cautioned that it is better to cut off our hands and pluck out our eyes rather than to sin with these body parts.

* We are told that a star came to rest over the place where Jesus was born. The last time I looked, stars were fantastically large masses of gravitationally bound gases burning at thousands of degrees Fahrenheit.

I'm sure you get the point – or at least the question. How can we say of these obvious falsehoods, these foolish — some immoral — instructions that they are the word of God? But then what does it mean that the Scriptures are inspired?

I am comfortable with this answer to the question: the wisdom of God finds even our human stupidity, our prejudices, our lack of understanding useful in communicating fundamental truth to us – which is why we should rarely stay on the surface of what we are reading or hearing in the Scriptures, but rather dig down, sometimes way down, to encounter the message these words, these ideas – many of them false in themselves – carry for our benefit.

For example, whether or not Jesus performed the miraculous cures the Gospels say he did, the real intent of the stories is to highlight for us the unconditional compassion of Jesus and to invite us to act similarly in our lives. The stories, whether factual or fictional or both, are simply the vehicles that bring this overriding point to our attention.

A priest whom I deeply admire and respect observed once that we can't possibly pay attention to all the "stuff" that presents itself to us in the course of an ordinary day. The thousands of things our eyes can see, the thousands of sounds our ears hear: no way can we take notice of them all and remain sane. He used the analogous example of someone standing next to a highway and trying to count and identify every single car that passes by. I thought of a fellow I frequently see along the Parkway in Essex County, NJ, who appears to be doing exactly that. He stands there hours at a time, just scanning the vehicles that pass by. I assume he's mentally ill or challenged. Well, no more than that poor fellow can give his attention to everything he is seeing and hearing can we give our attention to everything around us. We are left, then, either to make a chance sampling of it all according to the impulse of the moment, or to be deliberately selective in what we attend to.

Every morning when I open the newspaper delivered to my door, I realize that I cannot possibly read all that it contains, but at the same time I find myself getting into this or that article or captioned photo and then asking myself, Why am I wasting time on this? Let it go, and move on to something more significant.

And that's the way our entire life must go: an unending series of value judgments about what is worthy of our time and what is not.

An especially interesting aspect of this principle is that it applies to our religion as well. There is a solid core of belief and practice that defines our religion, but there's also an awful lot of "stuff" that has been added and compounded over the centuries that may or may not merit our involvement and commitment.

How easily we dismiss some of the most important words of Jesus. Let's keep in mind always that it was he who reduced all of religion to two basic commandments: to love God with all our heart and to love others as we love ourselves. He said that all other laws are rooted in those two. I think that means that if we are living in genuine, uncompromising love, it is impossible for us to sin. But that's an unacceptable risk for many of us: how much safer to observe scrupulously all the particulars of the law. How much easier to be told what to do and then to obey the command precisely, as if one were thus obeying God.

Although neither we nor our well-meaning teachers knew what was happening 50+ years ago, it turned out that we priests-to-be were being trained in seminary to be the third employee in one of Jesus' popular stories (Matthew 25:14-30), the man who dug a hole for his traveling master's treasure rather than invest it for profit. When the master returned, he praised the two employees who had carefully risked his money and succeeded in making more for him; the third servant he angrily condemned for his timidity in playing it safe. Well, we seminarians were skillfully conditioned, in essence, to play it safe. We were to take no risks for the sake of the greater good; make no personal, prudential judgments that come from the heart as well as the mind. We were taught to conduct our ministry according to the letter of the law and were assured that if we kept the rule, the rule would keep us.

How neat. How nice. And how deadly. Yet, all along we had the example of Jesus, who praised, not the one who acted cautiously, but the ones who took chances in pursuit of something greater than safety and security and good order. Jesus was no anarchist; he was that unique human being who conducted his life not according to a pre-ordained plan, not in slavish conformity to the expectations of others, including the institutional religion of his day. No, he lived in moment-by-moment response to the Creative Spirit that he knew lived within him and within every human being. He is not the bridge between us and God; he is not someone divinely appointed to make recompense for our sins. No, he is the one who pointed out to us the ever-present God and showed us how a truly good life here on earth can be only an ever-growing awareness of the divine presence and the never-ending effort to live in harmony with that Spirit of Wisdom and Love.

That's pretty risky business because it demands of us imperfect creatures total responsibility and uncompromising integrity. But we can be sure of this: had the risk-takers in his story failed, partly or completely, Jesus would have praised and honored them just the same.

"MYTH" UNDERSTOOD

We're appreciating more fully these days the function of stories and myths and fables in our Judeo/Christian tradition. Great minds like that of Public Broadcasting's late Joseph Campbell help us to understand that. A cold, factual, scientific or historical statement doesn't usually find its way into our memories and emotions as a really good story does, which can last for thousands of years, maybe forever.

The bible contains much of the most exquisite fiction, all of it designed to preserve and pass on the most important truths and principles of our religious tradition. What a mistake it is to try to change fictional accounts into fact and then dissect them as if we were analyzing a news report on CNN or in the *New York Times*.

The Epiphany of the Lord is a perfect case in point. For us in the Western Church it is a rich story about pagan astrologers who read messages in the stars (a practice strictly forbidden and condemned by the Jews of Jesus' day) and through a star find their way to the birthplace of Jesus.

They bring gifts of gold, frankincense, and myrrh. The story has evolved into there being three wise men, although ancient works of art show as many as 12 – an unimportant detail except for the fact that it suggests that the fable was altered and nuanced over the passage of time.

What is the truth this unforgettable tale contains and carries from generation to generation? A convenient way to start toward an answer is to consider the word "cellophane," the ancestor of Saran Wrap. The *p-h-a-n* in cellophane is the same *p-h-a-n* we find in Epiphany, and they both mean "to reveal," "to see through," "to show forth." The cellophane reveals or shows forth the lamb chop or the club steak in its package.

What we remember and honor in this feast is the showing forth of Jesus as God's loving outreach to all people in the entire world for all time. The gifts the mythical visitors brought to the Christ Child have been understood in Christian tradition in these ways –

GOLD – to acknowledge the benign royalty of Jesus, who loves and provides for all members of his kingdom, who rules gently, who secures life especially for the needy and the weak, who places his own life at the total service of others, who gives his life on their behalf.

FRANKINCENSE – to honor the presence of divinity in Jesus, who would say some 30 years later, You ask who and what and where God is; simply know me and you will know God. This is the Jesus who reminds us all that we, too, are to live in such a way that we can say the same.

MYRRH – (an embalming substance) to predict the inevitable death of the human Jesus, a death decreed not by God but by those evil persons who found it advantageous to get him out of their way.

The message of the three gifts drives home to us what the original disciples of Jesus found almost impossible to accept and what led them to such infighting that the very existence of the early church was seriously threatened: THAT GOD IS NOT PARTIAL TO ANY NATION, ANY RELIGION, ANY CULTURE, ANY RACE. God's love, presence, and action are always for all people.

If Jesus is the special gift of God, he is for everyone, no matter of what nationality or religion. God's love is never partial to anyone, never prejudiced. Because of our long training to think of Catholicism as the "one, true church," we considered it blasphemous to say that there are many paths to God. But now we know that not only is that true, but also is it true that there are many paths *with* God, for the Spirit of God is in all people, and our religions are different ways of living in and with that ever-present God.

In the complex situations that have developed between us in the Western World and those in the Middle East and elsewhere, there is much to be regretted on all sides, much to be forgiven, much to be reformed. Even while these terrible conditions endure, we must do whatever we can, no matter how little, to provide for the innocent, suffering victims who are caught in them. With such an attitude and such action on our part, the Epiphany is extended to the most unfortunate of earth's people, and they will come to know through our hearts and hands that God is not a god of military might and victory but the God of compassion and mercy.

FAITH-FILLED DOUBTS

My mother used to love hearing this story; it was about one of my brothers when he was in 4th or 5th grade in Catholic school. What happened was that his teacher, a Sister of Charity, was giving the catechism lesson of the day when he raised his hand to voice an opinion on the subject that was not exactly in accord with the official version. Sister looked at him scathingly and said, "Well, listen carefully, everyone. Rome speaks!"

Actually, I give my brother credit: he was ahead of his time. There wasn't much dialog in those days when all a Catholic was expected to do was to listen without questioning, give complete assent to what was taught, and obey what was commanded. A totally authoritarian church it was, neatly divided between the teachers and the learners, the rulers and the subjects.

In those days, the question "Do you believe?" had to do mainly with the *content* of Catholic teaching. For the ordinary Catholic that meant the catechism and the Apostles' Creed. A "Yes" that signaled *conformity* was the hallmark of the good Catholic.

The situation is so different today in an increasing number of Catholic communities. Faithful Catholics very openly and respectfully express doubts and difficulties concerning certain teachings of the church.

Should such persons, speaking and acting with the convictions of their consciences, be condemned as renegades and heretics? Shall we regard them as a threat to the church? Is it sinful to doubt about matters of faith and morals as presented officially by the church? And is it immoral, therefore, to live according to one's own well-formed conscience? Does being a good Catholic have to mean always submitting one's conscience to another authority, namely that of the church hierarchy?

Our belief as Christians is not primarily in statements and definitions, but in a person: Jesus of Nazareth, who is himself the Good News, concerning whom the vast body of teachings has developed over the centuries past. Ordinarily, those teachings are, as the Australians would say, "spot on." Sometimes, on the other hand, they don't quite express the mind of Jesus and need to be reformed. Scholarship and conscience are the major tools involved in that process. In this connection it would be well to point out that the words of the disciples, "We've seen the Lord!" do not suggest that they enjoyed a privilege reserved for a few. Those words, instead, point to a grace shared by all Christians: somehow we all find it possible to believe that Jesus lives and that we can and do converse with him personally in prayer.

That said, we must say also that since living bodies of all kinds must have organization and direction, the church has them too. It has the Holy Scriptures, a long and vibrant tradition, and also a stabilizing teaching authority in the person of the bishops, whose head is the pope. Occasionally it has worldwide councils, like the two Vatican Councils, that attempt to define or refine the basic beliefs of the church.

> *The authority of the church is meant to be exercised as humble service to all, never as power over others.*

The Spirit of God, that invisible presence of the Creator, leads the church always in the direction of truth and love. The authority of the church is meant to be exercised as humble service to all, never as power over others. That authority is at its best when it tries to discern where and in whom the Spirit has spoken – not only in the leaders of the church but in any person, anywhere, of good will and loving heart.

56

Authentic and faithful authority then shares that newly-acquired truth with the whole church throughout the world.

Think of the famous Apostle who has come to be known as the "Doubting Thomas" because of his hesitance in acknowledging the resurrection of Jesus after his crucifixion and burial. Recall that the scripture tells us that Jesus invited him to put his fingers into the nail holes in his hands and his hand into the spear gash in his side – and to be no longer unbelieving but believing. As Monsignor Ronald Knox, mid-20th century English convert to the Catholic faith, writes in his small but powerful book, *Lightning Meditations*,[9] Jesus was not condemning Thomas for doubting. He was simply acknowledging that for some people, like Thomas, belief is more difficult than for others. In fact, he seems to be saying that a special reward awaits those for whom belief in Jesus is often burdened with the never satisfied desire to see more clearly.

All of us together, those who never doubt and those who do doubt, profess our faith in Jesus, who was put to death but whom we believe to be alive among and within us now. Amen!

SALVATION

W hat do we mean by terms like "salvation" and "redemption"? Saved from what? Redeemed from what? We are not a fallen race; we are a developing race. There never was a Garden of Eden. Humans were not created in some idyllic state of perfection; the human race has evolved, we know now, from the most primitive life forms. Death did not enter human history as a result of sin: countless trillions of living beings had died over billions of years long before Homo Sapiens walked this earth.

The process of evolution, which even the rather conservative Pope St. John Paul II has endorsed, demands a whole new theology. We know now that much of what was once assumed to be fact because it was in Sacred Scripture is actually myth, story, symbol, conceived originally in scientific ignorance – "holy fiction" that carries a divine and eternal message. Yet writers, preachers, teachers, even at the highest levels of the church's structure, continue basing theological understanding and religious teaching on that outmoded cosmology, that discredited world-view, which, paradoxically, even they know to be false.

It seems to me that is the fundamental weakness, for example, of *The Catechism of the Catholic Church*, and all similar documents: they flow from an antiquated, false, unacceptable cosmology. And, because they are thus grounded in obsolescence, they facilely resort to such corresponding concepts as a "God above" who sends down to earth a redeemer to assuage God's anger toward offending creatures, etc. Locked into that scenario, so thoroughly anthropomorphic, these pronouncements must necessarily conclude that the one magnanimous gesture of mercy on the part of God and the one sacrificial appeasement achieved by Jesus' death, given on behalf of all humanity, are absolutely unique and unrepeatable and totally sufficient. "Redemption" in Christ is viewed as the one saving event on behalf of fallen humanity.

But what if we proceed from another base, one that we know to be a fact of scientific discovery? Scientists have determined that the universe came into being 13.8 billion years ago in a singular event called the "Big Bang" and has been evolving ever since. We humans are a very recent development in that marvelous chain of events. Our evolution continues to this day and will take us to levels of humanity we cannot now even begin to predict. In terms of this evolutionary process, it was only a moment ago that Jesus lived on earth. Faithful, contemplative, prayerful Jew that he was, he became uniquely conscious of the presence of the Creator, whom he envisioned as "Father," in all persons, in all things. So filled was he with the acknowledged divine presence that he could say that to know him was to know God. He claimed this intimacy with the divine, not as an exclusive personal prerogative, but as a phenomenon that any person could and should experience. He claimed to be "the way," the model for all.

In that context, Jesus shows us how to be human and how to journey from life to Life. In that context, Jesus is not "redeemer," for to redeem means to pay back, to ransom. Pay what to whom? Ransom from whom? The very questions are possible only in that primitive, unscientific world-view in which humans were created in perfection, sinned against the Creator, were banished in anger from the place of happiness, waited for a reconciliation they could not of themselves accomplish, and were finally rescued by the God-Man sent from above to appease the Creator through his suffering and death.

It is all myth, figment of human imagination, posited on an understanding of human and universal origins we know today to be completely false — a feeble, noble, perfectly understandable attempt to explain the phenomenon of evil in a world believed to be created by a good God.

And yet the theological teachings that derive from these falsehoods persist, as they do in the *Catechism of the Catholic Church*. What are we to do? What are we to think and believe?

It is time for us Christians to rethink our images of God and to face the undeniable fact that much of what has been handed down to us was the natural conclusion of a false concept of the world, its beginnings and its development over time. As we make and pursue that admission, the way will be cleared for us to see Jesus and the church that sprang from the Christ-event in a new and more revealing light.

We will begin to grasp that Jesus does not redeem us; he does not restore us to God's love and friendship, because God's love is unconditional, was never lost and can never be lost. God IS love! The absence of God's love would be the absence of God – absurd. There were no "first parents" whose sin condemned their progeny and made necessary a rescuer. The death of Jesus is not the price of our ransom. Jesus was ready to die for what he believed. Moreover, living as Jesus did would set people free from the bondage of fear, despair and all the "isms" that plague humankind.

We will see that all human beings have one common vocation: to be good human beings, loving creatures of a loving God, and we will continue to believe that in all of human history no one has as perfectly exemplified human life as has Jesus. In that sense he is savior, for he saves us from false notions about ourselves and our creator; he saves us from frustration and despair; he saves us from ever believing that evil

60

and hatred are, after all, more powerful than goodness and love.

Are we going to be saddled with those false notions of atonement forever? Is it not past the time when we should have moved beyond them, while honoring their authors for their integrity and sincerity? Do we not have the same obligation and privilege to apply the knowledge and the insights of our day to the mystery of God's creative, loving presence in the universe as our forebears did in their day? Do we honor them, do we honor the Creator, by continuing to treat what is patently false as though it were true? And if new knowledge leads us to new and different conclusions about God and our relationship with God, is that not to be expected and desired? We possessed, after all, intelligence and reason long before being blessed with religious revelation – and both are rooted in the same Creator.

A man told me once about a Lenten Mass he had been to. In the homily, he said, the priest pursued the theme of his hearers' sinfulness, their unworthiness, and their need to do serious penance, especially during Lent. He didn't say anything about their efforts to lead good lives and to serve others generously; instead, he kept hammering away at the sins he took for granted they were guilty of.

The man expressed to me his reaction with a kind of "give me a break" attitude. Life is difficult enough, he said, but despite our human faults we do generally try to do what's right. We don't need to be told how miserable we are and how displeased God is with us. I know that my reaction would have been much stronger: I would have been tempted to walk out of that church.

I may be somewhat naïve, but I've been assuming for a long time that that sort of preaching doesn't exist anymore; but every once in a while I am reminded that it does.

61

There are countless Christians, among us Catholics too, who think of Jesus' death as the ultimate sacrificial offering that made peace with the offended God. And those who still think that way urge us to combine our sacrifices with Jesus' incomparable offering.

I know I'll never win over great numbers of persons who remain mired in this old way of thinking, but I do entertain the possibility that some who are on the fence can be persuaded to jump over to a different way of thinking. I'd ask them to consider this: Jesus' life and death took place at a time when virtually all people believed that God, or the gods, could be won over to clemency by sacrifices — the bloody or burnt offering of one's animals, crops, wealth, even children. It's easy to grasp that when we consider the frequency of suicide bombings in today's world – believers killing themselves in expectation of immediate reward from God in the afterlife.

When we refer to Jesus as the Lamb of God, what do we mean? That he is the ultimate sacrificial victim, whose suffering and death were pleasing to God? That our sins have been expiated, paid for, by his cruel death?

That's an ancient, still popular belief of many Christians, and it's going to be around for a long time to come, you can be sure. But we can rethink it and discover that there is another way of understanding and interpreting the death of Jesus. In essence it is that his death was not the price of our redemption demanded by God but rather the price that he was willing to pay for remaining steadfast in his revolutionary teachings about the mystery of the unconditionally loving God. Jesus could have avoided that indescribably painful ordeal and lived to old age and died in peace and comfort. On the other hand, he knew that if he continued

62

his novel preaching and teaching and healing and confronting, he would pay with his life. This was so, not because God wanted his death, but because evil persons and institutions who viewed him as a threat desperately wanted him out of the way. We see with hindsight how easily they succeeded.

Our annual season of Lent is not a time for us to be scolded and humiliated. We are being reminded that, shabby as our lives may be at times, our Creator loves us passionately and unconditionally – even when we do not love others or even ourselves.

Jesus' journey is about leading and luring. We experience this with special focus during Lent. This is the season when we are being led into the desert of contemplation and prayer and fasting, as Jesus was, only to appreciate more how much we are loved. It is then, also, that we are being emphatically lured into making our own lives more loving and compassionate. Our personal crosses and how we carry them are, like his, the sign of how much we are willing to do for the sake of love.

THE PASSION OF JESUS: *A MATTER OF LIFE, NOT DEATH*

Our emotions are never the most important components of religion and faith. We have all seen the rituals of certain religions in which emotions are fanned to white hot intensity, and most of us would conclude that there's not much, if any, engagement of the intellect or the spirit in such frenzy. It's an orchestrated "high" that makes the participants feel they are in an other-worldly state of being – and that's all.

Genuine appreciation of Jesus' passion and death takes the form of deep gratitude for the totally unselfish gift of himself and of committing ourselves to join him in the transformation of the world into the very Kingdom of God on earth.

That gratitude does not have to be accompanied by tears or emotional affect of any sort. It is proven, it is validated, by our personal involvement in the cause for which he offered and gave his life – which was what? That we, God's human creatures, would all be one, living in peace, harmony, and mutual respect - that we would know beyond all doubt that we are loved unconditionally by our Creator and are called into existence primarily to love all other creatures; that we are to be about the business of building the Kingdom of God here on Planet Earth by every constructive, supportive, forgiving, healing, life-giving word, action, and attitude that we can contribute.

The life/death/resurrection of Jesus is so full of meaning, of mystery, and of important consequences for the human race that it will be explored as long as life exists. We're only a little more than 2000 years from it, and we see that our ideas about it are in some ways different from what earlier believers understood, and we cannot even imagine what Christians 10,000 years from now will find in it and how their views will differ from ours today.

As mentioned here earlier, we have to admit today we are questioning, even rejecting, an interpretation that has held sway for many centuries, namely that God sent Jesus into our world to suffer a terrible death in payment for the sins of humanity. You can be sure that many persons who saw Mel Gibson's movie, The Passion of the Christ, took away from it exactly that. They're saying, "Look how much he suffered to make up to God for my sins and the sins of the world!"

I always recall in this connection my last visit to a beloved uncle of mine who was in the last stages of a vicious cancer that moved relentlessly through his tortured body. On that occasion, he said, "How can I complain when I look at that cross and see what Jesus was willing to endure to save me?"

But more and more of us are challenging that position and saying, "Wait a minute! How could an infinitely loving, compassionate, forgiving God demand the painful torture of a loved one as the condition for forgiveness? Certainly not the God whom Jesus called Father and who inspired Jesus to teach us to love our enemies and to do good to those who hate and hurt us.

This early view of the significance of Jesus' cross originated at a time in human history when class distinctions among persons were absolute, i.e., when persons were born into high class or low and knew that would be their permanent lot. No upward mobility for the poor or the disenfranchised in those days. In that system, the seriousness of an offense was measured by the status of the person offended. If one, say, slapped a child,

65

so what? It's only a child. Or slapped a peasant? Again, it's only a person of the lowest class. But if one slapped the feudal lord or the king or the bishop or the pope – the very same action, mind you – ah, that's a very grave offense because of the standing, the dignity, of the person offended.

Now, just extend that line of reasoning to its logical conclusion: what if it is God that is perceived to be offended? In that case, the offense must be regarded as infinite, because God is, by very definition, infinite.

And so, the dilemma as measured against the just-described scale: human beings have committed countless infinite offenses against God by their sins; but no human being, not even the whole race together, can make infinite satisfaction or reparation for that immense load of sin. No one can make up to God for the sins of humanity. That's the logic that has prevailed for centuries.

And the solution, that we find still very much a part of our thinking: God alone can perform an action of infinite merit; therefore, God alone can save the human race from eternal punishment for its sins. Enter Jesus! God sent God to earth in the person of Jesus Christ, understood to be both human and divine. His atoning, redeeming suffering and death satisfy our otherwise irreconcilable debt.

Lest you think this is a museum piece I have described to you, something from the distant past and no longer in circulation, I hasten to tell you that it is exactly what I was taught in college and in seminary and exactly what I myself taught for many years as a young priest. It is safe to say that it is what most Christians still believe today.

Must we maintain this interpretation of the life and death of Jesus? I don't see why, not when we are aware of a much more reasonable, compelling, and beautiful interpretation, one that does not reduce God to the level of a sadistic, vengeful ogre, one that does not make of Jesus an item of barter – God saying, "Give me the cruel death of Jesus and I'll give you your long-awaited absolution." To more and more of us today it seems so absurd.

Let's rejoice in the knowledge that what Jesus' death signifies is not his payment of any debt of ours but rather his acceptance of death out of fidelity to what he believed and preached. Even when he knew that his teaching and preaching, his healing and confronting were going to lead inexorably to his death by crucifixion, and when he knew also that if he were to abandon his ministry of compassionate love, he could live peacefully to old age and a natural death, he chose to remain faithful to you and me and to God, despite the consequences.

The cross is the sign of the immensity of his love! No matter our troubles, let us rejoice!

THE RESURRECTION

I n one of his brilliant weekly columns, the late Father Richard McBrien, longtime professor of theology at Notre Dame University in Indiana, wrote that it seems more and more difficult to say something original about the Resurrection. What we hear, he said, is very predictable, often riddled with clichés. Even the Easter messages of popes, he added, have a completely familiar ring to them, as do the words of whoever the homilist is at Mass anywhere.[10]

I'm so glad he expressed those thoughts, which every homilist will easily connect with. It's true: there is an unwavering sameness to what we hear preached during the 50 days of Easter. We have to wonder if anyone is paying attention.

But, Father McBrien went on to say, we mustn't forget that we listeners are never the same persons from year to year. A seminary professor of his made the point years ago, he recalled, that the liturgical year is more like a spiral than a circle. By this analogy he was saying that, while we celebrate the same familiar feasts at the same time every year and in pretty much the same words, we are not in the same spiritual place that we were any year before. For good or for ill, that insightful teacher emphasized, we change from year to year, and therefore so does the impact of the feast upon our consciousness and our spiritual development. What a valid and helpful observation that is. What I hear this time around, I was not able or ready to hear last year or ten years ago. How true!

Let's first admit that there is no scientific proof of Jesus' resurrection from death. Almost certainly, there never will be. We believe in his resurrection, however one defines it, because faithful people of his time believed that he was alive after having died, and excitedly they expressed to us that firm conviction. A profound change came over them after Jesus' death: they could feel his real presence among them, not physical but spiritual – and nonetheless real. They bravely and boldly and publicly proclaimed their conviction that he was somehow alive and active among them.

It is very difficult to distinguish between what should be taken literally, word for word at face value, and what is to be understood as metaphor or figure of speech or allegory in the post-resurrection accounts we read in the Scriptures. Therefore, the way is open for us to be not overly strict in interpreting what we find there. For example, consider just the matter of their "seeing" Jesus: when we are told that Jesus' followers saw the Lord after his death, does that have to mean that with their physical eyes they saw him? I don't think so. It can also mean that they were simply aware of his mysterious presence among them in a non-physical way.

The placing of Thomas's finger into the nail holes in Jesus' hand and his hand into the spear wound in Jesus' side are, I admit, more difficult to explain – unless one allows that even the Gospels were embellished by the original believers in order to support the unusual claims they were making about this unusual person.

And how does all this differ from our own experience of the Risen Jesus? Really not at all. Unless our imaginations step in and produce images for us, we don't anymore see him with our physical eyes than our ancestors in the faith did. Yet we believe as firmly as they did that he is truly alive and intimately present to us. When we utter as simple a prayer as "Jesus, have mercy on us," we are not addressing a memory or an historical figure or a concoction of our creative minds. We are speaking directly to Jesus, whom we believe to be eternally alive and always with us.

We find Jesus wherever we are, whatever we are doing, and in whomever we are with. Who knows whether it was actually by some magic-like miracle that his first followers learned this or by their simply being in the ordinary circumstances of work and family, love and sex, social activity, quiet contemplation and noisy discussion, eating and drinking, recreation and sport, politics and government, and so on?

I turn again to the late Monsignor Ronald Knox's views on the gospel's account of the conversation between Jesus and Thomas.

He said he was sure that Jesus was not scolding Thomas for not believing in his resurrection, as we might have assumed. He felt that Jesus was merely stating a matter of common fact: namely, that there are two categories of believers. On the one hand, there are those who find it not at all problematic to accept mysterious, unexplainable religious teachings and accounts of supernatural happenings told to them on good authority. That doesn't make them gullible fools who would believe you if you said you saw a cow jump over the moon, but their respect for authority is so deep and trusting that it just doesn't occur to them that what is proposed for their acceptance could be either false or deceptive.

I imagine that this is the faith that most of us were raised in, the faith of our mothers and fathers and grandparents. It certainly was the faith imparted to us in our parochial schools and from the pulpits of our parish churches. We learned early on that it was not our place to question or waver the slightest bit in our belief; after all, this was the voice of God we were hearing in the voices of those who gave their lives to being God's spokespersons on our behalf. At the dinner table at the end of a

Catholic school day, the definitive discussion clincher was, "But, Mom, Sister said…" Case closed!

But then, Msgr. Knox went on to say, there is another category of believers, and these are those good people whose inquisitive, searching, scientific minds are constantly looking for proof of absolutely everything and anything before they will accept or assent to it. For such persons, Knox reminded us, religious faith can be extremely difficult, appearing to them to demand a kind of intellectual suicide: "How can I believe something for which I find no solid evidence?"

They are not sinners or infidels. They are not being obstinate in their refusal to believe or impertinent in entertaining their doubts. That simply is the way they are, and we can only praise them for their integrity. I remember in this connection a brilliant man, a few years older than I, whose wife was a scrupulously obedient Catholic but who himself was constantly doubting some of the pronouncements of the church as unscientific, unreasonable, downright insulting in certain instances. I could not help but like and respect him, because he was so completely sincere as well as super intelligent and very articulate. It really was amusing when his wife would "deliver" him to me as if he were a piece of drapery in need of dry cleaning! For sometimes two or more hours, we would discuss the issues he – or she, before leaving us! — had chosen for the day, and always we parted with a firm handshake and expressions of friendship and mutual respect. As I look back on that long, ongoing dialog, I see more and more clearly how right he was in so much of what he said, and how he was helping me to refine my own faith, as I hope I was doing for him. There are countless persons of good will in his category.

Msgr. Knox assured them that there is a special reward reserved for them, who have to throw back their shoulders, grit their teeth, clench their fists and trudge forward in a faith they find in some ways so hard to hold on to. Often enough I find myself among them. The church has never claimed that it is infallible in everything it teaches. The church acknowledges that there is wisdom among the people that comes also from the Spirit of God and sometimes is closer to the actual truth than what the official teaching in a matter of faith or morals may be at a particular time. It is the duty of authority to tap that wisdom and eventually make it available to all.

In such a case, the sincere, faithful, patient doubter renders an important service to the whole church because often faith grows under the stimulus of honest doubt.

But the point here is that belief cannot be forced or commanded or imposed; either we believe because we see reason to, or we do not believe because we see reason not to. We must do our best always to be open to the truth, whatever it is and from wherever it comes. Whether people struggle with the literalness of the body rising or not, our common faith is that Jesus' death was not the end. He is still with us in spirit and will remain with us always. In any event, our baptismal commitment means that we will be faithful to Jesus in the community of the church, where we will try to resolve our doubts with open hearts and minds, with humble prayer, with respectful attention to our appointed teachers, with trustful sharing, and above all with fidelity to the Eucharist, which, more than anything else, makes us one.

THE ASCENSION

I doubt that any of us can fully appreciate how conditioned we are to expect factual, accurate reporting in what we are told. Jack Webb, of Dragnet fame, made his slogan a household word: "Just the facts, Ma'am." The president or the pope makes a plane journey to a foreign country, and we are told the exact time of the departure and arrival, down to the very minute. We are flooded with so many facts that they become an annoyance, especially when they are repeated over and over again, and not on one station or one channel or in one newspaper, but on many at the same time and, it seems, all the time.

It's hard for us to appreciate how different it was in Jesus' day. I suspect factual details, for whatever reason, were of much less importance to people back then. Maybe one reason was that it took so long for reports to get from one place to another that the details diminished in importance or got so contaminated in the process of transmission from one time and place to another that they were regarded as unreliable. If that is so, then contradictions in the accounts of two or more witnesses of the same event would not have troubled the people at all; no one would be accused of carelessness or deceit. The conflicting accounts simply resulted in a better, richer story.

You can immediately see that we, with our conditioning in factual accuracy, can easily and unwittingly create a huge problem when we interpret and judge the scriptures according to our standards, not the standards of the people for whom they were originally written or uttered. But that's what we've been doing for centuries. A glaring example of that is what we've done with the first book of the bible, Genesis, in trying to make scientific sense of its narration of the creation of the world. There are countless people today who still believe that the world was created in six days and that God, weary from all that work, had to rest on the 7th day. They don't understand, or they won't accept, that that whole section of the bible is pure conjecture, written by persons who had not the remotest idea of how the world came into being. Remember, it would be a couple of thousand years after their time that Christopher Columbus would discover that the earth is a globe! (To the people of Jesus' time it was more a gigantic table supported by four immense legs positioned over water and fire and covered by a dome.)

So they concocted a wonderful, lyrical, mystical, enduring tale, injecting into it what they knew about production: how a potter, for example, makes a vase out of the clay of the earth, and so on. There was absolutely nothing factual or scientific about what they said; its purpose was only to proclaim that there is one God, that God is love, that God is the creator of all that is, and that human beings were created to resemble that God in ways not possible for any other creature.

Again, it is the meaning of the writing, not what facts it contains or doesn't contain, that counts. But fundamentalists even today insist that the bible can make no error of any kind, and they calculate, therefore, that the universe is only 6,000 years old – while authentic science tells us that the universe is nearly 14 billion years old!

What is written in the bible about the ascension of Jesus "into heaven" after his death and resurrection is another significant case in point. Consider that, of the four gospel authors (Matthew, Mark, Luke, and John) and St. Paul, out of those five, Luke is the only one who has left us with a chronological theology, a step-by-step account of the events of

Jesus' life, death, resurrection, and ascension. Nowhere else in the bible will you find the supposed "facts" that he offers. John bunches up the resurrection of Jesus, his ascension, and the coming of the Holy Spirit upon the disciples all in one brief day. Mark and Matthew make no mention of ascension; they tell only of Jesus' resurrection. And Paul, the first New Testament writer — before Matthew, Mark, Luke, and John — treats the two events, resurrection and ascension, as if they were one and the same.

So, we're not going to get much in the way of factual reliability from those five! But I stress again: it is the *meaning* of what is passed on that is the important thing, not the historical accuracy of it. These scriptures are not history books; they are not biographies; they are faith documents. They are the joyful proclamations of a people who had come to know and believe in Jesus as the way to life, and they used every device at their disposal to make that story heard and loved by all.

But there's a message in these ascension accounts and references: we who have heard and accepted Jesus as the ultimate life-giver, the very word of God, are called, not only to believe, but to imitate! We are to carry on what he began, a ministry of love, healing, forgiveness, and peacemaking. We are to act, not depending on our limited human resources alone, but on the Spirit whom he would share with us always. His "ascension," even though it may not have been the physical lifting of his living body skyward, implies that he is with God in a total union of the most intense love and that we are here to be Jesus to others by allowing the Spirit to work through us as that same Spirit did through him.

CELEBRATING THE BREAD OF LIFE: EUCHARIST

The character "Sportin' Life" in the Gershwin musical masterpiece *Porgy and Bess* had it right when, with devilish glee in the song, "It Ain't Necessarily So" (whence the title of this book, with a grammatical correction), he cautioned that often what we read in the "Gosp'l" simply "ain't poss'ble!"

But don't get me wrong, please. I am not in any way trivializing or discrediting the bible; I am simply restating the underlying principle that if we refuse to interpret the Holy Scriptures in the broad context of the time, place, and circumstances of their composition, if we don't grant to the authors of the scriptures the same freedom of literary expression with which we speak and write, we reduce the sacred writings to ultimate absurdity and we miss the Spirit's authentic message.

As we are reminded in John's Gospel, it is really impossible for us human beings to communicate without using figures of speech. Jesus calls himself the living bread. We are inclined to say, "Oh, we know what he means. We're not taking his words literally." But that's precisely the point: Jesus is, strictly speaking, no more bread than he is a vine, which he once also called himself, or a spring of water, another name he applied to himself.

Jesus is using metaphors, figures of speech, analogies — call them what you will — and we do understand what he is saying. However, there are countless thousands of Christians who still refuse to trust human beings' ability to interpret correctly. And so they resort, for safety's sake I suppose, to literal interpretation, taking the words in question at their face value.

Anyone who knows anything about the many branches of Christianity today knows that we are in for one big fight, to put it bluntly! Fundamentalists — those who do not allow for any accommodation or "adjustment" in our understanding of the words of the bible — are rapidly gaining in strength and in number, mostly outside the Catholic Church but also, it seems, to a lesser degree, within our church as well. I am urging my fellow Catholics to summon the courage to use their intelligence, their God-given powers of reasoning, their common sense, in their approach to what is called the written word of God.

All of the foregoing is by way of coming to grips with Jesus' graphic references to himself as the bread from heaven, the food that we are to eat and then never die. What are we to make of this? How much of it, if any, are we meant to take literally? We ask again, what is the message?

How often have you seen in the newspapers or on TV coverage of humanitarian efforts to bring life-saving food supplies to the destitute people of war-torn nations? It is not ready-made "meals on wheels" that are delivered; it is most often sacks of wheat flour and corn meal and rice, the equivalent of bread. To hungry, starving people, bread is life. In the poor Hebrew society to which Jesus ministered you can be sure that bread was synonymous with life and survival. We, who sometimes throw out as much as we consume, can find that difficult to understand. Intellectually, we know it is a fact, but emotionally we may not be able to feel it. We may have to struggle prayerfully to grasp what Jesus is saying: that as necessary as food and drink are to life, so is he necessary, absolutely essential, to our deepest well-being.

No matter our state in life, our occupation, our financial situation, or our social standing, we eat and drink of him mostly by absorbing his words and trying to incorporate his values into our lives. We receive him from each other in the course of our ordinary daily encounters. We experience him in our midst when we gather to pray together. He comes to us in sacramental reality in the sacred ritual of Eucharist. Our Creator is not distant or remote. God is with us in an endless variety of ways, but in none more intimately or intensely than in the person of Jesus, the nourishing, healing, life-giving bread of our lives.

BECOMING LIKE JESUS: "OTHER CHRISTS"

It was St. Augustine, sinner-turned-saint, who, more than 1600 years ago, said that when the minister of the Eucharist holds the sacred host in front of the person about to receive it and says, "Body of Christ," that person is not being asked, "Do you appreciate the difference between this and ordinary bread?" Nor is he or she being asked, "Do you believe that this is the real presence of Jesus?" No, St. Augustine said; the question is, "Do you know that *you* are the Body of Christ?" And, when the communicant answers affirmatively, he or she is actually saying, "Yes, I do know that I am the Body of Christ."

For some years now it has pleased me to find in the worshiping congregations that I am privileged to serve more and more persons who say, when I put the host in their hand, "I am" in response to the words "the Body of Christ."

Augustine expanded his excellent insight into Eucharist by putting on the lips of the minister the beautiful admonition, "Then receive more of what you already are."

This is a valid, time-honored, sacred tradition in the Catholic Church. It's really too bad that it strikes some of us as something new while it actually comes from a time very soon after the church's beginning. How did we lose this awareness and the practice that has grown out of it?

Well, it seems that another tradition has dominated for many centuries, a tradition that is based on *adoration* of Jesus, whom we believe to be uniquely present in Eucharist. And so we have customs like

Benediction of the Blessed Sacrament, Forty Hours Devotion, and a variety of bodily gestures made at Mass, all of which are expressions of worship in the presence of divinity.

Among us Catholic Christians there have always been, as there are today, two sides to this issue, not at war with each other, but peacefully coexisting. It is, after all, not a matter of either/or; it is, rather, both/and. Jesus was not given the name "Christ" by Mary and Joseph. "Christ" in Greek, means "anointed," which in turn means "called." The earliest followers of Jesus attached that name to him to express their belief that he was chosen, or called, by God for a special mission among them. The record of his life and ministry shows clearly how he consistently sought and followed the guidance of that Spirit. Christians believe that Jesus is the perfect human embodiment of the Divine Spirit. In imitation of him, we are literally anointed with oil in our Baptism and Confirmation and commissioned to be moved by that Spirit as he was. Therefore, all of us are "alteri Christi," "other Christs."

> *The same divine Creative Spirit that activated Jesus activates us, if we are willing. In that sense above all, I should think, are we "other Christs."*

The same divine Creative Spirit that activated Jesus activates us, if we are willing. In that sense above all, I should think, are we "other Christs."

But common to both of these parallel historical strains is the notion of feeding: eating, drinking – spiritual nourishment. After all, the setting has everything to do with dining, and we relate what we do in that setting to Jesus' Last Supper. We stand or sit or kneel around a table. A plate, a cup, and various other pitchers and bowls are the primary appurtenances that we use. We gather together in one place, we converse, we sing and pray, we tell and hear stories old and new; we eat and drink after reaching out to those around us with a gesture of peace and love. It does seem that what we are doing is less an act of adoration than it is a ritual of preparation for further and more dedicated living in our world in the very same Spirit of love and generosity that motivated and energized Jesus, whose life-giving, saving ministry we carry on.

The feast of Corpus Christi is an annual celebration of the sacramental presence of Jesus in Eucharist. People in every nation in the world carry the sacrament in festive processions, and worshipers along the way kneel and bow and strike their breasts. At the deepest, most fundamental level of conviction and faith, they are acknowledging with gratitude and humility the presence and action of God, the Creative Spirit, in our world. And then there are others who will eat the sacred bread and drink from the holy cup quietly, gratefully acknowledging that in Baptism and Confirmation they were anointed and became "christos" people and in their celebration of Eucharist pledge themselves again to be faithful to what that means.

ORIGINAL SIN?

We grow accustomed to rash promises and empty assurances. We pacify one another by stating as fact what we know deep down is really only a hope or a wish. We announce what we'd like to have happen rather than what we intend to do. Most of the time we don't mean any harm; the deception rolls off the tongue carelessly and with little or no serious consideration. And then we get used to decoding each other's messages and making adjustments that will reveal the actual truth. Often we wish that speech would be more direct and dependable; we praise those who are known for the unfailing truth and reliability of what they say. We remark that they speak bluntly or that they don't mince words.

In times past, not all that long ago, this peculiar human characteristic would have been noted under the heading "original sin." We would have regarded it as one of the curses for which we need a savior. Big Daddy, from "Cat on a Hot Tin Roof," would have scornfully called it mendacity. Exposed as we are today to the endless conversation of the entire world, disgusted as we are with its duplicity and dishonesty, we get weary of the whole mess, tired of living in suspicion of so much of what we read and hear, sick of having to examine and select, judge and reject. We think of heaven as that state of being in which, at last, yes always means yes, and no always means no – period!

It's possible to talk to God deceptively, too. Jesus saw that and said that it isn't those who cry out "Lord, Lord!" who enter the Kingdom, but those who do the will of his father. "Say yes," he insisted, "when you mean yes; say no when you mean no. Everything else is from the devil."

And in his crisp parable found at Matthew 21:28-32, he tells of one son who gave a perfect response to his father's order but had no intention of complying, while the other son flat out refused to obey but then repented and did what his father had commanded. Good answer/bad action in one case; bad answer/good action in the other.

Repentance is a process; it's what can happen between the bad answer and the good action. That bad answer can begin very spontaneously, almost thoughtlessly, and can last a long time while the process of thinking things over goes on. Reason and grace shed brighter light, emotions cool and change, vision sharpens, the will begins to bend. Finally repentance has been achieved and a new decision is firmly in place.

I have the impression that many people do not understand this phenomenon, or at least don't recognize it as applying to them. They remember only that their lives were once a No to God, and they can't put that aside. They torture themselves with an endless accusation. But the Spirit of God was in them all along, gradually turning wrong into right, No into Yes. And that is all that matters. The first book of the bible tells of the Spirit of God presiding over the chaos that preceded the formation of the universe; so does that same Spirit hover over their lives – our lives – ever drawing new life in closer union with God.

Hearing the first confessions of little children helps me to recall my own some 75 years ago and how I prepared for it. Armed with a calendar, paper and pen, I sat at the dining room table and calculated the number of sins I had committed since I had attained the use of reason, which, I was carefully taught, occurs when we reach 7 years of age. To my puny mind, that meant that on the morning of my 7th birthday, I awoke suddenly equipped with the use of reason! All my misbehavior up until that pivotal day was only that: misbehavior. But from that birthday on, any such conduct was sin! I reckoned, with a bit of scriptural prompting, that I had sinned at least seven times a day and in at least four major categories: disobedience, fighting, omission of prayers, and disrespectful talk. Even in those pre-electronic calculator days, the number reached something in the neighborhood of a whopping 30,000 sins! Not too bad for a young kid.

And, by the way, I carried into the confessional my list of sins. When the priest, a very kind and gentle man, opened the shutter to greet me and hear my confession, he saw gleaming in the darkness my list of sins carefully inscribed on a sheet of white paper. He said, "What is that you're holding, sonny?" I said, "My sins!" He said, "You can hand it to me; you won't need it." A big arm reached over from his booth to mine and took my sins away!

Well, as absurd and funny as all that sounds, so is it equally absurd that we should continue to think of our "first parents," as we call the mythical Adam and Eve, as instantly invested with the use of human reason, capable of both virtue and vice. Since we now accept the theory of evolution as more than merely a theory but rather as the fundamental fact of the origin and history of the human race, it makes no more sense for us to say that our most distant ancestors jumped from non-rational to rational life, from purely animal to basically human life, than it does to say that we wake up on our 7th birthday with the newly-bestowed power to reason and to make moral judgments for which we are accountable.

Yet, that's what we believed until too recently. We believed that human evil came into existence in a moment through a selfish decision of a brand new, first of his kind, human being and his companion. We have called ourselves ever since a "fallen race," and our whole Christian theology is based on that totally unscientific, unhistorical notion.

St. Paul believed that. What other choice did he have? He writes that death entered the world through the sin of one man. Paul could not have known about the lives or the deaths of countless millions of animals and prehistoric humans over millions of years on earth long before the human race emerged. Even though his facts are dead wrong, he makes the statement in order to set up a comparison, namely, that the healing, restorative, life-giving work of Jesus is overwhelmingly greater than all the sins of the human race as represented in that one, presumed "original" sin of the fictional Adam.

Stumbling down the corridors of history for eons, we humans are nonetheless not a fallen race; we are a *developing* race and still are that. We have emerged from lower forms of life through a process too complex and too marvelous for us to appreciate fully. Like 2, 3 and 6 year-olds on their way to moral responsibility, our ancestors struggled and experimented and made countless errors in their efforts to achieve maturity. The struggle goes on today and is unconditionally warranted, as we know from the sinfulness, selfishness, and violence of our present world. We've come a long way, but we have a long way to go.

No more than the 7-year-old has reached the full use of reason have we as a race achieved as yet our destiny as completely *human* beings, as persons created in the image of God. We are still in the process of development. Who can predict what we will be a half million years from now? It seems beyond question that our race will look back and find us to be as primitive as we today regard prehistoric humans to have been. We can expect that distant successors will live in a totally nonviolent society, a gentle, peaceful, and loving society formed by the teachings and example of Jesus. We can envision them in an updated Garden of Eden, not the imaginary one we have mistakenly thought we came from, but the one toward which we are progressing, even in difficult and dangerous times.

The lesson here, it seems to me, is that we are blessed to have come into existence and to have not only our natural instinct to live and to live well, but also the tremendous advantage of the leadership and abiding presence of Jesus. He directs us unerringly to become what we have been created to be.

The ancient biblical story tells us the first humans, whom it named Adam and Eve, were not faithful to the God who created them and, because of their sinful disobedience, they were excluded from the Garden of Eden. From that time on, instead of their carefree life of unmitigated joy, they were condemned to suffer the hardships of the world as we know it still today. They were also punished by being denied the presence of God both in this life and beyond death.

So serious was their transgression that it infected their very nature, which meant that they would inevitably pass on to future generations the guilt and shame of their sin — the original sin. And so all of us, the story had us believe, are born in a tainted condition, bearing the sin that we did not ourselves commit but that our progenitors, our "first parents," as we call them, committed.

But think about it: the "immaculate" conception of Mary has meaning only in the context of the biblical account of creation. Take away the mythical Adam and Eve, the talking snake, the tree of good and evil, and all its other impossible ramifications, and how can we then speak about the universal transmission of an "original sin" of two mythical persons and the privilege of immunity or exception granted to Mary?

So, if one takes literally this ancient story of the creation of the world, and the fall from grace by the first two human beings, and the passing along of original sin, the doctrine of the Immaculate Conception makes perfect sense. But if one is persuaded instead by the overwhelming evidence available in our day that the universe has been in evolution for billions of years, and that we humans were not created as we see ourselves today but rather have evolved through a long, long process of development; and that we are therefore not a fallen race but an evolving race; and that we are born, not in the guilt of someone else's sin but into the sin of an unfaithful human race, an often violent and loveless world; what then can we say about the Immaculate Conception? What does it signify?

What we can say is that, based on the absence of scientific knowledge at their time in history, our ancestors used whatever was available to them to celebrate and to honor the great woman who gave birth to Jesus and nurtured him in preparation for the task of his life. Their cosmology, their view of the universe, how it began and how it progressed over the centuries, was completely incorrect and devoid of fact. It was an ancient myth and understandably infantile. Recall again that 15 centuries had yet to elapse from Jesus' time before it would be discovered that the earth, spherical in shape, revolves around the sun; and that the cause of rain is the process of evaporation and condensation; and that the union of sperm and egg is the essence of conception; and on and on and on. They knew nothing about any of that.

In a scientific vacuum our predecessors spoke of the holy ones, especially Mary and Jesus, praising and honoring them in the loftiest terms they could summon, unaware that many of their accolades were based on factual error.

We do not dismiss or ridicule them. As we do, they did the best they could with what they had at their disposal. Instead, we must get to the heart and intent of their acclamations.

To attribute "Immaculate Conception" to Mary is simply to say, at rock bottom, that she was an extraordinarily cooperative instrument of the Spirit of God, "marked out," as it were, from her earliest days for a life of service to our race. That life was guided by the Holy Spirit, whose active presence she was always supremely conscious of and whose direction she unfailingly sought and eagerly accepted, no matter the personal cost to herself.

And so, as we respectfully say the traditional words our liturgical books provide for us, we are thereby honoring the sincerity and the deep faith of our forebears. We do this even though we are aware of what they could not have known in their time, and we join with them in praising and thanking the holy mother of Jesus.

MARY

A priest friend of mine told me once that he'd rather prepare 100 Sunday homilies than prepare just one for Mary! I share his sentiments.

To begin with, how could countless thousands of books, poems, prayers, litanies, plays, etc. be written about a person of whom so little is actually known? What part — major, obviously — has popular devotion played in the production of this flood of pious literature?

When a person or an event seems larger than life, we humans resort to poetry and fable, hyperbole and creative imagination, symbolism and figurative speech in our attempt to express what is ultimately inexpressible.

Think of the made-up stories concerning or attributed to the beloved Pope St. John XXIII. We hardly care whether they are fact or fiction; we simply appreciate them because they provide insight into the character of this great figure.

Or George Washington and the cherry tree tale.

How about Moses and the parting of the Reed Sea, commonly mistaken for the Red Sea in popular culture? (Cecil B. DeMille made it look like a million tons of Jell-O!)

Scale the issue down and consider the gross exaggerations with which we regularly express our emotional reactions. For example, "My heart sank!" If my heart really sank, I should be in a morgue, or at least an emergency room. But the factually untrue words handily make the point that I was stunned or disappointed or whatever.

And so it is with our efforts and our need to express, to celebrate, and to share our experiences of the God who lives within and among us. We resort to the most colorful, concrete, descriptive, imaginative images we can conceive of in order to articulate as well as we can what we know we cannot fully grasp.

Examples:

* How better to say that the power of God was uniquely active and accessible in Jesus than to picture him as walking on water?

* How could we miss the assertion that Jesus was fully human when we are given a dramatic account of his battling with the devil – his being tempted to exercise power selfishly, as we all are?

* Can anyone fail to recognize that the story of Jesus having fed some 5,000 persons with only a handful of food at his disposal was really about, on one level, generous love and on another the Eucharist?

This is all the language and the imagery of poetry and creative storytelling, a language that all cultures, all peoples of all time can understand. It is perfect for the handing down of what we call the Word of God!

So too with the words, "Immaculate Conception." We analyzed this description of Mary when we looked at the concept of Original Sin. We discovered that the words are based on the notion that all human beings are born with a sin that they have inherited from Adam and Eve, the "first human beings" but that Mary, because she was to be the mother of Jesus, savior of the world, was exempted from that inevitability and was born instead in the perfection of absolute sinlessness, a purity that would endure throughout her life and would even transform what should have been her natural death into assumption into heaven.

What do we do with such a longstanding belief when we today know that human beings were not created in our present form but are rather the current result of a long, long, beautiful process called evolution? If, in that context, there were no Adam and Eve, no Garden of Eden, no tempting snake, no angry and punishing God, and so forth, what are we celebrating under the title "Mary's Immaculate Conception"?

Some suggestions:

* Mary was her own person and chose her own destiny by assenting to what she discerned was the direction of the Spirit within her, aware also that her yes would cost her dearly.

* Mary's humble life of faith had an enormous effect on the development of the human race and in particular on the status of women.

* Mary had a deeply personal relationship with God and asked to be guided in all things by the Creative Spirit.

* Mary chose good over evil, love over hatred, nonviolence over revenge.

* Mary trusted in the loving and powerful presence of God even when there was no reason to trust and when she saw her beloved son horribly and unjustly crucified.

* Mary now and forever lives in the most intimate union with God as visible to her, having lived her earthly life in uncompromised union with the invisible God.

Once again, the story is for our benefit: what happened to Mary we also are destined to experience in our own unique ways! What more do we need in order to endure with lively hope the trials of our human lives?

I reached the point of no return on December 8, 1999, the feast of the Immaculate Conception of the Blessed Virgin Mary, when I knew that I believed in neither the Immaculate Conception nor the virginity of Mary. This was not a sudden, unpremeditated act of apostasy; I had not been spiritually deluded and ravaged by some lurking evil spirit catching me in a moment of weakness and luring me into the exhilaration of emancipation from doctrinal servitude.

No, I had been thinking along those lines for many years, while cautiously, provisionally hinting at new interpretations of the totality of Christianity – boldly, unreservedly to trusted friends and soul mates; more guardedly to congregations, retreatants, audiences in general. I was always testing the climate of acceptance or resistance and always finding some who understood what was being said and what was being hinted at, and who welcomed the long-awaited opportunity to say that they agreed. I recall fondly the beautiful woman in an affluent town in New York State who came up to me at the close of a retreat I had given, her eyes glistening with tears, her hands reaching out to grasp mine, and said, "I am 86 years old, a lifelong Catholic, and I have waited all my life to hear what I heard today."

What did she, what did they, hear? Let's go back to the beginning of this apologia and say that on that commemoration of the Immaculate Conception, they heard this:

I ask your complete and undistracted attention to what I am about to say to you. To some, perhaps to many, it may sound more than a little disturbing at first; to some it will come as good and welcome and long-awaited news. But to all, I hope, this message, more than any other you have heard on a feast of Our Lady, will bring peace and joy. So, let us walk through this together, asking the Spirit of Wisdom to enlighten us.

In Jesus' time, and for many centuries beyond his day, in those pre-scientific times when human understanding of the universe was hardly distinguishable from that of a small child, it was universally thought that the whole of the new human being, the baby in the mother's womb, came from the father. The mother contributed only space and warmth and nutrition and security – but nothing of the substance of the child. After all, you could see the semen which the male deposited in the female body; how could its meaning and function be any different from that of the seed which the farmer places in the womb of the ground? From within the female, there was nothing to see but occasional blood. Conclusion: whatever this child will be is contained seminally in the father's contribution. The mother is but the holding place, the incubator, the oven in which the finished product is processed.

Move ahead with me now, beyond what the church assures us are the fables of the Christmas story, invented and written decades after the actual birth of Jesus, and consider those years after Jesus' death and resurrection, when his followers were saying that he was God. (Recall that he himself never said that, although we are accustomed to interpreting some of his statements as meaning precisely that. Each of those statements has been decisively treated by countless competent theologians who do not view them as unequivocal assertions of his divinity, but rather as predications that can be made of all persons in general and of certain prominent persons in particular.)

93

If Jesus is God, then it must be that his father is God, since the whole person, in the primitive understanding of these people, comes only from the father. Hence, the "Virgin Birth": Mary conceived, not through the participation of a male human being in normal sexual intercourse (How can a human being be the father of God?), but by having the seed that would become Jesus placed in her womb by the very Spirit of God – God is the progenitor, the only generative parent of Jesus.

All's well thus far. But wait! Doesn't a child frequently, almost always, resemble its mother as well as its father? The father is tall and has black hair; the child grows to be quite short and to have red hair – just like the mother. The child has its mother's placid disposition and sense of humor, neither of which is found in the father or in his original family. How to explain this?

Easily. Nine months of such intimacy with the mother, nine months of living on her blood, nine months of being closer to her heart than her own limbs are, has to have some effect. Of course her characteristics, both physical and spiritual, inevitably must rub off on the child. No great mystery here.

Yet there is still a dilemma. Every human being is imperfect, faulted, inclined toward selfishness and sin. Even the most virtuous of us is not without such shame. How can it be, then, that a God-become-human-being can have, in his embryonic formation, anything of human imperfection, any tiniest influence of sin in his gestation? It cannot be. On the contrary, what must be is that this one human being, this woman whose womb has harbored the embryonic Jesus, must herself be absolutely perfect, with not the slightest trace of or connection with sin in her. In a word, she must be entirely free from "original sin." She must be the human race's singular exception to the universal rule of our tainted conception and birth. In other words, she was immaculately conceived!

94

What I am telling you is that many sincere and loyal Catholics, both scholars and ordinary folk like ourselves, are taking another and critical look at this popular belief and are concluding that, on the one hand it was an admirable attempt to grapple with the mystery of who and what Jesus really is, but on the other hand is a completely false notion because it is founded on a scientific absurdity. It is no different a case, they insist, from that of the origin of the world as we find it described in the Book of Genesis and as we are understanding it more and more clearly through the investigations of scientists. In other words, there is no more reason for us to accept the idea of Mary's preservation from a universal state of sin presumed to be passed on genetically to every human being than there is for us to believe that God created the universe in six days and rested on the seventh.

Doesn't that suggest an interesting state of affairs? Ask the same set of two questions twice and see what happens. Ask, "Do you believe in God as creator of the universe?" Answer: "Yes." Ask, "Do you believe that the creation happened as we read about it in the Book of Genesis?" Answer: "No, of course not. That's a pre-scientific attempt at explaining something that human beings did not at that time have the means to comprehend. After all, they didn't even understand something as elementary as evaporation and condensation, much less the original creation: they thought that when it rained God had opened the portholes in the dome above the sky to let the waters pour through!"

Good!

Now try those same questions in a New Testament setting. Ask, "Do you believe in Jesus of Nazareth, his life of preaching and healing, his ministry to the poor and needy, his ministry of hope and love and universal acceptance? Do you believe that after his death he lived again and continues to live both in the eternal life of God and in unfailing union with us?" Answer: "Indeed I do." Question: "Do you believe that all the events of Jesus' life happened exactly as they are told to us in the writings we call the New Testament?"

Ah-ha! The response is very different this time! Many will be inclined to say a firm and unquestioning yes. Some fewer will admit to doubts and reservations. A few, but an apparently growing number, will say no. And those last will express their understanding that the writers of the New Testament were virtually as unscientific as their ancestors of several centuries before and that everything they wrote was conditioned by a worldview that we know now to be false. And they are convinced, this last group of thinkers, that we must forever re-interpret Jesus against the background of more realistic premises as these come to light in contemporary research.

So why do we worship on the Feast of the Immaculate Conception? We simply honor a good human being, a woman by the name of Mary, who became involved in a life that would make a profound difference in the lives of many. Her son's journey and theirs together progressed from day to day, without reassuring angels or voices to direct and console, she stayed with the whole confusing, demanding, often terrifying thing, giving generously, sacrificially even when she was not at all sure of the purpose or what return could reasonably be anticipated. Her faith in the loving and powerful presence of an unseen, unheard God was her strength, her wisdom, and her lifeline.

It is no different for us. We are gift to each other as Mary is gift to us all. As a beloved seminary priest-teacher of mine told us 60 years ago, what Divine Wisdom did with her, Divine Wisdom is doing with each of us. Some things in life really don't change: we suffer, we rejoice; we fail, we succeed; we live, we die. Mary is one of our best guides, among our chief inspirations. Her relationship to Jesus is certainly unique, but it is not exclusive. We are meant to enjoy the same, albeit in a somewhat different manner: she was his mother; we are his brothers and sisters.

During its very short run on Broadway, I saw the one-person play, "*The Testament of Mary*." I wish it could be seen by all. It's an entirely different look at the mother of Jesus: she's not the unflappable, plastic figure we have known from our infancy. She doesn't glide smilingly above the uncertainties and horrors of real life, impeccably dressed in blue, her unsullied hands reaching out to welcome the afflicted.

Not this Mary. Quite the opposite: in crude peasant attire we find her in her hovel, angry, disappointed, fearful. She worries about this strange son of hers, who is both idolized and demonized by the crowds. She suspects that his dangerous life will end in his execution and wishes that he had chosen another, safer path. She calls his band of closest associates "misfits" and holds them in suspicion. And when the final curtain comes down, we feel the pain of her lament as she wonders aloud whether it was all worth what it cost her and him — and them all —or not.

The Irish author of the play, Colm Toibin, helps us to view Mary much more realistically than we are accustomed to doing. As I've already observed, when a person or an event seems larger than life, we humans resort to poetry and fable, hyperbole and creative imagination, symbolism and figurative speech in our attempt to express it, realizing that it is ultimately inexpressible. We have done that with our image of Mary, the mother of Jesus, perhaps more than with any other person. From that somewhat altered vantage point, what can we make of the feast of the Assumption of Mary "into heaven" when even Pope St. John Paul II, conservative theologian that he was, taught clearly and emphatically that there is no such place as heaven? Heaven is not, he said, a geographic location — like New York or the South Pole, we might add. It is rather a personal state of being. It is something that happens within the human being at the time of death – in St. Paul's words, a lifting of the veil through which we see God only dimly and darkly in this world. But with the transformation that takes place in us, with the removal of that veil, we see God directly in what we learned as children is the Beatific Vision.

Let me repeat: the Assumption of Mary proclaims that during her earthly life her awareness of the presence and love and power of God was so keen and so constant, even when there was no clear and obvious reason to trust, she *did* trust in the unseen God. Because of her unfailing trust, it is a foregone conclusion that beyond her death, without purification of any kind, she was totally united with her Creator. A popular way of saying this is that she was "assumed into heaven."

FAITH HOPE AND MIRACLES

T he apostles asked Jesus to increase their faith.

Every once in a while I make myself watch one or another of the abundant television preachers with their elaborate sets, their dramatic styles, and their theatrical presentations. What I've discovered is that there is one dominant message common to virtually all of them: If you believe strongly enough, if you say the right prayers, if you demonstrate your sincerity with a hefty money donation, you can obtain anything you want; you can conquer or eliminate anything that disturbs you or causes you pain.

Want a million dollars? Then follow the formula. Hoping to overcome your cancer? Get out of debt? Find the perfect mate? The answer is the same.

Faith, these preachers would have us understand, is a belief in God so uncompromised that it enables you to control everything in your life. Believe intensely enough and there isn't anything that will master you, there isn't anything you can't either obtain or vanquish.

I don't believe that, and I hope you don't either.

Consider, by way of contrast, the following three vignettes:

One: A priest friend of mine, much younger than I, has become blind in one eye and is struggling to maintain some vision in the other. I dared to ask him how he is dealing with the prospect of complete blindness. He replied with a short burst of laughter, then said, "If it happens, it happens. But the God who brought me this far in life will have no problem, I'm sure, taking me the rest of the way, whether I'm sighted or not."

That's genuine faith! He's not asking 600 people to make novenas and say rosaries in petition for a physical miracle; he neither expects nor requests one. He's simply confident that in good times and in bad our gentle, loving God is with us constantly to strengthen and sustain us.

Two: I know a married couple whose baby was born with very serious abnormalities, both mental and physical. The physician immediately advised them not to take the baby home but to put her in an institution where she would receive appropriate care. She would be too much for them to handle without disastrous consequences to themselves and their other children, he said. But a wise and inspired priest counseled instead, "Take her home and love and care for her. She'll be the joy of your life." I know the family well enough to tell you that she has become exactly that.

That's genuine faith. They weren't demanding the total reconstruction of their baby's body and brain, but only the grace to trust in the empowering presence of a loving God.

Three: I come from an alcoholic home. For 35 years I prayed that my father would overcome the terrible disease and be always the good and loving man he was in sobriety. That recovery never occurred. The miracle my family and I so ardently sought through prayer was not granted; however, there was another one: out of that tortured family, with all its pain and all its love, came four pretty good persons, of whom I am the eldest, who have lived basically happy, productive lives — not in *spite* of our shared cross, but in some ways *because* of it, or at least *with* it.

I think we learned what true faith is and what it accomplishes in our lives.

> *True faith is a relationship with God so intimate, so*
> *firm, that even when uncontrollable things happen*
> *to us, we are not dehumanized, we are not denied our*
> *human destiny.*

What is a miracle? Not necessarily something spectacular or supernatural. A miracle is something in which we see the divine power, divine presence, divine love – like the sight of a beautiful newborn baby. That is the faith we can hope the apostles were asking for, simply the constant awareness of the presence of a loving, caring God. It's one of those either-you've-got-it-or-you-haven't-got-it things. Jesus had it to the full and urged us to cultivate, and ask for, the same sensitivity.

At virtually every marriage at which I officiate, I end with the words of the Jewish/American musical playwright, Alan Jay Lerner: "I don't believe in miracles; I've seen too many of them." This curious statement requires a bit of analysis: we can't believe in what we see; we *know* what we see. We believe in what we can't see and accept it on the testimony of others. Religious faith is the acceptance of unseen truth on the testimony of God. Mr. Lerner was saying, I don't have to believe anymore; I *know* now – there have been so many miracles in my life.

The basic "miracle" of faith is the unyielding awareness of the intimate presence of our loving Creator.

In 2003 the safe return of the kidnapped Elizabeth Smart to her family was wonderful news for everyone; we all shared the relief and joy and gratitude of her family when we saw them over and over on TV with their beautiful daughter.

101

Please don't think me a Scrooge if I point out one aspect of this happy conclusion that I find very disturbing: Several persons, including members of Elizabeth's family said that her rescue was a "miracle of God" granted in response to the prayers of people around the world. I just can't accept that; I think it is a false conclusion that can be reached only by persons who cling to the primitive notion of a God who sits in some super-managerial position, dispensing both favors and punishments according to who-knows-what criteria.

This is anthropomorphism at its most basic level: attributing to God the ways and the characteristics of human beings. It is a popular concept, unfortunately corroborated by all the words found in the Scriptures that are attributed directly to God, words written by human beings like ourselves and from which we get the idea of a bearded Charlton Heston somewhere above the clouds.

I have not the dimmest hope that I can convince even one fundamentalist Christian, Catholic or Protestant, that such an interpretation of God is passé and false, but I do want to confirm what I believe to be the right thinking of you who have come to see that God is the Creative Spirit that lives at the core of all that exists throughout the universe. God is the love that calls creation into being and sustains it. God is the "Ground of All Being." God does not watch and manage from some distant place; rather, God experiences existence in every form, at all times and in all places.

Elizabeth Smart was identified and rescued because of the hard, patient, often discouraging work of thousands of caring persons, beginning with those in law enforcement. God, I say again, experienced with them everything they went through, including the discouragement and near despair. It was their intelligence, their love and concern – all of it sustained by the presence of the Spirit of God – that brought about the final resolution.

If that were not the truth, what could we ever say about those countless children and adults around the globe and in our own country who have never been found and may never be? They are prayed for also. Does God play favorites? Can God be swayed or convinced or won over by the most appealing prayers or by the volume of prayers? Does God's interest wax and wane? Is God moody and capricious? Are these kidnappings that never end, or that end in murder, arranged by God as a way to punish or to instruct or to test?

Foolish, meaningless questions, all based on an idea of God that primitive, even prehistoric, humans concocted because they had no other way to think about the invisible reality we name God. But we know now — we cannot say it often enough — that we are not a fallen species, but a developing species. We know now that the universe is in process of an evolution that spans billions of years. We see now that God is the Spirit whose life and love are expressed in that fantastic, marvelous, exciting process!

When Abraham raised his dagger, was he ready to slaughter his beloved son as an act of obedience to God? Pure, sacred fiction! A timeless fable. An ingenious story containing little if any historical fact, but carrying the truth of an essential lesson for life: never abandon faith in God's sustaining presence, no matter how absent God may seem, how inactive or uncaring; no matter how contradictory, hopeless, and confusing the situation at hand may be. God is there, in love and in power, and, whatever the final outcome will be, the love of God will provide strength and support and will triumph in the end.

Elizabeth Smart, like so many other kidnapped persons, might never have been found. Had the nine month nightmare gone on for the rest of her life, God would have remained present to everyone involved, not producing "miracles" as we are conditioned to think of them, but supplying a context of love far surpassing our limited human capacity, a nurturing love to which faith is the connecting link. That's miracle enough for me.

CHAPTER THREE

When Life Happens...

TRAGEDIES AND TRIUMPHS

I vividly recall reading in the *New York Times* a sickening article about the torture and murder of a two-year-old child by her parents. I remember choosing not to finish the piece, which already had saddened me and caused me to brood over how such things can happen.

Instinctively I resorted to my Christian faith, to the beliefs I've lived with all my life, which told me that the child was now completely happy in eternal union with her Creator. The horror was over and would never return; she lives now in the fullness of light and love, I kept telling myself.

But I also instantly recognized the trap, the pitfall, which lurks in that kind of religious thinking, valid and commendable though it is. It's this: we can easily move from it to assuming that what happens here on earth isn't really all that important, not if there's a heaven waiting for us all. And so we put all our eggs in the basket of eternity and regard the things of earth as less and less valuable or worthy of our time and effort. We tell ourselves that all that really matters is that we work at qualifying for the prize that awaits us in the Great Beyond, what unbelievers call Pie in the Sky – and they're not entirely wrong.

I knew a misguided young nun years ago who lived on a strict subsistence diet, obviously severely malnourished. Apparently she was communicating to God that she cared nothing about this world and its pleasures and that her sole delight was in a purely spiritual relationship with God in anticipation of her death and the heavenly life that would follow. To my way of thinking, that's a good example of how absurd Christian religiosity and piety can become.

So, yes, we have the tremendous advantage of believing that, no matter how our lives here on earth should turn out, there will be for each and all of us complete happiness in our union with God after our death. However, that ought not to be our first concern: that realm belongs to the Creator alone. Our concern must be for this present life, God's here and now gift to us, the only life we know by direct experience.

That means we must do whatever we can in our small sphere of influence to prevent human suffering of any kind in any place at any time. That blessed afterlife is assured us all, but it's for us to create the humane conditions in which no parents would ever resort to murdering their child, no soldier ever go to war, no person be forced to live on the street or eat out of garbage cans. We must not say or imply to such persons, "Be patient with your present lot and just remember that there's a heaven waiting to receive you."

But, in effect, that is what we do when we lose consciousness of our personal responsibility for the quality of life on Planet Earth for all its inhabitants. Father Roger Karban, the eminent and down-to-earth Scripture scholar whom I often quote, once remarked that Jesus never encouraged his followers to shun the world and find blissful solitude in a cloistered convent or monastery, something he could have chosen for himself but did not. Jesus appears to have taken for granted that they would live his teachings and follow his example in the ordinary circumstances of their everyday lives – in the stresses of their work, the tensions and worries of their homes and families, their struggles with health and finances, and so on. He didn't ask them to be different from other people by splitting off from them but, as he so simply put it, by staying awake.[12] Awake to what? Awake to the active, loving presence of God in and among them. And why? Because to remain aware of that mysterious, real presence and to offer themselves as instruments of God's love among the people is to achieve the very changes that a hurting world desperately needs and doesn't know how to acquire.

How else but in those terms can we explain a Pope St. John XXIII or a Martin Luther King, Jr. or a Sister Ita Ford, M.M. or (you add to the names). They were constantly awake to, alert to, the divine presence within and around them and by their yes to it were empowered to act in extraordinarily life-giving ways.

At the core of the Gospel message, I think, is Jesus' expectation that, in the particular circumstances of our individual lives, we would stay awake and responsive to the promptings of the Divine Spirit.

It can't be denied that Jesus' words, "This happened so that the works of God might be displayed in him" (John 9:3), do say that God caused the man to be born blind for a purpose; however, words must always be understood in their context. For example, the two words "Kill him!" mean one thing in the carrying out of a murder, but they mean something very different when shouted by an excited fan at a ball game or a prize fight. Words are always conditioned by the situation in which they are uttered. Jesus' words are no exception.

So, what is the context that can reveal to us the true meaning of these words of Jesus? It is simply this: In Jesus' day religious people thought that everything that happens on this earth is caused directly by the all-powerful God. It was God who caused your baby to be conceived and born and your enemy to be killed; it was God who brought up the crops in season and sent angels to the dome of the sky to open portals for rain to fall on the earth; it was God who raised the sun in the east every morning and retired it in the west at night. (Interesting, isn't it, that we still pray to God asking for favorable changes in the weather: old habits die very slowly!) It is God who puts thoughts in human beings' minds and gives them the words to speak. A very managerial God indeed!

It was perfectly consistent, then, with the thinking of his day that Jesus should say that God caused the man to be blind so that he, Jesus, could demonstrate his divine power by healing the man and thus lead people to believe in him as the word of God.

But we have grown past such thinking. We know that things happen in this world for a variety of reasons, mostly because humans make them happen, or nature does, but often also purely by chance or by accident. If a medical doctor of today could go back in time and examine that blind man and his history, that doctor could likely identify the chain of events that resulted in his congenital blindness. And we would say that the man's condition is a pure tragedy, but that Jesus will use it to bring about even greater good than the restoration of a person's sight.

The late Protestant minister, William Sloane Coffin, lost his 24-year-old son to drowning when the young man's car accidentally went off a

Boston wharf and sank to the bottom of the bay. Sympathizers spoke of the mysterious will of God, something, the grieving father said, that infuriated him. He wrote, "The one thing that should never be said when someone dies is 'It is the will of God.' Never do we know enough to say that…when the waves closed over the sinking car, God's heart was the first of all hearts to break."[13] I think Rev. Coffin had it right. And consider the good that has come from that tragic, accidental death, even just through the helpful reflections of a faithful father.

This gospel episode concerning the cure of a blind person is not primarily about physical healing or even about Jesus as a healer; it is about willful spiritual blindness, our tendency to ignore the light that Jesus is for us – the "light of the world" we call him, even when we turn blind eyes to him.

I like that bumper sticker that comes from Alcoholics Anonymous: "Keep It Simple." We do have a way of complicating things unnecessarily, including Jesus' words of wisdom.

A flyer was put out a few years ago announcing the coming talk of a popular theologian, a priest whom I very much respect. The presentation was being given a distance from my home and, much to my regret, I was not able to go to it. The mailed promo included the title of the talk and beneath it a subtitle which read, "Teachings of Jesus That We've Never Taken Seriously." What a truth that points to! We've obscured some of the most important parts of his message by cluttering them up with too many words, distinctions, and laws. He said he is the light of the world, which suggests to me that every problem, every uncertainty, every fear, every prospect in my life will benefit by exposure to him.

A TANGLE OF WITS

Would that it were so simple! You get a message from God, often through a divinely appointed individual, and all you have to do is listen and obey. Whenever I hear anything like that, I recall the words attributed to St. Thomas More, once Chancellor of England, who was put to death by his former friend King Henry VIII for refusing to acknowledge Henry as the head of the church in England. Thomas is reported to have said, while awaiting his execution in the Tower of London, that while all other creatures are directed by instinct — programmed, as it were, by nature — it is the high destiny of us human beings to figure out life's course in the "tangle of our wits." I've always loved that term – the tangle of our wits.

We are constantly hearing from self-appointed "prophets" who claim to speak for God and who tell us that they have been anointed to be carriers and spokespersons for the living God. They pass on to us, they say, what God has commanded them to tell us. My response is "Absurd!"

The truth is too obvious for us to fall into such a trap. The truth is that, unlike our fellow creatures of the animal kingdom, we have been gifted with the powers of observation, judgment and free will. Because of that, we humans have the responsibility of discernment, that process of intellectual analysis by which we can and must decide on what is right and what is wrong, what is to be done and what is to be avoided. Our Christian belief is that we are not left alone and unaided in that often difficult process; rather, that those gifts of observation, judgment and free will also enable us to know that the Creative Spirit lives and acts within us, enhancing our natural wisdom and increasing our power for good. Your dog, your cat, or your parakeet cannot experience that; only you can.

Jesus is the supreme prophet, the very Word of God. Yet, to many of the most important and vexing issues of our day he has spoken little or nothing. So we come to discover what is right, not by a simplistic appeal to the bible, but by the delicate, difficult, frequently lengthy process of discernment. It demands of us that we be faithful to our tradition, that we understand as best we can the mind and the message of Jesus, that we be eager to receive the light of what may indeed be God's truth from whatever immediate source it happens to come, and then we pray earnestly and humbly.

Against that background, what do we do with that disquieting passage of St. Paul's First Letter to the Corinthians (chapter 7, verses 32-35) in which he is encouraging unmarried persons to remain unmarried so that they can devote more of their time and energy to deepening their devotion to God through their following of Jesus? It certainly gives the impression that Paul is ranking at least the two states of life — singlehood and marriage — and concluding that being single is a holier way of life than being married. I can't resist admitting my strong feeling that Paul is displaying a rather jaundiced view of marriage, which we regard as a sacrament, a source of grace to the couple and to all whom their lives touch. And I can't refrain from suspecting that Paul was mightily influenced — biased, I'd say — by his conviction that the world was about to end as the Kingdom of God, following the death and resurrection of Jesus and within Paul's own lifetime, was moving in to take its place on Planet Earth. Against that background, Paul seems to be asking, why think of anything regarding the future except the Final Coming of the triumphant Lord Jesus that is about to take place momentarily? So this is one of those passages from the powerful writings of Paul which have led to false conclusions down through the ages: in this case, that the single life is spiritually superior to the married life. That is simply not so. To say yes to whatever one's conscience leads one to select as a worthy lifestyle is an admirable and holy choice. There is no rank ordering among the various states of life; there is no superior or inferior among them. To be a priest, for example, is not in itself a more saintly choice than to be a married person or a single person or a religious. Marriage is not a compromise, a concession to human weakness. One does not ever have to choose between loving another person and loving God, because to love another is precisely to love God. To love another in Christian marriage is to live a sacramental life, a life in and with Jesus.

We are still emerging from an era in which we accepted without question everything that was handed down to us. It's good news, I would say, it's comforting and encouraging, to discover that even great saints like Paul had their human limitations and prejudices — hang-ups we might call them today — and that the Holy Spirit continues to work in and with us, refining and clarifying the Word of God more fully with each succeeding generation.

ANSWERED PRAYERS

A Methodist minister was counseling two young children whose mother was gravely ill and thought to be dying. He urged them to pray and to trust in God. Raised in a good Christian home, the children eagerly accepted his advice and continued to pray, as they had been doing for a long time, but with increased hope based on his assurance.

Weeks went by, during which time the illness became a desperate struggle for survival and ended in her death. Around the time of the funeral, the article from which I got this story went on to say, the grieving children said to the pastor, "We thought that if we prayed faithfully God would make Mommy well, but God didn't do that. God let her die." The story ended with the pastor's reply: "No, only her body died. God made your mother so well that this world wasn't good enough for her anymore. Now she is living with God, and when that happens to you someday, you will be with her again and forever."

That account impressed me deeply; however, I repeat it with both respect and caution. It contains an important truth; but at the same time, just as in the case of the scriptures, it has to be interpreted with care. It suggests and reinforces the notion that God manages our lives, decrees when we are born and when we die and everything in between. More and more of us find such a conviction no longer possible. Yet, in the minister's words about God making the woman so well that this earthly existence was no longer good enough for her, we recognize the phenomenon of transformation – a radical change in the person that moves her from one level of existence to another. And that's about as good a definition of the spiritual aspect of death as we can come up with. We believe that is what happens in our biological death: the cloud that surrounds and permeates our entire being here on earth is lifted, enabling us to see all things as God sees them, even to see God as we cannot in this life. This is the transformation that we call heaven.

So again, even though the good pastor's words are not to be taken literally, that is to say, God was not engineering the progress of the fatal disease, his words do express in a very attractive and appealing way a fundamental truth at the core of our faith, namely, that we do pass over from life to life in death, a life that is pure light, grace, peace, love, and joy.

Now consider Jesus' words: "Ask anything you want, and it will be granted you" (John 14:13). Those two children who lost their mother and the billions of others around the world who have prayed to no avail for relief from their painful tragedies would find Jesus' words impossible to accept, or at the very least extremely confusing. Their experience doesn't seem to validate his promise. But maybe this is where the minister's words are most helpful. He has his finger on something we are apt to miss: the wisdom of the Creator of this universe far surpasses our own, and that God's care for us is infinitely more tender and comprehensive than our own care could ever be.

When we ask for something in particular, as the two children did, which is perfectly natural for us to do, it should always be with the understanding that we see only the smallest part of the total reality embraced by God's vision. The response to our plea will often enough not immediately satisfy our specific request. But our living in faith means that we really do believe that God loves us unconditionally and is wise beyond our comprehension and that in the end everything will work to our welfare. Jesus' way of praying supports this point of view: "Not my will but your will be done." And I think again in this connection of my high school classmate who said at the funeral of his 19-year-old daughter, "In this, too, God is only loving and merciful."

The old song had it right: *"Que sera, sera."* What will be, will be. I doubt that the author knew what a profound theological statement that is. Our prayers don't change anything outside of us; they change only *us*. They broaden our vision and understanding so that when terrible things inevitably happen to us and those we love, we do not despair, because we know that the power and love and wisdom of God are never absent from the human scene. Jesus might have said, "Ask anything you want, and in the end you'll get a thousand times more. Be patient – and trust."

> *Our prayers don't change anything outside of us; they change only us.*

But what shall we do with that assurance of Jesus (Matthew 18:19) that if we join our voices on earth to pray for something, it shall be granted us by the God he called Father?

What is granted to us in prayer are not miracles of power over nature – subduing of storms, curing of disease, restoration of sight, awakening of the dead, etc. No, what is promised is the unfailing gift of the Spirit of God, a divine presence within and among us, whose power cannot be overcome by any calamity, but who enables us to endure whatever comes and to see a bright future ahead in this world or in the next.

ABOUT HUMAN SUFFERING AND DEATH

Y ears ago I read an article by a priest extolling the value of suffering. He confessed that he prayed every day that he would have the "privilege" of enduring excruciating pain on a long journey to death. His point was that suffering is meritorious and redemptive when it is deliberately undergone in union with the remembered agony of the crucified Jesus.

This sounds at first like the description of the perfect Christian. But I suggest to you that it is wrong, terribly wrong. It is the end result of confused and muddled thinking — bad theology, bad spirituality. Why? Because, to begin with, it places far too much emphasis on the redeeming aspect of Jesus' suffering and death and suggests that God, the Creative Spirit, is actually a petty tyrant who demands excessive reparation for the sins of the human race. But it was not God who ordered or desired the death of Jesus; it was rather the jealous, evil forces of his day, both religious and secular, that considered him to be a major threat that had to be exterminated.

The truth is that suffering of any kind is an evil and should be prevented as far as possible. It is the absence of health and good order and wellbeing; it is to be conquered and vanquished wherever it exists. But, at the same time, it is to be endured nobly and hopefully when to avoid it means to abandon the pursuit of a significant good. In other words, while we don't seek suffering as a good in itself, Jesus teaches us by word and example that we are to accept it when it stands inevitably between us and the good that we must pursue. To put that still differently: we accept it when the only way to avoid it is to quit the path to a good that our conscience tells us we must achieve.

116

That was the experience of Jesus. He was fully aware that it was precisely because of his radical preaching and teaching that he was becoming a hunted prey. His message was pure truth. He and his message were offensive and threatening to those who had established their own kingdoms, and they wanted him out of the way. Jesus could have submitted to their demands and retired to a peaceful old age; instead he stayed the course, knowing full well that that decision would lead to rejection and condemnation, to torment beyond description. His loyalty to us and to the one he called Father won the day. He embraced the anguish because to avoid it would have meant abandoning us and the Father.

Living in love often exacts a great price, as anyone who has ever loved deeply knows from personal experience. The price comes in the form of suffering – mental, physical, spiritual, emotional. Suffering that ought never to be sought for its own sake but ought never either to be refused or circumvented at the expense of the beloved.

Hundreds of years before Jesus' time, there was, even among his Jewish ancestors, no belief in a life after death. The life that Moses talked about was life right here on earth for the brief time that each of us occupies this planet. Our tendency today is to interpret the words "that you may live and take possession of the land" as a reference to eternal life after death in a place called heaven. But that was not their understanding. They thought they had one chance at a happy life, and that was here on earth, and they were certain that the Author of Life meant them to enjoy it and would help them to achieve it if they remained faithful.

I keep on a bookshelf in my living room a booklet that was assembled a few years ago as a touching tribute to a deceased friend of mine, a seminary classmate, a fellow priest with whom I spent a year at Catholic University in Washington, D.C. just before our ordinations.

117

Jack Conway became a hospital chaplain, the best there ever was. To meet him was to love him. He was invariably kind, unfailingly patient, always cheerful and full of fun, a "people person" to the nth degree. He was humble, almost self-effacing, never boastful, a great listener. Jack was sensitive, a feeler, a realist, and also extremely bright and perceptive. He possessed a disarming combination of shyness and outgoingness. A skinny guy, but an enthusiastic athlete, he was willing to try anything.

Once, when we were both in one of our first assignments, I remember his saying to me with his characteristic penchant for understatement, "Let's face it: my pastor just isn't a very nice person." But that pastor, I'm sure, never had an unhappy moment because of Jack.

I can't help but wonder what this giant of a priest, this man whom Jesus would have been so pleased with, would be contributing to the image of the priesthood and the church, so tarnished at this time in our history. I can't think of any priest I've ever known whom I've loved and respected as much as him, and few deaths in my life have saddened me as his did.

One of the many tributes the booklet contains was written by his colleague, a Protestant chaplain at the same hospital, who asked him, some months before his death, how he was really feeling. The chaplain wrote, "He took his hand and shook it…and said that, whether he lived or died, he belonged to the Lord."

The chaplain continued, "He talked a lot about the Resurrection during the last few weeks. In fact, I understand that he offered a half-hour theological dissertation on the Resurrection to Father McNulty when he visited him with the Eucharist. He told me that he hadn't been preaching the Resurrection all those years without believing it. And that he looked forward to whatever surprises God had planned for him."

Another friend of Jack's, a resigned priest, said in a homily shortly after his death that since Jack was such an incurable romantic, his faith "was something of an adventure. He believed that the tenets of faith were far too profound to be described by the limitations of theologians. Only the limitless imaginations of artists, musicians, poets and storytellers could adequately tell the tale of God. He often used the poet's story of the dancing God to describe the Resurrection of Jesus."

It's impossible for me to think about my friend without smiling and at the same time feeling a lump in my throat. And I have known for more than a half century that the unquenchable joy in that good man was rooted in his belief that the Creator is a playful God, whose bag of surprises is larger than the universe.

I last saw him the day before he died. He spoke only with his eyes and the feeblest movement of his hands. I reminded him that he owed me a dinner, and he smiled wanly as if to say, "You can count on that."

The people asked Jesus theological questions about what happens after our biological death. They wanted him to reconcile our earthly experiences, like relationships such as marriage, for example, with what happens in the life to come. His response could not have satisfied them any more than it satisfies us. And Jack was right: theology can't handle such sublime mysteries. They are grasped, however incompletely, by poets and artists and musicians and dancers.

Preoccupations about what happens after death are never conclusively resolved. All we need to know is that **love loves to surprise the beloved** and that God is boundless love! What can there be awaiting us but happiness beyond our wildest imaginings?

119

I have read that in the body of a newborn baby there are many miles of DNA. Not one tiny particle in that wondrous network exists independently of all the others; they are interconnected, complementary. They are in relationship with each other: action and reaction, corporate effort, communication. Simply fantastic!

That all of that superb organization should begin in the microscopic form that it does is absolutely mind-boggling. It's a wonder – almost incredible – that the process of such development ever succeeds.

We live in a world that appears to have design and purpose; at its core are intelligence and, beyond that, love. But it is also composed of random forces that seem to have, as we are accustomed to saying, a mind of their own: the hurricane that ravages and kills, the raging fire that consumes a village, the cancer that incapacitates and eventually takes a life, the pregnancy that ends in death.

There are still many religious persons who attribute this entirely to control by God, a God whom they imagine as administering a detailed plan containing both good and evil, making things happen sometimes to please us and sometimes to distress or test or punish us – or only to leave us so bewildered that, to preserve our sanity, we say things like, "We must accept this; it is God's will. It is not for us to understand but only to accept."

I don't believe that, and I hope that you don't either. If we were to say or to suggest that an infant's death, so soon after birth, was actually the will of God, then where shall we draw the line – or is there a line at all? Was World War II God's will? Is drug addiction God's will? Are earthquakes and the incalculable human suffering and death that follow in their wake God's will?

Reason – our participation in the divine intelligence – shouts a firm and uncompromised No. And faith, our Christian faith, supports that judgment. An infant dies at birth without any chance of a human life on earth, without the possibility of here and now returning love for the immense love she received from her parents, because this is an imperfect world in which accidents happen, in which things sometimes go terribly wrong, and in which the irrational forces of nature often hurt cruelly but unintentionally, innocently.

Whether or not one is a person of Christian faith, or any faith, it is the same for all of us: to be human is to be vulnerable and to be hurt regularly and deeply. But we Christians have a distinct advantage, for we are aware of the abiding presence of the one whose suffering and death were turned into joy and life, the one who earned the right to say, "Come to me, you who are burdened, and I will refresh you."

No one has to explain to the risen Jesus the sorrow and the heartache of parents and a family at the death of their child; but neither can anyone know, without Jesus' revealing it, that death, heartless visitor that it is here on earth, is actually the gateway to magnificently transformed life exactly like his own.

St. Thomas More, just before his execution, looked out at the vast crowd of spectators and said, "Pray for me, as I will for thee, that merrily we may meet in heaven."

CAN GOOD TRIUMPH OVER BAD

I t is necessary for us to take the risk of a first, scary step if we're going to arrive at the good things that lie ahead. We'd still be crawling on all fours if we hadn't summoned the courage to stand up at one point in our infancy and take the chance of falling many times before mastering the art of walking.

The New Testament consistently relates this principle to our spiritual life as followers of Jesus, urging us to continue applying his values, his goals, his ways, his vision, no matter the situation we are in and no matter what painful consequences may occur in the immediate future.

But when we recall that the courageous decisions Jesus made led him to his unspeakable suffering and death on a cross, it's no wonder that we feel some hesitation about imitating him. Chances are that we'll get hurt in some way, too; and so our whole being shifts into an avoidance mode and tells us to play it safe.

A dear friend of mine, a fellow priest, has been deeply involved in the clergy sex abuse crisis for many years. He has written and spoken up boldly and confronted the powerful church leaders who have contributed to the scandal through their covering up and their denials. He has become a hero to the victims of abuse and an inspiration to all who are trying to address the problem honestly. But, at the same time, he has become an outcast to many who are intent on protecting first of all themselves and the institution of the church.

This priest-friend wrote to me at the height of his painful involvement in the shameful situation, "Despite my distaste for (Mel Gibson's movie) 'The Passion of the Christ,' I have taken great inspiration from the scene of Christ's personal agony in (the Garden of) Gethsemane. I can't tell you how often that scene has upheld me in recent days."

Jesus' decision to accept suffering and death the way he did out of loyalty to others was to this good priest, not only a hint of what he himself may yet have had to undergo in some way or other, but also an encouragement, because he realized how worthwhile that terrible experience of Jesus was. It's obvious that my friend was saying to himself, "I may have to undergo even worse suffering than I've experienced so far in this ugly mess, but I've got to remain convinced that great good will come from it, as it did for Jesus. With his example and with his help, I can and will do it."

In our own lives, similar choices often lie before us. We can stand pat, deciding not to do something new and different because it makes us feel uncomfortable even to think about it; or we can summon our courage and then speak or act differently, resolve to do what frightens us, not at all sure what the results will be, but hoping against hope that something good, something better, will come from it. And then we find that usually it does!

Maybe the most frequent example of this is found in our relationships with others, especially those who are closest to us. We can, if we decide to, speak more gently and kindly, more attentively and respectfully. We can be less judgmental and more forgiving. We can express affection more often and more tenderly; we can accept the other's weaknesses and "funny" ways without comment or criticism.

There's risk involved, no doubt. The gesture, the words, could at first be misinterpreted and make us feel foolish for the moment. Like

123

the toddler learning to walk, we could fall flat on our face. But it's all so worthwhile because always it will move us from crawling to walking, and life will be so much better for all involved!

NO FAILURES IN JESUS

Did the *real* Jesus (not the Jesus manufactured by piety and religious imagination over the centuries), have any idea that his life of loving service would end in rejection and violent death? I don't think so.

I gather that, during those three years of his work among the people, when they came flocking to him from all over, listening to every word he spoke, singing his praises, wanting to crown him king, he could never have imagined that he would soon be crucified as though he were a criminal. It was only when he was very near his death that he saw clearly the handwriting on the wall.

The greatness of Jesus is found in both periods of his life: in the first, when he gave himself totally to God in unselfish service to the people; and in the latter, when he did not run away from the terrible ordeal he then knew awaited him.

I think that is what we are honoring when we remember his Baptism at the age of about 30: that he was committing himself to something largely hidden from his view, trusting that the One who called him would, in the end, make all things right and happy and beautiful and would provide for him along the way, especially at the most difficult times.

Like the wedding vows of a couple in love, Jesus was saying a firm Yes to both "better" and "worse" and was certain he'd complete the journey successfully because its ultimate outcome lay in the wisdom and love and power of God.

125

I'm aware that among my readers there are many who are separated or divorced from a once-beloved spouse. There are also many others who were formerly committed to religious life or priesthood who have moved on to other ways of life.

I don't want any of them to consider themselves failures, when that is most probably not true at all. There are marriages so badly broken that they cannot be repaired, especially when the partners have become destructive to one another and to others and there is no possible basis for a new start.

There are priests, and men and women in the consecrated religious life, who discern that they no longer fit into the choice they once made in all sincerity, and they believe that the only reasonable thing to do is to change course toward a newly bright future.

The separation, in either case, must be made as a dictate of right reason and good intention and love; the person or persons involved must move on, confident that they are driven and accompanied by the same Spirit of Love whose guidance they had previously sought, despite the tragedy that followed.

But persons who have experienced the death of their marriages or a radical change in their life commitments still have lives to live, commitments to keep, love to share, and faith to practice. In all of that, they are still destined to be led beyond anticipated or foreseen limits, just as Jesus was.

For all of us Christians, the focus of existence here on earth is our Baptism, in which we affirmed the direction and the ultimate meaning of our lives, just as Jesus did.

With the baptism of Jesus in mind, and considering the relationship between his baptism and ours, I wish you happiness and peace and hope on the next lap of your journey – no matter the unexpected and disturbing detours it may have taken in the past. All is well. God is love. We are born and baptized to live in love.

MARRIAGE AND DIVORCE JESUS STYLE...

Interpreted on its own merits, St. Paul's letter to the new Christians in Corinth seems to indicate that marriage is an inferior way of life for the really committed Christian. Paul says that to have a mate inevitably pulls one away from devotion to God. That's one of the standard arguments, you know, against a married priesthood: that the priest who is married could not possibly at the same time devote himself adequately to his ordained ministry. I'm among the many who do not subscribe to such thinking.

And how different that line of reasoning is from what an Episcopal priest said to me many years ago. He told me that his wife is so much a part of his personal, professional and prayer life that if she were removed from the equation, as he put it, he would not know how to be a priest.

But actually St. Paul was not denigrating marriage; he was only trying to establish an order of priorities in the lives of his fellow followers of Christ. To get this, we have to remember his conviction that the world as he knew it was coming to an end. He was certain that within a very short time Jesus, having experienced death and resurrection, would return to establish the Kingdom of God on earth. I believe I am correct in saying that this was Paul's point: Why pay more attention to things of this life than is absolutely necessary and unavoidable? I guess that made perfect sense to Paul: this is no time to be thinking about marrying or starting a business or traveling or whatever. All that should be done now is to prepare as best we can for the glorious, triumphant return of Christ, which could occur even as soon as tomorrow.

Well, we know that Paul was mistaken about a second coming of Christ; it hasn't happened yet, 2000 years later. But that doesn't strip his words of relevant meaning, not if we see in them a more general plea that we take seriously becoming more and more attentive to the voice of God within us. A professor of mine told us seminarians decades ago that when we are searching for a clue to the meaning of the Sunday readings — why these three were chosen and what we are supposed to be getting from them — we should look to the responsorial psalm that follows the first reading. He said that, uncannily, the psalm will almost always identify the core message of the scripture passages. I have found that to be true, not always, but time and time again. One of those familiar responses comes to me as I write these words. It has us say, "If today you hear his voice, harden not your hearts."

I grant you that this is very subjective: two persons can hear the voice of God very differently, even with opposite interpretations, as is the case in the present time among good people who are concerned about grave moral issues like abortion and wars in the Middle East and various sexual matters.

But God doesn't speak as we do; there is no "voice" that any ear can hear. This is a metaphor. The Second Vatican Council, over 50 years ago, put it very well: It said that we discover in ourselves a law in our consciences which calls us to love and to do what is good and that we will be judged on how we observed that law. Of course that too is subjective, inevitably so; but what all authentic religious teachers, Jesus first of all, are saying to us is that on the journey of life we have to be guided constantly by an inner compass which gets its orientation from the Spirit of God present in all of creation. Each of us is responsible for learning to use that compass so as to deal successfully with the persistent distraction and competition that we encounter along the way.

How many times I have heard distressed parents agonize over a son who is gay or a daughter who is divorced and remarried, for example. To help them resolve their sorrow, I begin always by asking two questions:

* Is your child a good and loving person? Invariably the answer is Yes, without question or doubt.

* Is it clear that he or she is acting, not thoughtlessly or selfishly, but in good conscience after a long period of consideration? Again, I have rarely heard anything but a resounding Yes.

A moral decision can be costly for the person who makes it when it disappoints those whom he or she loves. But, if it comes out of heart and mind and conscience, it is perfectly in accord with the time-honored tradition that we are to be directed ultimately — in the final analysis, as we say — by the Divine Spirit present within us and speaking through a well-formed conscience.

"If today you hear his voice, don't harden your heart."

In the time of Jesus, divorce was strictly a male prerogative and was a powerful instrument of female oppression. A man could divorce his wife for even the flimsiest reason, after which she was left absolutely destitute – no money, no home, no livelihood, no claim to any property, no good name, nothing. She invariably turned to begging or prostitution just to remain alive. Surely one reason for Jesus' strongly negative position on divorce was his sensitivity to the plight of these discarded women and the evil of the system that allowed men such shameful liberty.

Virtually all Christian churches today hold that divorce is sometimes unavoidable and that persons who divorce for good reason have not thereby sinned. Unfortunately, the Catholic Church stands virtually alone in forbidding divorced persons to move on to a new marriage and remain members of the church in good standing.

Jesus emphasized that marriage is not the unaided invention of humans, not merely a convenience or a regulation that society has adopted, but a way of life that is rooted in the inner life of the Creator.

"If today you hear his voice, don't harden your heart."

TILL DEATH (OF MARRIAGE) DO US PART

Dear Reader: As we pursue, however briefly, this sensitive subject, let me remind you that I am not a canon lawyer or a professional theologian. I express my long and well-considered convictions only as an ordinary priest formed by the traditional teaching of the church, the writings of contemporary theologians, and more than a half century of dealings with married persons.

Several years ago, a faithfully practicing Catholic told me of his recently ended marriage and of how his parish priest had urged him to seek an annulment. He replied, "Never! My marriage was sound and beautiful for almost two decades and produced three children conceived in love. It is broken beyond repair now, but no one will ever convince me that it was never a true sacramental union." An only too common story.

After nearly 60 years in the priesthood, I am increasingly disappointed with our Catholic Church's overall policy and process of marriage annulment. Granted, there are some open-and-shut cases in which significant deception or defect on the part of one or the other spouse clearly indicates that what appeared to be a valid marriage was not at all that and needed to be declared so. (The husband had a wife somewhere else, for example, or the wife made it known to friends that she never wanted children even while telling her husband that she did.) In such a case, an annulment is both reasonable and appropriate, maybe even imperative.

However, the Catholic Church allows only two acceptable alternatives regarding the resolution of a failed marriage. One is the obtainment of a civil divorce, with the clear understanding that the couple is still sacramentally married to each other and will remain single until the death of one of them. And it should be noted here that a divorced Catholic who has not remarried is not barred from the sacraments, including the Eucharist. The second, as mentioned above, is to seek and be granted an annulment by the church, after which both parties would be free to marry someone else if they desired to do so.

But, as I see it, what the church fails to acknowledge is a third possibility: that a perfectly valid marriage can disintegrate to the point at which there is no longer a bond of love between the two partners and they become in a variety of ways destructive to each other and to others whose lives their dead marriage contaminates. In this third instance, if the church were to honor it, a civil divorce could be followed by a new marriage within the church. In such instances, a *church* divorce — not an annulment — seems to me to be the appropriate course of action. Jesus called his disciples to the *ideal* in all things, including permanence in marriage, but he was compassionate and accepting toward those who could not achieve it in practice. Divorce is regrettable, of course, but we human beings still do not always attain the ideal. Besides, a marriage in which husband and wife do not really love each other does not seem to be a marriage at all; it is the corpse of a once-living marriage.

It has long seemed to me that the church unintentionally further wounds and burdens some of its members who seek release from hopelessly failed marriages when it requires them to say that those marriages were never true sacramental unions from the start. Eager to be free and to enter new, mutually satisfying unions, they agree to that judgmental pronouncement, although they are aware that, while they were once very much in love and committed to each other, love and commitment, on the part of one or both of the spouses, are irretrievably lost.

It is important to keep in mind, I realize, that the complexities and characteristics of broken marriages are many and varied, and that the corrosive forces involved come from multiple sources — no one-size-fits-all solution or methodology here. No matter by what process or decree the marriage formally ends, the possibilities of both hurt and help are numerous. A subsequent marriage can be worse than the first; the need for healing of both parties and the protection of their children must be carefully addressed. Growth in psychological health is likely to be necessary in preparation for a future, more wholesome relationship.

But I wish that my church would at least abandon the position that when a marriage is judged to be invalid, it has been invalid from its very beginning, and acknowledge instead that a marriage *validly* begun can become sick unto death, despite the sincerest efforts of at least one of the partners (including a generous "cooling-off period," extensive counseling and earnest prayer), and at that stage declare it a defunct marriage and grant a divorce.

I think it is not in the true nature of the Christian community to demand of its members what their consciences find offensive.

GAY AND STRAIGHT-*FORWARD*

A couple of years ago I read an excellent statement written by a priest to his parishioners on the subject of homosexuals' activity in Catholic ministry. A regular churchgoer had challenged him with the question about whether it is right for gays to be distributing Holy Communion.

The priest reminded his readers that the question and the issue had nothing to do with pedophilia, the sexual abuse of children, but apparently everything to do with homophobia, a fear or a hatred of homosexual persons. He suggested that the cure for such an attitude is to meet gay men and lesbian women as fellow human beings, as friends, contributors to our communities, as our brothers and sisters in faith.

He noted that the bishops of the United States, in a now famous document entitled *Always Our Children*, urged parents not to turn the church's teachings against their homosexual children, but to accept them for who they are. He quoted the bishops as saying, "Generally, homosexual orientation is experienced as a given, not as something freely chosen...(and therefore not sinful in itself), for morality presumes the freedom to choose."

The pastor closed his article with a reference to the bishops' encouragement that homosexual persons be given leadership opportunities in the church, and he asked if we can ever think of the tragedy of 9/11 without the image of the heroic Father Mychal Judge or think of Catholic spiritual writing without remembering Father Henri Nouwen, both good men born with homosexual orientation.

135

To consider the foregoing seems a perfect way to grab hold of St. Paul's teaching as we find it in his celebrated letter to the rather new Christians in the city of Corinth, Greece. That young church of the Corinthians was in trouble – there were all kinds of factions, quarrelling, jealousy, and so on. Paul was very concerned that the community was going to destroy itself because the people did not understand what it meant to be Christian. What they weren't grasping was that the Risen Jesus was in each one of them and that they had to recognize and honor that presence, no matter who the person was. He wasn't expecting them to build shrines to each other or give each other the showy obeisance that royalty demands; all he was demanding was that they love each other.

And again, not love in a romantic or emotional sense. Most often, that's not possible, nor is it essential. Properly, that's reserved for very few persons in our lives of relationship and most of all for someone in particular in a bond of intimate friendship and commitment such as marriage. No, the love he speaks of requires work, effort, hard decisions, self-sacrifice. It doesn't come from, or usually produce, fuzzy, warm feelings. And so, Paul describes it as consisting of patience and kindness, the lack of jealousy, pomposity and egotism. He says it means not being rude or selfish or quick-tempered or brooding or mean.

That's a tall order! Anyone who can accomplish it fully deserves a lifetime achievement award. But the truth is that we are called to precisely that. The reason that we do Eucharist every week, listening to sacred teachings and receiving Jesus in sacrament, is mainly to strengthen and nourish us for the exhausting, difficult job of living together in such disciplined love.

Think of some of the persons you have reached out to who are not considered by the world to be important or worth anyone's attention. The *New York Times* had an unusually beautiful and moving front-page article on just such a person, a dying old man, one of God's little people, not rich, not famous, not well-placed, not good looking, not highly educated. But he was befriended by a retired corporate lawyer, who, in our terms, saw Jesus in him and accompanied him to a happy and hopeful death.

That's what Paul knew Jesus had in mind! That's what our being Christians is mostly about. There are no unimportant people, no human throwaways. The Spirit of God is in each of us, without exception. Jesus tells us not to miss that presence but to connect with it through thoughts and words and acts of love.

There is a gospel passage that tells us the people in Jesus' own home town took offense at what he was saying to them. It doesn't explain why; in fact, it's preceded by exuberant praise for him: "Where did he get all this knowledge he's sharing with us? What kind of wisdom has been given to him? And how do we explain the miraculous things he's doing with those hands of his – placing them on the sick, the near dead, only to make them well?"

The people were astonished. Keep in mind that the older folks among them saw Jesus grow up; knew him well, probably as a bright, fun-loving little boy. Some were wondering what wonderful thing had happened to him. Others were asking sarcastically, "Who does he think he is?"

And then a sobering, down-to-earth reality kicks in when the very same "astonished" persons attempt to put Jesus in his place, reminding him and the crowd that "he's just one of us, so don't be too taken by what he says. Remember, we know his brothers and sisters; they're our

137

friends and neighbors. We've grown up together…"

Hearing that, it's Jesus who then takes offense, which must have gone deep into his soul. He reminds them all that while the world may praise and glorify someone who speaks the very truth of God, when that person gets back to his home and family and friends, he's very likely to be dishonored, ignored, scoffed at. "Jesus," we are told, "was amazed at their lack of faith."

Because of this painful dissonance that had occurred between them, Jesus was unable to exercise his ministry of healing among these people with whom he had close ties and whom he respected and dearly loved. Love is meant to be shared, to be mutual. A one-sided love can be a tragedy that causes deep sorrow. Surely Jesus knew what that experience was like, not only when he was dying on the cross, but throughout his ministry among the people that he loved so much.

This idea of reciprocity, of mutuality, applies also to what we *believe* as Catholic Christians. By that I mean that a teaching of the church in order to be authentic requires not only competence and authority on the part of the teacher, the official church, but also understanding and acceptance on the part of those who are taught, the ordinary members of the church. This is so because the Spirit of God is present and active in both the teacher and the taught. I have heard it called the "Doctrine of Reception."

I have in mind on the one hand the recent astounding decision of the United States Supreme Court to honor same-sex marriage and on the other hand the condemnation of that decision that expectedly and immediately came from church leaders, including our own bishops. At the same time, from my own rather wide circle of respected friends and family members, I've been hearing nothing but approval of the decision. The point I make is that with regard to this present critical matter, it already appears that the church's official teaching is not being generally received by the people. At the same time, there are not yet signs that the official church recognizes and honors that non-reception. Surely this suggests that the matter needs to be widely discussed with open hearts and minds in the expectation that it will ultimately be resolved.

"Come, Holy Spirit, and renew the face of the earth."

Very shortly after same sex marriage was made legal in New Jersey, I was asked, not to officiate at their wedding, but to give a blessing to the male spouses at the reception that immediately followed. I said to the assembled well-wishers:

> I have known John and Mark for 37 years, having first met them as their new pastor in 1978. From that time until my retirement in 1998, I recognized them as men of honor and integrity, devoted to their families and to one another in bonds of faithful love.
>
> So exemplary were their lives, that our pastoral team eagerly agreed to commission them as Eucharistic Ministers, which means that they were delegated to distribute to the people assembled for Sunday and other worship what we Catholics believe to be the sacramental presence of Jesus in Eucharist – commonly called Holy Communion.
>
> I applaud this step that they have just taken in the long journey of their relationship, and I appreciate the

privilege of being asked to pronounce a blessing upon them on this occasion of their formal and public betrothal as legally wedded spouses.

Let us pray.

Creator God, Author of all that is, Energy of the Big Bang 13 billion years ago, Spirit of the process of evolution from which we humans have come, God whom Jesus called Father, we welcome with gratitude and joy your blessing upon John and Mark, who have pledged themselves to one another this day in a bond of human love patterned after the love that Jesus has for you and for us all.

In the unpredictable circumstances of their life ahead, may they remain aware of your loving presence to them and committed to the values that Jesus has uniquely taught us.

May their lives together be filled with joy and peace, and may they embrace lovingly also those who look to them for comfort, healing and compassion.

We ask this of you, Father, through Jesus, who lives within and among us now and forever. Amen.

IN VITRO FERTILIZATION

In that portion of the church's year called "Ordinary Time" we concentrate on what membership in the church involves. The fact that we show up for Sunday Mass together, say the prayers in common, and all receive the Risen Jesus in Holy Communion really doesn't guarantee that we are thinking or acting alike with regard to the demands and expectations of our Catholic life – nor should it. The pronouncements of popes and bishops notwithstanding, there is and will forever be that fact of individual response to church teaching and discipline that varies from person to person.

I'll give you a good example. A friend of mine, an elderly nun, now deceased, had a grandnephew who is a paraplegic, married but unable to father a child. By a method forbidden by official church teaching, his wife conceived and bore two beautiful baby boys about two years apart. Along with a photo of the children, I saved the note that my dear friend sent me. She wrote, "Who could ever deny life to these beautiful children and the tremendous joy they have brought to their parents, especially their quadriplegic father? If you know anyone who has difficulty conceiving and is concerned about the church's ruling, show them this picture."

Not long after, she wrote: "Another picture of (the) boys. Show it to anyone who hesitates having *in vitro* (fertilization). These two children have brought so much happiness to everyone. Our church has to go back to the compassionate Jesus. What would He say?"

Imagine! This from an intelligent, deeply involved, life-long Catholic nun! We mustn't pretend that this sort of thing is not happening. It is happening – all the time and all around us. And it isn't a form of rebellion or apostasy or malicious disobedience. It is simply a case of good and faithful Catholics faced with difficult moral situations who are turning to every resource they know of in their attempt to arrive at a decision in good conscience. They hear openly and they respect deeply the official teaching of the church, and they want to comply. They listen also to other voices of responsible persons, voices that have the mark of reason and authenticity. They consult, they read, they agonize, they pray – and finally they reach a conclusion that forms their conscientious decision.

I am well aware that such talk as this can be upsetting to Catholics who believe that what is expected of us as disciples of Jesus is unquestioning obedience to every law and teaching of the official church. But that cannot be so. The church itself, at the highest level of its authority, teaches that each of us must be guided ultimately by our own individual conscience. We have the duty, she makes clear, to work at developing a conscience that is as correct, as good, as we can humanly make it to be. And then we must take a courageous leap of faith, trusting that what we have determined to be the right thing to do is in fact precisely that.

In St. Paul's letter to the newly-baptized converts in the Greek city of Corinth, he expresses the fond hope that there will be no divisions among them, but that they will remain united in one mind and in one purpose. He says he is disturbed over the rivalries among them that he's been hearing about. But the rivalries are based on by whom they were instructed and formed for their commitment to the new way of Jesus – some by Paul himself, others by Apollos, still others by Cephas. This situation of an almost cultic loyalty to the person who led them into the reform movement started by Jesus and his apostles gave the impression that their allegiance was not primarily to him but to the messenger who introduced them to his way of life. And Paul says, in effect, Hold on there! Remember, it wasn't I or any of the other missionaries who died for love of you; it was Jesus!

On that point, the centrality of Jesus and his Gospel, Paul insists there must be absolute unity. But that cannot mean that disagreements concerning what Jesus taught and what he meant must never occur. It cannot mean that in areas that Jesus never spoke about all must be of one conviction. Quite the opposite, the infant church starts out with a verbal brawl between a couple of the apostles, one of them Peter himself and the chief of them all, over a major requirement for prospective converts and whether it should stand or not. Peter, the one we think of (not entirely accurately) as the first pope, took the conservative side but soon enough became convinced that he was wrong, that he had misunderstood the mind of Jesus and of the Spirit of God, and willingly, even eagerly, gave in to his opponents.

Trained, as we are, to be obedient, the very notion of such freedom can be unsettling to some of us. But the truth is that Christian discipleship — being a faithful follower of Jesus as a member of the Catholic Church — does not demand that we abandon our God-given capacity to reason and to decide. While we must listen with an open and receptive mind to the official position of the church, we have also to weigh the options before us carefully and with much prayer. We have the duty to consult broadly in every way possible to us. And then we must finally make a decision and live with it in peace. We remain firmly united with the Christian community especially through our weekly Eucharist, in which we can always be of one heart, though never totally of one mind.

WHEN DEATH HAPPENS

A nd then, in a shattering shout of joy, it turns out that the vast silent emptiness we experience as death is filled with the mystery of mysteries that we call God—filled with God's pure light and all-embracing love! ~ Karl Rahner[14]

The *New York Times* carried the obituary of the great Protestant New Testament scholar, Marcus Borg, who died at the age of 72. By all accounts, along with his total immersion in biblical theology, he was a very human, kind, gentle, loving and compassionate man. His widow, incidentally, is an Episcopal priest. His contributions to our understanding of Jesus and his times were enormous and will be a guiding influence in modern Christianity for decades, if not centuries, to come.

But how often it happens that out of the voluminous teachings that extraordinary minds like Dr. Borg leave us, there stands out, above all the rest, some simple statement that even a child can understand. One of those from Dr. Borg caught my eye and remained with me. The topic was the afterlife – "heaven," as most people refer to it. Dr. Borg wrote, *"So, is there an afterlife, and if so, what will it be like? I don't have a clue. But I am confident that the one who buoyed us up in life will also buoy us up through death. We die into God. What more that means, I do not know. But that is all I need to know."*[15]

My dear friend, Australian theologian and author, Michael Morwood, has said words very much like Dr. Borg's. He wrote: *"**God is not present in some places and peoples, absent in others. Our death will not mean travel somewhere else.** (I add "…to an imaginary heaven or to an imaginary hell.") **Rather it will be a transformation into a completely different way of living in God – the God who is always present in**

144

creation. We live in God and we die into the love that is God, and nothing can change that."[16]

As we're so fond of saying, "Let's face it": no one knows what happens after death. The beloved Cardinal Joseph Bernardin said several years ago, when the question was put to him by a young man, that he didn't know any more than the young man himself did. Not even Jesus is of much help to us in this regard, assuring us only that these mysteries of life belong to the God he called Father.

But notice, in particular, that one small sentence of Dr. Borg's: "We die into God," and almost the same from Morwood, "We die into the love that is God." Of that they are sure. Borg admits, and I'm certain Morwood would agree, that the full meaning of that belief statement escapes him, but that the little he does know is all he needs to know.

It is, after all, a matter of personal choice. We are free to believe or not to believe, according to whatever seems more likely and plausible to us.

I choose to believe – although, like the theologians, I don't have any idea of what the afterlife will be like. Believing in a life that awaits us beyond death gives me courage to live life here on earth with all the energy and zest that I can give it. It helps me to accept present failures and disappointments and limitations as mere potholes in an otherwise trustworthy road. It keeps reminding me that there lies ahead a total sharing in the life of the creator of the universe, an experience that will satisfy me beyond my wildest aspirations and desires.

Let's not waste any opportunity to think often and deeply about who we are, and who Jesus is, and how we have been granted the grace to catch a glimmer of what lies ahead, just enough to fill us with eager anticipation!

RESPECT FOR LIFE: ALL LIFE

In the spring of 1972, the Catholic bishops of the United States passed a resolution that during the month of October, every year and in every diocese of the land, there will be a week dedicated to respect for life. Through prayer and study the bishops hoped that we all would come to a clearer vision of the sanctity of life and would pledge ourselves to defend and promote life in every way available to each of us in our particular circumstances.

I think it is fair to say that the threats to life in our day are more varied, pervasive, powerful and subtle than ever before in human history. That is true not only because of the availability and stockpiling of weapons of mass destruction; it is also certified by the existence of evils such as pollution, widespread poverty, abortion on demand, drug abuse, hunger and homelessness, domestic violence, and so on.

Let's be clear on this point: not every attack on life is necessarily evil; sometimes it is unavoidable and may indeed serve life in a broader context. I am aware that there is another, opposing opinion on what I am about to say, and I respect it; nonetheless, I'll say anyway that the soldier who goes to war against a truly evil enemy and kills only as a last resort does so in the cause of life and the essential properties that belong to human life, including freedom and security and the pursuit of happiness. His/her situation is somewhat analogous to that of the surgeon who kills a part of the body only so that the whole body may live and thrive.

But another question belongs here, too: Do we realize adequately our personal responsibility for the stewardship of life? Are we convinced that we must not leave war completely to the government and the military? We must not leave abortion on demand to the clinics, the

146

hospitals, and the courts. We mustn't regard the slaughters on our over-crowded roads as solely the business of Detroit or Ralph Nader. We should not consign our elderly to institutions, or the poor to welfare, without our involvement.

All of the above are our problems too, because life is God's gift to all of us. Together we cherish and preserve it, or together we waste and destroy it.

As a Catholic and a priest, I will continue to express publicly my opposition to abortion — except in the most critical and extreme situations. However, I think it is a mistaken notion that legislation banning abortion can be effective. On the contrary, as our recent history has proven, it can only drive abortion back to crude procedures in alleyways and hidden rooms. Our tools must instead be wise counseling and generous, tender care.

As a full-time hospital chaplain for five years and then as a pastor for twenty, I learned how desperate can be the plight of the woman who feels compelled to have an abortion. No law would have prevented the actions that eventually placed her in such dire circumstances; but it is likely, indeed probable, that a law prohibiting abortion would not have dissuaded her from seeking one from anyone, anywhere. Wealthy women can travel great distances, even overseas, into temporary obscurity or make other arrangements to guarantee the safety and success of the procedure, but these are possibilities beyond the reach of the poor.

In 2000, two Catholic philosophers from Seattle University, Daniel Dombrowski and Robert Deltete, wrote *A Brief, Liberal, Catholic Defense of Abortion*. I chanced to read it and was deeply impressed by it. I made contact with Professor Dombrowski in my attempt to bring the work to the attention of both sides of the national debate, at least in my limited circles.

The book's thesis is simple, direct, humble in tone, and well documented: It presents without bias the centuries-old conflict between the two opposing views on the morality of abortion, while highlighting the major subthemes that supported each, e.g., the point in the fetus's development at which it receives a soul and becomes a person. It informs us that with the invention of the microscope (ed: in the 1590s) the fertile imagination of Catholic scientists had them believing that they saw miniature human beings in the fetal tissue. The authors neatly outline for us how there came about the present unequivocal and inflexible teaching of the Catholic Church on the matter.[17]

The book's point of view seemed plausible to me, and I treasured it mainly because it dealt so compassionately with the plight of women who bear a life within them that not only brings them no joy, but causes them to experience profound sadness and even horror and fear, especially when that life originated through brutality and/or gross violation of their personhood. I applauded the courageous authors for assuring those women that to terminate that life in its earliest stages cannot be murder. I entertained the hope, as I still do, that once we can get past the super-charged emotionalism surrounding that judgment of innocence, we can then insert the issue in the broader context of respect for all life and apply the same principles to the early embryo as we apply them to animals or trees or any other life form. In other words, just as I may not cut down a Sequoia tree for pleasure or whimsy, or shoot animals solely for recreation, so may I not attack early life in the womb unless there is a compelling and undeniably just reason to do so.

St. Augustine believed that abortion is evil — but on the grounds that it perverts the meaning of sexual intercourse: persons enjoying the pleasure of the act but rejecting the attached responsibility and purpose of sexuality, namely, to produce offspring (only *one* of its purposes, we would emphasize today). According to St. Thomas Aquinas, the evil of abortion in the later stages of pregnancy is the unjust killing of an innocent person. But neither of these two most influential thinkers believed that an early embryo was a human person. Today there appears to be consensus among those holding a variety of opinions on the thorny matter that to abort the embryo or the fetus before what is thought to be the onset of ensoulment or sentiency is not the killing of a person, although it is the ending of life on its way to humanness and is justified only by serious cause.

Can we not hold the hope, however slim, that there will ultimately be agreement on this between the pro-life and the pro-choice camps? Can we not concur that, since for most of its history the church believed that "hominization" (the process of becoming human) goes on for months, we are, therefore, not dealing with murder when the life of an embryo developing up to that point is terminated for compelling reasons?

The authors also remind us that nature itself produces far more "abortions" (e.g. miscarriages) than people do. That also has to be respectfully factored in, I should think.

What should we say about late-term abortion (commonly and incorrectly called "partial birth abortion")? Considering both the advanced development of the fetus at that stage and the nauseating cruelty of its surgical execution, I am utterly and unalterably opposed to it in any case. And I admit that I find it impossible to answer the question in an unemotional state of mind. But remember: I am not a self-proclaimed oracle; I am a Christian, a Catholic priest, eager to share my thinking with you and grateful that you allow me to do that.

The fundamental question, it seems to me, is not whether or not there is life in the womb, but whether or not it is truly *human* life. When does that human life begin? No one knows for sure, and we may never know with absolute precision and certainty; but neither should that invincible ignorance prevent us from doing what is humane and reasonable and "natural" for compelling reasons, at least up to the point at which we are morally certain that there is a truly human person in the womb. (Of course there's life in an acorn, and it is full of potential, but the acorn is not yet an oak tree.) I hope I'm recalling correctly that many scientists suggest that the point (of viability) has arrived when the spinal cord and cerebral cortex are adequately developed and functioning, implying that at that stage the body has begun to be capable of supporting human personhood. In other words, "ensoulment" can now take place.

Most of what we believe and think is solidly based on both the wisdom and the ignorance of those who came before us. What each age does is to scrutinize what has been handed down and, using the best tools available to it, as their predecessors did in their day, retain what seems to be valid and modify and reject what appears to be invalid. In the case at hand, I am convinced that the insight of our ancestors was correct, despite their lack of scientific knowledge. But then again, I cannot imagine that science, however sophisticated it may become, will ever be able to determine *exactly* when a fetus has become a human person, even if there were agreement that the full development of the spinal cortex is that determining point. We have to be content with a degree of inexactitude in this puzzling and sensitive matter. That said, while making it clear once again that I am neither a scientist nor a theologian, I remain on the side of those who insist that we proceed in favor of preservation of the life and well-being of the fetus unless and until it becomes evident that there is reasonable cause for its termination.

My personal conviction is that we have to move past sentimentality, emotion, religious prejudice, etc. and recognize that all life is to be respected and that there are countless circumstances in which humans, as well as animals and plants, take life in the service of life. We slaughter millions of animals every day, for example, so that we can eat meat. We fight wars and kill our fellow human beings to defend the innocent. We cut down acres of trees to build houses and roads. And so on. All life is precious and is to be respected; but there are circumstances in which that right is seen to be not absolute. That's a matter of human judgment, granted, and humans are not infallible, but we must try to do the best we can.

Our stewardship means not only that we protect life in all its forms from wanton destruction, but also that we do our part in guiding life to ever greater fullness and richness. The potential of life seems limitless. How many melodies or symphonies can be composed? How much beauty can artists create? How many different human faces can there be? How deep can human love become? How far into the heavens can humans explore? How long can human lifespan be? How healthy can we be? These are questions that will never be fully answered since there is no limit to life's potential.

Commitment to life, respect for life, necessarily demands of us that we act for God in our responsibility for life.

The bible tells us we are "made to the image and likeness of God." That means that we stand in place of our Creator and that we are charged not only with preserving life but also with keeping it growing into its unfathomable potential. The fact that we are exercising that responsibility poorly in some significant areas does not take away this sacred trust in which we most resemble God. Through humble prayer and the counsel of all good persons, let us learn in our day what respect for life really means.

151

CHAPTER FOUR

Where Did It Go Wrong?

CONFRONTING THE SEXUAL ABUSE CRISIS IN THE CHURCH

Easter means life, new life, resurrection, hope, the best of good news. That joyful optimism has been more than a little muted as the church has undergone for several years at the time of this writing the crisis of the sexual abuse of minors by its clergy. Even now, we await further disclosure of shameful, scandalous charges almost every day.

In some important ways, it's not a good time for the church; it's a dark and depressing time. A whole range of emotions pulses through the community of Catholic Christians – anger, disillusionment, resentment, disbelief, frustration. "How could this have been happening right under our noses without our being made aware of it?" people are asking. "How could those to whom the leadership of the church has been entrusted have known that these crimes were going on in so many places for so long a time and have done virtually nothing about the situation except cover it up? What was in their minds? What did they think they were accomplishing? To whom or to what did they think they were being faithful and accountable?"

These are among the puzzling questions Catholics are entertaining these days. And we all look for answers, we look for some sign that we can and will emerge from this terrible situation purified, strengthened, wiser, more virtuous than we were before.

We are disappointed in the lackluster performance and the bland statements of our bishops, and we see them more clearly as men who are conditioned to make their first priority unquestioning obedience to higher authority. I knew well, and loved dearly, a priest much older than I whom I had many reasons to respect deeply. His long years of training, however, beginning at a very early age, enabled him to say to me after one of our many theological battles, "Dick, if the bishop required me to say that the white wall behind me is green, I would obey and agree." Sounds absurd, I know, and surely it is, but that's how far untempered obedience can go.

As one beloved bishop said to me long ago when I urged him to make a pastoral decision that would have required bending church law a bit, "Remember, my friend, I was made a bishop not because I am smart or holy, but because I'm safe." Translation: "I am obedient."

We are demoralized at the undeniable truth that the laity, especially women, are not yet recognized as full members of the church, who possess the ability to contribute to its recovery and to its more vital life at every level of its mission and existence.

That's not yet what we seem to be experiencing in this unprecedented crisis the church is in.

I can't tell you what shame and embarrassment I felt several years ago at a newspaper headline that read: *"Protect Our Children from Pedophile Priests..."* Imagine! Protect our children from us who are called Father! We've come a long way from Bing Crosby's Father O'Malley in 1943!

In my 58 years as a priest, as I write these words, I have never experienced a darker time for the church.

What can we do to address this situation effectively? I think we all know something about what we must do, but here's my suggestion for a start:

- Take every means possible to prevent further damage to other children.

  > We must report to the proper authorities any signs of suspicious behavior, especially as they become more credible when observed over a long period of time.

  > Church authorities must remove offending priests from contact with children.

- Help victims however we can to be healed of their psychological wounds and to move on to normal, well-adjusted lives.

  > Not too many years ago, an elderly man told me outside the Sacrament of Penance that as a child he

had been routinely abused by the respected pastor
of his church over a considerable period of time. He
said that somehow he went on to a happy marriage,
fatherhood, and a successful professional career. I'm
not a psychologist, and in no way am I treating such
a weighty matter cavalierly, but that anecdotal evidence given to me makes me hopeful about the
recovery of those who have been scarred by such
abuse in their early and formative years.

* Support the decision of church and civil authorities
to remove offending clerics from all contact with children. I think it was in the mid-80s that I read the statement of a United States government office that
pedophilia is an incurable condition or disease and that
all that can be done is to create and maintain those conditions in which abusive behavior is kept in check. I
think "containment" was the word it used, not cure.

My own good father was an active alcoholic who
loved his children very much and provided hand-
somely for them. But for most of his life I did not
understand that alcoholism is a disease. I thought
my father drank simply because he wanted to and
decided to. It was a moral weakness, I was convinced, that he could overcome if he willed to. After
his premature death, I learned the truth. There is an
analogy between pedophilia and addictive diseases
like alcoholism: they are incurable and need to be
treated with understanding and compassion.

In the middle of Lent is the day that we call "Laetare" or "Rejoice" Sunday, because that is the first word in the ancient introductory invocation of the day's Mass.

The idea is that we lift our heads up from the penitential mood of the season, with its focus on sin and repentance and death, and remember that, in the end, light wins out over darkness, life over death! Accordingly, the church decorates our places of worship with splashes of color, like rose-colored vestments. Good teacher that she is, the church says, "Take a break – go back to your penances tomorrow. Don't forget that the journey is to Easter and resurrection."

In the darkness of a terrible scandal, we may not feel like rejoicing as a church; therefore the order, the command, to do so is appropriate. The darkness, felt especially by victims and their families, priests who have the disease of pedophilia, falsely accused priests, anguished leaders of the church, loyal members like you, dear reader, will inevitably give way to the light of Jesus!

Much good will come from the present travails, I am convinced, as the church shows clearly her human weakness in having to be forced by such shameful circumstances to take a fresh, hard look at her attitudes and laws concerning human sexuality across the board. While many have been hurt by policies and teachings that are seen now to be not really conducive to personal and relational wholeness and growth, many more persons will benefit from a renewed theology.

Let us look forward with eagerness to the light that has already begun to dawn!

GIVING GOD A BAD NAME

Television, over the past several years, has brought into our homes the images and the messages of some prominent American atheists, one of them a popular and brilliant comedian; another a recently deceased author/essayist and philosophical critic. I've listened to them several times and have read some of their writings, and I have to admit that I find truth and irrefutable fact in what they are saying — not in everything they are saying, mind you, but in much of it. In essence, what I agree with is *their rejection of the very God that I too reject* — a God that is so human as to have been created by humans. A God who sulks, a God who threatens and punishes, a God who argues things out with us humans and bargains with us, a God who sent Jesus to suffer and die a painful death, etc.

We religious people can give God a bad name mostly by taking the Scriptures literally when they should be understood as metaphors or symbols or allegories. I say it again, it's the mistake of not realizing that very often the true message is to be found, not in a literal reading of the Scriptures, but *as carried by the images that the words produce.*

A perfect example of that is the ancient Book of Genesis, which tells about a man of faith, Abraham, who is commanded by God to kill his only son on an altar as a sacrifice to God. You know how the story goes and how it ends: Abraham does what he's told, only to be stopped by an angel — also at God's command — before plunging the dagger into his son's heart.

The image that the words produce is of a father who believes that God has commanded him to kill his son. The question is, what message

158

does that image have for us? We mustn't make the mistake of interpreting the story as factual truth, as if it actually happened. I don't believe that it did, and in increasing numbers neither do Scripture scholars today. But don't throw the story out either! It's been doing a great job for almost 3,000 years – but we've got to know the "code" so as to unlock its meaning.

Look at it this way, if you will. The story of Abraham and Isaac is couched in a time when human sacrifice was an accepted part of pagan worship. Against that background, the story can be seen as a teaching that human sacrifice is wrong, sinful, immoral, and unacceptable to the one true God.

Second, just as the George Washington cherry tree fable was created to proclaim and to celebrate the perfect honesty of our first president, so is the fable of Abraham and Isaac a powerful and unforgettable way of celebrating Abraham's unyielding trust in the presence and the love of the one and only God. It is also a challenge to all believers ever since to hang on with unwavering hope when they are facing frightening trouble and it seems that God doesn't care if they perish or succeed.

Third, in this bit of Scripture we are in touch with the beginnings of the faith that we Christians live by today. But how did Abraham come to know that there is only one God? What convinced him that there is a God at all? What were the signs that eventually revealed to him that God is loving and compassionate? I don't think we'll ever know the answers, but I am certain that this fictitious story of a trial that God put him through stands for the great conflict he had to endure as he committed himself to faith and trust in the God he would never see or hear. Doesn't that remind you of Jesus' reputed encounter with the "devil" who, we are told, tempted him to abandon the God he called Father and to follow him instead and become wealthy and powerful beyond imagination? Another example of sacred fiction that carries a divine message.

In Scripture we read of the faith journeys of Abraham, Paul, the apostles Peter, James and John, and many others. They were all thoroughly human beings like you and me. They all struggled to know and to accept the personal challenge of faith in the unseen God. They were all supported by occasional, however infrequent, glimpses of the realness of the God in whom they placed their trust.

Hasn't your faith experience, like mine, been somewhat the same? It's helpful to realize that our story has been lived over and over again before us and that we celebrate *it*, too, as we read the Scriptural accounts of "God-with-us."

After Mass one Sunday, a woman stopped on her way out of church to tell me about a terrible tragedy that had just occurred in her family. It was unquestionably a heart-wrenching ordeal that she and her family were experiencing. I listened attentively while she poured out her story with remarkable discipline and control. She appeared not to be asking anything of me except to listen and to pray for them all. And then – I don't know whether to say it was to my surprise or not (I can give reasons for both) — she summed up her story by saying, "Well, we know that God does not ever give a cross too heavy for us to carry and that we must simply accept this as God's will for us."

I tried, as I have tried over and over again with so many good people, to lead her into thinking the matter out differently and not any longer making things worse for herself and her family by assigning to God blame for the tragedy.

There are so many of us Christians who believe that the troubles that have befallen them were arranged and decreed by God. Most of these good people don't seem to have the slightest idea why they have been so punished. They either make the sad statement that, if only they did know what sins they had committed to deserve the penalty, they would never commit them again or, in contrast, confess that it must be for a particular sin they could not deny they may have committed.

That same kind of thinking makes its appearance on the world scene as well. Christian ministers like the Reverends Jerry Falwell and Pat Robertson told us that the tragedy of 9/11 was an act of God in punishment for the sins of us Americans – in particular, for what they called the sin of homosexuality. Unfortunately, we are still stuck with a long and strong tradition that would have us believe that the Creator is in charge of what happens in this world, when actually there is so much more reason to reject such thinking.

There are reasons that many of us are so quick to assign to God responsibility for our troubles: to begin with, we get comfort from assuming that there is a rational cause for the terrible things that happen to us, and that the cause is God. That belief enables people of faith to shrug their shoulders, grit their teeth and say that God must have caused or allowed the tragedy for a reason that they cannot comprehend. Something deep inside them tells them that they could not survive in a world of pure chance; someone's got to be in charge, there must be some sort of intelligent design, otherwise this is an absurd world, and we are all its hapless victims.

But that's a dead-end street; it is simply false. If we could get rid of those old notions about the supposed "will of God" in our lives, we would free our minds to understand that our strength and consolation come from the presence of the Divine Spirit, the Creative Spirit, within us in both good times and bad. We must tell ourselves over and over again that that is enough and that we need nothing more other than our own personal resources and the support of those who love us.

The truth is that life is full of accidents and human violence and disease in addition to the irrational, often deadly, forces of nature, enough to produce a climate in which all living things, including us human beings, are only too likely to get hurt — not just occasionally, but often.

And so we go on, people of faith, expecting rain and storms as well as sun and cool breezes, all the while knowing that the Creative Spirit is with us every step of the way.

RESPONSIBILITY OF AUTHORITY

I t has long seemed to me that the function of church authority is not only to facilitate the passage of authentic tradition from generation to generation, but also to observe respectfully and to call forth eagerly the contemporary works of the Spirit wherever they occur. A good pastor does precisely that: he honors and elicits from the people their well-considered perceptions of the Spirit's direction. And why should his own pastoral sense not be trusted to present the teachings and the guidelines of the church in such a way that they become more understandable and acceptable to his people? Take the liturgy, for example: why should not the dictates of common sense, courtesy, and practicality encourage him to invite the people to participate maximally, not minimally, in the flow of the liturgy — which is defined as the "work of the people"?

What could be more stultifying and more boring than the same words and gestures repeated endlessly? Is uniformity really to be exalted over life-giving creativity? Can we not depend on the corrective faculties and mechanisms within the Christian community to discern if and when, occasionally, individual expression has gone too far and missed the mark? Is the church meant to be an engraved stone or a living organism?

It saddens me to conclude that our bishops sometimes regard themselves, not as catalysts of vigorous growth in the church, but as defensive keepers of the status quo. I respect their zeal, but I could not feel more strongly that it needs to be redirected. Their instructions may be based on the highest ecclesiastical authority and thus mark them as obedient bishops; but do we all not owe Rome more than mere obedience? We owe the exercise of reason, graceful adaptation, and sometimes respectful opposition when it is clearly called for.

The Vatican now stipulates that lay persons are not to handle the sacred vessels (the usually gold cups and other containers used at Mass). About 40 years ago I happened to be in the chapel at Yale University and to hear a wise and far-sighted Catholic chaplain ask two young ladies to bring the bread and wine to the altar at the offertory. Dutifully instructed in their "proper place," they demurred, to which he said, for all present to hear, "For goodness' sake, those vessels are pieces of metal or glass shaped by human hands. You are the living tabernacle of God. Please, pick them up and come!" A moment of clear thought and sound theology that has stayed with me ever since.

And we all know the status of women in our church, maintained at such a low level. Well, among the best homilies I have ever heard have been those conceived and delivered by women, religious and lay. I think it is wrong for us and our people to be denied such a font of wisdom and faith. How can I ever forget the night that I met in the hallway one of my fellow resident priests coming home to the rectory and being eager to tell me about the good day he had had. Best part of it, he said, was the funeral service he had attended in a Protestant church for one of his chaplain colleagues at a local hospital. What made it special, he said, was the homily given by a female minister. "What she said, and the way she said it," he exclaimed, "could have come only from a woman's heart and mind." I remember punching his shoulder and saying, "Attaboy, Frank! You're learning!"

Polls indicate time and again that the number one complaint Catholics make about their ordinary Sunday experience in church is the poverty and irrelevance of the homilies they are regularly hearing from their priests.

I always enlist lay ministers of the Eucharist to serve their brothers and sisters at Mass, no matter how many priests may be present, because I believe that this is a very effective way of bonding these good people with the priests they love and also giving public witness to the servant status that befits every true follower of Jesus. Their role must not be allowed to become more and more passive, yielding exclusively to a priestly caste what should instead fall within their own responsibility.

ORDAINED FOR SELF OR FOR SERVICE?

On the day of my ordination, one of my father's employees, a simple, uneducated man, something of a diamond in the rough, dared to darken the cathedral doors and enter the venerable building to witness the event. At its conclusion he waited for me on the sidewalk beyond the iron gates. He approached me; stuck out his hand to this young man he had known since he was a teenager and said, "Congratulations, Father Dick (special emphasis on "Father"!). I hope you like it." (My family and I have ever since been amused by the recollection of that moment!)

I *have* liked it. There's not been a day in the past 58 years in which I've not felt grateful to have found my way to priesthood. With all its to-be-expected ups and downs, it's been uncommonly satisfying, shared as it has been with some of the most beautiful human beings ever created.

That said, it must also be acknowledged that hardly a week has gone by these past several years without our reading in the press or hearing on radio and television disturbing reports about Catholic priests behaving immorally and even criminally: Sexual crimes on the one hand, financial on the other. It's amazing how forgiving Catholics are. They far more frequently react to these scandalous exposures with remarks like, "Oh well, we're all human" than with words of scathing condemnation. In no way am I excusing these crimes or making light of them, but nonetheless I dare to suggest that there is another area of clerical abuse that seems to have been equally if not more important to Jesus and to which we all ought to pay more attention.

What I have in mind is the priest who seems never to have learned that he was ordained to be a servant of the people and who, rather,

166

guards carefully his own convenience, making it known to everyone when he is going out of his way, however begrudgingly, to minister to the people. There may be relatively few such men, but they stand in very obvious contrast to the far greater number of generous, self-sacrificing priests whose purity of ministry often goes unnoticed.

The matter is fresh in my mind as I write this, because only recently a friend of mine told me that she had called her parish priest to the bedside of her dying mother and that what happened in that sacramental setting was not only not consoling but rather an added burden to a family under stress and in sorrow. What this priest did, she said, was to punctuate his soulless, rote recitation of the sacramental ritual with complaints about being called out of the rectory on such a busy day. This visit, he made clear, would have been unnecessary if the family had taken the ailing woman some weeks before to the parish communal celebration of the Sacrament of the Sick.

An attitude like that is a distortion of the meaning of priesthood — the priesthood of the ordained and the priesthood of the people. Jesus made it unquestionably clear that he was calling his followers to a life of generous service. The invitation had nothing to do with personal convenience or wealth or fame or status.

In the world of Jesus' time, when there were so many people who were desperately poor because of the greed and oppressive practices of the wealthy and the powerful, when there were so many poor people who wanted to be better off and could not help envying the lifestyle of the more fortunate, when there were so many religious people who had been taught by human authority (which claimed God's endorsement, of course) that high status in this world was a sign of God's approval – in such a climate, Jesus did what no ordinary politician is likely to have done: he told the people the truth that they did not want to hear!

He didn't say it is a sin to be rich or a curse to be poor. He said that it is God's will that all human beings serve each other generously. What the people of his day did not see, and what we may still not be seeing, was that, if human beings really acted that way, there would be no poor people. There could not be the violent class warfare that we are so accustomed to.

St. Mark (10:35-45), it appears, aims the words of Jesus in this regard, not first to all of us, but to the leaders of the movement that Jesus was starting – the movement that would eventually become the Christian church. He was targeting the leaders of the newly emerging "Way of Christ," forerunners of today's priests and ministers. He was addressing the twelve apostles, commanding them, above all, to serve humbly and generously, leaving them with the initially puzzling equation that the path to genuine greatness is simply humble service to all.

A newly ordained priest once wrote to me with thanks for the gift he had received from me. His letter suggested that his theology was ultraconservative, which disappointed me because I am convinced that the church needs most of all today priests who are progressive in their thinking and are alert to the directions of the Spirit of Truth and Love in our troubled times. My return letter to him contained the following lines:

The souvenir card you sent me I regard as representing the church of the 1940s and 50s. That was the church that Pope St. John XXIII said needed to open its windows and let in some fresh air. For that purpose, he summoned the Second Vatican Council as a mighty instrument of reform. The vestments of the priest pictured on the card represent that dying church also, as do the orientation of the altar, the items on it, the bowing of the altar boy, etc. Why that choice?

I was ordained before you were born, in 1958, and I remember those days only too well. I don't want to see them ever again!

You say that you are committed to teaching only what Jesus commanded his disciples to teach. But Jesus knew nothing about organ transplants, nuclear energy, same-sex marriage, in vitro fertilization, labor/management issues, weapons of mass destruction, etc. He said nothing about abortion, homosexuality, married priests, etc.

You get the point, I'm sure. While you hope "never to fall in the error of teaching my own personal opinion," that is precisely what you must do at times simply because Jesus did not tell us what his opinion was on the matter at hand (if, indeed, he could have an opinion at all). It will be from your mind and heart, immersed as they are in the spirit of Jesus, that truth will be shared with others. And you will do that, not independently, but in collaboration with the best thinking available at the time both within the church and without. The Spirit has not been silent and inactive for the past two millennia; on the contrary, the Spirit always does what Jesus said the Spirit would do: teach us what he did not, or could not, during his brief ministry among us.

You seem to be such a good man, a good priest. You are blessed with intelligence, grace, an appealing personality, and a generous spirit. If you were to devote your priesthood to a narrow conservatism, I would judge that to be a lamentable loss to the church that eagerly awaits your enthusiastic leadership into a beautiful new birth!

Your brother in the ministry of Jesus,

CLERIC-ISM

In one of the earliest centuries of the church, Pope Celestine I wrote to all his priests a letter of correction because it had come to his attention that they were dressing in a distinctive way, setting themselves apart from the people they served. He said that priests should be distinguished not by what they wear but by their conversation and their charity.

Now, surely that is not to be interpreted as a proscription against religious habits or clerical collars any more than Jesus' statements about scandal are to be taken as instruction for us to amputate our limbs or pluck out our eyes as a safeguard against sinning. No, it's a matter of emphasis and priority.

A priest acquaintance of mine said rather publicly some years ago that we Catholics are permitted to be only as charitable as the law permits. We should not succumb to such legalistic distortion. Quite the opposite. Our commitment to the Gospel values of Jesus and our courageous willingness to risk disapproval, when unavoidable, for the sake of what is right actually purify the law and make it more reflective of the divine presence.

The rules of our lives are the invention of humans and contain human wisdom, but the law of love comes from the Creator of all. What matters in the end, therefore, is not so much whether we have observed the rules perfectly, as admirable and desirable as that may be, but whether love for all, without rejection or exception, has grown and matured over the long course of successes and failures.

Everything human is subject to failure despite our best intentions and highest hopes, despite the degree of energy we generously expend. Much of the time we do not see very clearly what is right before our eyes. When the heart, with its wonderful instincts and spontaneous emotions, gets in the way, vision is even the more impaired! Many good persons like us find ourselves for a time on the wrong path, one we never fully intended or sought. In such a case, it is love that endures, taking on new forms. In particular, forgiveness of self and others and the daring decision to make a new departure lead us to experience life in depth and color and vibrancy that we may otherwise never have known.

I'm certain that you have discovered as I have that many persons have strange notions of what priests and religious are as consecrated Christian servants of the people of God. It was only a couple of months after my ordination to priesthood that I was at my parents' home on my weekly day off, installing an overhead door on my dad's garage. I was dressed appropriately for the somewhat greasy job when a neighbor came sauntering down the driveway. Pleased to use my new title, he greeted me courteously and then after a minute's small talk said, "Tell me, Father, are you supposed to be doing that?"

"Doing what?"

"Working with those tools the way you are."

"Well, why might anyone think that I should not be doing this?"

He said, "You know... I mean your consecrated fingers and all that."

I remember his words better than my own, but I hope that I reminded him that Jesus worked in his father's carpenter shop, and St.

Paul was a tent-maker, and the apostles were fishermen, and Mary labored hard to keep a good home for herself and at least two very hungry and grateful men.

And then there was the barber to whom I went for a decade or so. One day, I suppose summoning the courage to say something he'd wanted to ask for a long time, he stepped back from the cutting and the grooming and said, "So, tell me, Father, what do you actually do all day? Do you say Mass in the morning and then meditate and pray the rest of the day?"

I remember my response: "Tony, it may be hard for you to understand this, but my day is every bit as busy as yours; however, my busyness is in many more than one place."

Jesus referred to his disciples as being like the leaven, the yeast, which is small in quantity but makes the whole loaf of bread rise. He also referred to another kitchen staple, an ingredient of most foods, salt. Jesus calls his disciples — us — the salt of the earth and asks, rhetorically, what can season the salt if the salt itself loses its flavor.

I never understood that reference until I learned some years ago that salt in Jesus' day was not the pure white crystalline substance that we know today. Instead, it was a dirty lump – literally "dirty" because soil was mixed in with it. It was taken from the lake shoreline and then placed in a cloth bag. The bag was dunked into the food, either at the table or on the stove, and therefore its contents had a limited useful life; at some point, the salt would have all been dissolved, leaving only a residue of dirt. It's about that residue that Jesus asks what can be done to make it enhance the flavor of food once again. And, of course, the answer is "Nothing." It remains useless and should be thrown out to function only as dirt.

Jesus is talking about us, his committed followers, and passionately reminding us that we have a job to do in association with him and in imitation of him. As salt brings out the flavor of virtually every food, enhancing that unique flavor without subduing or destroying its individuality, so are we to live and speak and act in such ways as to brighten with hope and clarity of vision the lives of our fellow human beings, especially those who are discouraged to the point of joylessness and even despair by the cruel and oppressive circumstances of their lives.

My late pediatrician brother returned from a two-week medical mission in a remote area of Brazil, and thereafter often told of the beauty of the people, their abject poverty, their deep faith, their gratitude and graciousness. What struck me most among his personal reflections was his conviction that he received more from them than he gave to them, more in the way of human values and fundamental lessons for life. In such cases, who is the salt? It must be both the visitor and the host. And that is the way it should be, because no one is excluded from being an agent of the compassionate Jesus.

I have in my files the personal testimony of the late William E. Simon, Treasurer of the United States, concerning his ministry to the sick in my own Diocese of Paterson, NJ. For many years he took the Blessed Sacrament to sick people in hospitals and in their homes. In several typewritten pages, he felt compelled to say what those visits meant to him, how privileged he was to take to those suffering people the sacramental presence of Jesus and, while they thanked him profusely, how much he was enriched by their strong faith at a very difficult time in their lives. Again, who was the salt?

But there's a fly in the ointment. We continue to be plagued by the disease of clericalism. In other words, we still tend to think that the work of the church belongs primarily, even exclusively, to the clergy and the religious. The official church itself added to that heresy when it taught, only a couple of generations ago, that Catholic Action is the participation of the laity in the mission of the hierarchy. That is not so, and we must put it to rest once and for all. Jesus had no such thing in mind; he never could have envisioned a church of unequals, of owners and tenants, of masters and servants. Jesus was intent on reforming that very misconception in his own beloved Jewish religion. We are all meant to be equal as his followers, from pope to peasant, each of us with a unique ministry defined by our own personal makeup and the circumstances of our life, all of us united by one Baptism, one faith, and one Eucharist.

I wish I were qualified to say much more than I am about to say, but we must let this suffice: We know that clericalism, a caste society, exists in the church when we recall how priests have been regarded as a class apart, a privileged minority, more than merely human, idols of a sort. The current sexual scandals certainly help to restore reality in that regard.

We see clericalism in our memory of the church into the 1960s that allowed its people to say not a single word in the entire Mass until it was over, when the three Hail Marys were recited!

Clericalism rules when intelligent men and women ask their priest, "Father, is it a sin for me to miss Mass because I will be traveling to Asia on the weekend?"

We are a clerical church as long as we have no say in the selection of our leaders.

We are all called to be yeast and salt and light in the real world of human beings; that is how we become the church of Jesus. Each of us – with no exceptions – is gifted in many wonderful, unrepeatable ways. Our task, our joy and fulfillment, is to share as generously as we can.

ME AT THREE IN 1933, Clifton, NJ. (Thank goodness I wasn't a style setter!) There would be seven moves up and down the East coast over the next 13 years as my father was pursuing his career in the textile industry.

MY YOUNGEST BROTHER DAVID, retired businessman, husband of Roberta and father of their three children, with me (right) in the early 2000s.

MY SIBLINGS AND I: (left to right) David, Bob (died 2012), Barbara (married to Charles and the mother of 6 children; died 2015). They have given me 17 nieces and nephews, among the greatest joys of my life.

MY LATE BROTHER BOB, husband of Beverly and father of their eight children, a compassionate, skillful and much loved pediatrician.

177

MY MOTHER, Margaret Pellegrine, on the day of her graduation from Newark Teachers College around 1922, the first member of our clan to have an education beyond high school in America. Her father had been a teacher (for a while, a seminarian) in Italy.

MY PARENTS' WEDDING PICTURE 1929. "As you advance in years and under-standing," my mother wrote in my grade school (1944) graduation autograph book, "may you read deeper mean-ing in the following thought: 'To thine own self be true. It followeth as night the day thou canst not then be false to any man.'" (Don't miss the part in Dad's hair - but how could you?)

I'M NOT A GOOD PHOTOGRAPHER, but this was a lucky shot I took at one of my favorite places in the entire world, the Trappist Monastery in Spencer, Massachusetts, where I made my annual retreat for half a century.

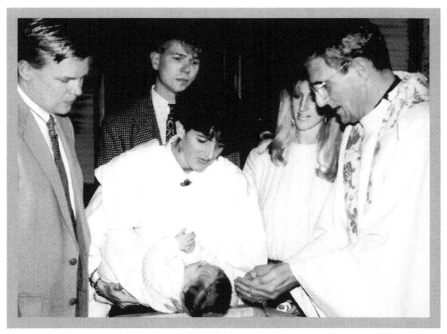

BAPTISM OF ONE OF MY GRANDNIECES at. St. Brendan Church, Clifton, NJ. Twenty happy years of team ministry with a responsive, engaged congregation — who never asked, "Who's in charge here?"

179

THAT'S ME, the food slicer for the 1988 celebration of 20 years of broadcasting the Sunday Radio Mass on WPAT, Paterson, NJ, into NJ, NY, CT, and PA. At the writing of this book, it was 48 years and counting. A ministry I very much enjoy.

FIRST PRIESTLY ASSIGNMENT, 1958. Full-time chaplain at St. Mary's Hospital, Passaic, NJ. Wonderful five years! Best imaginable introduction to priesthood.
Photo: Christmastime at 2nd floor nurses' station

MASS ON THE BEACH. For seven years every summer Saturday afternoon, as many as 250 participants. Little kids in April and May: "Mom, are we having Mass at the beach this summer?" Many adults returning to Mass and Communion.

THE ORIGINAL PASTORAL TEAM (c. 1980) at St. Brendan Church in Clifton, NJ, 1978 - 1998, where I requested that I be, not pastor, but pastoral team coordinator. The only formally established pastorship of its kind in the diocese, constant sharing and collaborating made it work well.

RELIGIOSITY VS. FAITH

I was in the parking lot of a church to which I had gone to give a retreat. A middle-aged woman drove up to me and asked if I knew where a certain Catholic church was located. I explained that I was a stranger in the area and was not able to help her. She somehow felt obliged to tell me why she had to find the church. She said, "I heard from a friend this week that the church is offering a plenary indulgence for only a few prayers and a small money donation, and I think that's a very good deal." I responded, with a hint of impatience, I'm afraid, that I was not "into" such practices and sent her off with a wish for her good health.

That is only one of the countless such pseudo spiritual absurdities I have encountered in my many years of priesthood, sure signs that our Catholic worship remains badly infected with superstition and pagan religiosity that we blissfully ignore or fail to recognize. People "buy" (I put the word in quotes, but it's the right word for what they think they are doing) — they "buy" Masses for the release of their deceased loved ones from Purgatory. Some light candles to ensure a safe journey abroad. Many promise God or the mother of Jesus or some other saint that they will perform sacrifices or charitable works, or say certain prayers, in return for the granting of a requested favor. These are but more indications of how corrupt our relationship with the Creator of the universe, with Jesus and Mary and the saints, can become. More proof positive that genuine Christian spirituality can easily — for a while imperceptibly — degenerate into the grossest ignorance and impropriety, however well intended it undoubtedly is. It's all around us and among us, and at least a smidgen of it is very likely to be found in the heart and mind of every one of us Catholics.

Jesus confronted this phenomenon in his day and urged instead a purity of worship that remains always solidly based on our awareness that —

we and all other living and inanimate things are creatures of the one and only God,

God is love,

God is compassionate and unimaginably generous and forgiving and merciful,

God is provident,

and we are to live in unwavering trust in our benevolent Creator.

The ancient scripture tells us that we are made to the image and likeness of God. We are made to live in gratitude for God's immeasurable goodness and to imitate God as we see Jesus doing. No bargaining, no "deals," no *quid pro quo*, no bribes or paying up. On the contrary, just an appreciation of the lavish generosity and unconditional love of God for us and, in response, our constant efforts to be good human beings who extend that loving concern to others without compromise or discrimination.

> *True religion, Jesus said, is taking care of orphans and widows.*

True religion, Jesus said, is taking care of orphans and widows. That says it perfectly: A human life pleasing to its creator is simply one of genuine charity toward others on our shared earthly journey. That's the heart of real religion. Our rituals and worship practices, our sacraments

183

and prayers are essentially for celebration and the expression of thanks. The true "stuff" of religion is not generated in the church building or at its altar, but in our daily lives, mostly in our relationships with other persons and with this globe we inhabit together. The bread and wine that we Catholics offer at every Mass have meaning and value only in proportion to what we have already given them in our day-by-day efforts to be Jesus to others.

That was emphasized and underscored for me in two visits I've made to the American Indian Museum of the Smithsonian Institution in Washington, D.C. The American Indians' traditional reverence for the earth and sky and their gratitude to the Great Spirit, who makes and sustains this marvelous universe, echo Jesus' passionate desire that we, his followers, adopt that same attitude toward all God's creatures. He wanted it to be that way with us especially in relation to our fellow human beings. He taught us to make our prayers not childish exercises in coaxing and bargaining, but rather outpourings of thankfulness and praise and absolute confidence in God's love for each of us.

REVELATION IN METAPHORS

I should think that not too many Catholics share with their bishops their dissatisfaction with "transubstantiation" as an approach to an understanding of Jesus' real presence in Eucharist, but many priests, religious and lay persons have admitted such to me. In essence, what the word means is that when the priest says the words of consecration ("This is my body...This is the cup of my blood..."), the substance of the bread and wine is changed into the substance of the Risen Jesus Christ, while the physical properties of "bread-ness" and "wine-ness" remain unchanged. I have expressed that colloquially (I hope not offensively) in this way: "transubstantiation" is like a table being changed into a chair while continuing to look and feel and weigh like a table. Thus are the bread and wine, we are told, changed into the substance of the living Jesus while retaining all and only the physical characteristics of bread and wine. Pretty hard to swallow, I say.

Doubters, I have learned, typically have great difficulty also with the classical definition of the Trinity (three Persons in one God).

For example, a very bright woman, mother of two married daughters and long-time employee of the church, wrote to me:

While I accept the "presence" of Jesus in the Eucharist, I always had trouble with the transubstantiation/"body and blood" thing. I reject the notion of the priest as some kind of wonder-worker who exercises divine power through his consecrated fingers, says the magic words, and Voila! we get to "eat His body and drink His blood." No, thank you. I'm a vegetarian! Besides, Jesus did say, as he broke the bread and poured the wine and then passed it to others, "Do this in remembrance of me," which in my mind means His presence occurs when the meal is SHARED. As for the Trinity: I have read John Dominic Crossan's books, in which he notes that Jesus referred to himself as the "Son of Man." The early Church called him the "Son of God" to counter Caesar's claim to the same.

I get lots of feedback like this, leading me to conclude that the *sensus fidelium*[18] of our church includes a strong desire for a reinterpretation of some old doctrinal formulas. Jesuit Father Thomas Reese made the excellent point that we must not go on merely repeating the teachings of ancient giants like Augustine and Aquinas; instead, he urged, we must do what they did: namely, use the sciences of our day to elucidate the faith as they used the available wisdom of their day to do the same.[19] I would add that we have long since turned an important corner: it is no longer Revelation that determines the validity of science (consider Galileo); rather, it is science (revelation with a lower case "r") that helps us to interpret Revelation correctly. My thoroughly Catholic, daily Communicant mother used to say as she would read the *National Geographic*, "Isn't God wonderful!"

Trappist Father Matthew Flynn repeats over and over that everything – everything – we say about God is pure analogy and metaphor, so incomprehensible is the mystery of mysteries we call God.[20] Trinity is metaphor. We make our best human effort, he emphasized, to say something true about God, and we do not really understand what we are saying; we merely take a stab at the impossible task of expressing the inexpressible.

It seems to me that some of the metaphors we have inherited from the past, at least in their traditional interpretation, cannot satisfy today's quest for a credible faith. Honoring the core concepts of such articles of faith necessarily involves a process of demythologizing – a pruning away of earlier, admirable attempts to speak of the mystery, in favor of more effective and acceptable ones for today.

A cardinal example: once we take seriously our awareness that our theology is based on ancient myths like the Adam and Eve story, we simply have to examine anew the conclusions that follow from such false premises and then reform and restate them. If we are actually not a "fallen" race (the inherited sin of our "first parents," etc.) but are instead a *developing* race, having come from lower forms of life (as Pope St. John Paul II told us is the case), then what do we do with the myth of an angry, punishing God, the need for a divine redeemer, the meaning of the life and death of Jesus, etc.? Christianity will never be acceptable and attractive to discerning people of the 21st century as long as it defies the obvious truth that has come from other compelling sources. The church must demonstrate a willingness to explore these fundamental issues.

Transubstantiation is simply incredible to me, but a presence of Jesus in the context of a shared meal (which implies that his presence is as much in the assembly – the Body of Christ – as it is in the elements of bread and wine) is both credible and appealing. "Three persons in one God" is to me pure human invention, but loving relationship as belonging to the essence of divinity I embrace as eternal truth.

I find myself in the terribly uncomfortable position of not being a qualified, competent, professional theologian and yet having to admit that I cannot accept some of the traditional teachings of the church and instead am searching for a different interpretation of Jesus in the light of a radically different cosmology.

I see Jesus as that uniquely sensitive and holy Jewish man who was so aware of the presence of God in all things and in all persons that he

187

could say that to know him is to know God. I interpret his crucifixion, not as payment or ransom for sin, but as the measure of his unconditional love for us and for the one he called Father. I call Jesus savior, not because he pays my debt of sin, but because he rescues me from false notions about the Creator, assures me of my worth, opens my eyes to an ever-loving God, and invites me to share in his paschal journey to eternal, transformed life.

> *I call Jesus savior, not because he pays my debt of sin, but because he rescues me from false notions about the Creator, assures me of my worth, opens my eyes to an ever-loving God, and invites me to share in his paschal journey to eternal, transformed life.*

EUCHARIST: MAGIC OR MYSTERY

E very once in a while, a concerned Catholic will tell me that he or she has been to a wedding or a funeral at which, just before Communion is distributed, the priest announced to the people present that only practicing Catholics in the state of grace may receive. Sometimes the announcement is blunt and to the point, and sometimes it contains an explanation, the most common one being that Eucharist is a sign of the unity, however imperfect, that does exist in the church and, since members of other religions cannot be thought of as totally united with us Catholics, it is inappropriate that we share at the Eucharistic table.

That whole phenomenon always distresses me deeply, and I feel strongly that there must be other ways of looking at the situation. To begin with, why must Eucharist be seen only as a sign of unity already achieved? Why not also a sign of the unity that we seek, the unity that still evades us? Isn't that one of the main reasons we begin our liturgies with a penitential rite, the admission that we are sinful and are in need of reconciliation? And, even when we are all good Catholics in the state of grace who are receiving, can we ever honestly say that we are completely united? It is obvious that we cannot claim that at any time.

On the other hand, cannot Eucharist celebrate whatever unity we have achieved? We may be of different degrees or different kinds of faith, but if we all believe in the one God, if we are all making a sincere effort to do what is right, if we are paying increasing attention to the neediest of our brothers and sisters, if we are trying to bring about peace and an end to violence, if we are all grateful for the gifts of life and love and share in appropriate ways, do we not then have much in common

189

and therefore have we not attained a respectable, though certainly not perfect, unity?

I believe that what we celebrate on Holy Thursday is the introduction to the world by Jesus of a new sacrament, a sacrament of table fellowship, in which we believe Jesus is truly present. Eucharist is not a sacred action that we perform only in church; it is rather a sacred action that we begin and celebrate usually in church – but not until we have extended it, by our own words and deeds, to our world, both immediate and remote. As St. Augustine said, in Communion we receive more of what we already are, the "Body of Christ." And then, energized with that increased or intensified divine presence, we are sent back into the world to bring Jesus — indeed, to *be* Jesus — to others.

The "Magic Moment" mentality about Eucharist has seen its day and must yield to a more enlightened theology. I refer to the moment of Consecration, when the presiding priest, holding the bread and wine, says the words of Jesus: "This is my body...This is the cup of my blood..." It is at that moment that heads are bowed and silence prevails and breasts are beaten and standing persons suddenly drop to their knees — all signifying that at that instant the transformation of bread and wine into the person of Jesus happens. Not so. It is the whole action of the Mass that brings about a unique and exquisitely intimate presence to us, for us, and in us.

But let's say again what we have been reemphasizing only lately: that Communion is primarily not a *thing*, however sacred, but an *action*, in which we are publicly renewing the pledge to make our lives increasingly conformed to the generous, unselfish life of Jesus. That's what he meant when at the Last Supper on the night before his execution he said, "Do this in memory of me." He said that while he was breaking a loaf of bread and passing it around to his friends at table.

The Mass:

- Our gathering around the table in response to Jesus' invitation.

- Our proclaiming and receiving the "word of God" in Scripture.

- Our prayers of praise, thanksgiving, repentance, and petition, especially on behalf of others.

- Our recalling reverently the suffering, death, and resurrection of Jesus.

- Our eating the sacred meal of fellowship with Jesus and with each other and with those who have gone before us from life to Life.

- Our anticipation of the "heavenly banquet" symbolized by this oft-repeated earthly meal.

- Our resolving to assist others in generous service, as Jesus did.

- And, most important of all, as we eat the bread and drink from the cup, our pledging, for all present to see and hear, that we will continue making our best efforts to imitate Jesus in everything we think and say and do.

In all of that, not just at the moment of Consecration, the Risen Jesus becomes uniquely present to us, not to be adored but to fill us with love and power for good works.

As I have come to understand it, the Last Supper is not the bestowal of divine power on a few chosen men, but the beginning of a ritual involving all of us, a ritual so intimate, so full of history and promise, so connected with and expressive of the life, death, and resurrection of Jesus, that it is true to say that we are never more fully church than when we are engaged in the act of Eucharist.

We must hope that the celebration will never end!

SPIRITUAL INSURANCE POLICY

A few years ago, a man by the name of Robert Kent, who had worked for the same company for 33 years, was given a grand dinner party upon his retirement. At that celebration, several of his co-workers noted that what they loved and admired most about him was his optimism. In an article in a Connecticut newspaper he subsequently wrote, "If indeed I am optimistic, I got to wondering where that sense of optimism came from."

And then, after noting that the firm had gone through some very difficult times during the years of his employment, he went on to say, "I finally concluded that whatever sense of optimism I have comes from my Christian faith. Christianity, at least as I understand it, is rooted in optimism. We are optimistic that God is with us and loves us; we are optimistic about life after death; and we are optimistic that God will be with us in good times and in bad. It seems to me that having a life based in faith leads to an optimistic attitude. Without faith, I don't know how anyone can be optimistic. One of the reasons I like to go to church is that I meet the most wonderful people there. By and large, they are optimistic and caring people, filled with love and concern for their fellow humans. Each Sunday our faith and optimism are renewed through our liturgy…"

We celebrate Mass every Sunday not to make installments on a spiritual insurance policy, not to beg God to forgive our sins and wrongdoing, and not primarily because we are required by church law to do so.

No, Sunday Mass is simply our time-honored way of thanking God for what we are and what we have, of being renewed and strengthened for the next lap of our earthly journey, of recommitting ourselves to following

Jesus, and, as St. Augustine so well put it, (already noted a few pages back) of receiving more of what we already are.

But *what* are we? We are the body of Jesus in the world of our time and place. Jesus said, "As the Father has sent me, so do I send you."

When we receive Holy Communion, it is not to be understood as reward for good behavior; indeed, it might well be that among our most thoughtful, most devout Communions are those that followed some of our worst behavior. It is not essentially an act of adoration we are performing. We are receiving into our hearts, minds, and entire lives more of what we already are — nothing less than representatives of the person of the risen Jesus, filled with the same Spirit with which he was filled.

The question arises then: What does our being the presence of Jesus to the world demand of us, do for us? It *demands* of us that we try to act in all circumstances as he would have us act and as he himself would act — WWJD (What Would Jesus Do?). It *offers* us the direction and empowerment of the same Spirit that directed and empowered Jesus.

Can you imagine how peaceful, how loving, how beautiful our homes and our lives would become if we were increasingly acting according to his example?

Christ has no body but yours,

No hands, no feet on earth but yours,

Yours are the eyes with which he looks

Compassion on this world,

Yours are the feet with which he walks to do good,

Yours are the hands with which he blesses all the world.

Yours are the hands, yours are the feet,

Yours are the eyes, you are his body.

Christ has no body now but yours,

No hands, no feet on earth but yours,

Yours are the eyes with which he looks

Compassion on this world.

Christ has no body now on earth but yours.

~St. Therese of Avila

THE "NEW" TRANSLATION OF THE ROMAN MISSAL

A cknowledging with respect the zeal and good intentions of those who labored to produce the translation of the Mass texts introduced on the First Sunday of Advent, 2011, I submit for the consideration of all who share my concerns about it the following critique.

To begin with, it seems to me that drawing the translation from the Latin text is, in more ways than the chronological, a step backward at a time when the church desperately needs to be forging ahead with all the energy and wisdom it can muster in the spirit of Vatican II.

In revising the Mass texts, why embrace the theology of former centuries *lock, stock and barrel*, without taking into account the brilliant theological insights that have been contributed in the intervening years by both theologians and the church's faithful membership?

And why would we not eagerly honor the scientific discoveries that have allowed us, for example, to image God and creation radically differently?

Why would we choose language that "retrojects" us into an age of scientific darkness from which, long ago, the world has emerged? Is it right for us, as a case in point, to continue speaking of Jesus as coming down from heaven when even Pope St. John Paul II, hardly a theological liberal, taught that there are no such places as heaven and hell, which, he said, are in reality "personal states of being"?

The church cannot possibly be taken seriously by a sophisticated world when it presents its fundamental teachings and tenets in archaic terms, no longer credible to scientifically enlightened minds. Instead of honoring those terms as venerable vestiges of the past, we err by endorsing them anew as creedal statements for today. We could have managed quite well with the forms we have been using for the past many years, making prudent modifications dictated by pastoral discretion; instead, we find ourselves forced to be spokespersons for an obsolete theology that more and more of us, lay persons as well as priests, can no longer subscribe to.

There are many flaws in the new translation that mark it as regressive rather than healthily progressive. Words like "consubstantial" are no improvement over their predecessors and tend rather to keep ordinary people at a greater distance from the holy mysteries rather than to draw them closer, while at the same time implying that the clergy possess a knowledge exclusive to themselves.

And what are the implications of "And with your spirit"? Does that response imply that the presence of "spirit" in the clergy is somehow different in kind or intensity from what it is in the lay responders? Is there not but one Spirit present in all of creation?

Is "incarnate of the Virgin Mary" really clearer and more appealing and more related to human life than "born of Mary"?

And in the Nicene Creed why should we say "I believe" instead of the former "We believe," when community and covenant are such time-honored, foundational concepts of Judeo-Christian religion and culture?

The 1985 Roman Missal spoke of the shedding of Jesus' blood "for all"; what has dictated the present change to "for many"? Who are excluded from his unconditional love?

Some of the newly revised sentences — *sentences*, mind you — are beyond 70 words in length. Has not something gone wrong when excessive verbosity and run-on sentences pass the test of "improvement"?

Since the current translation's introduction, I have discussed it with over 40 priests, in addition to many, many lay persons and professed religious. I have found *not one* who has anything good to say about what we have been given. They all agree that the new translation is sentimental, verbose, flowery, sanctimonious, archaic, obsequious and simply unprayable.

One older priest among the 40 said it best of all, I thought: "Required to say these distasteful words, I am made to feel that I am groveling before a capricious God."

If I were asked what can be done about the situation and if I were empowered to contribute to fixing it, I would suggest that two primary steps be taken: 1) that the optional use of the 1985 missal be authorized, and 2) that wider latitude be granted to the clergy and the faithful to temper what has now been prematurely presented as the norm for all to observe. Such a policy of trustful, expectant oversight would allow the *sensus fidelium*,[21] up to this point neglected in the process, its rightful role in the reformation of Catholic Eucharistic prayer.

CHAPTER FIVE

How Do We Make Things Better?

Dear Father Rento:

Thank you for the retreat you conducted in our parish last week.

I want you to know that my husband left the Church about 20 years ago. I left a few years later. But then I found it possible to return and to view the Catholic Church as an adult instead of how I had been taught as a child. You know: God is "mad" at you, you've "hurt" God, He (sic) is going to get even for all the bad things you've done, etc.

My husband has never been able to get past some of the things he has been taught and the anger he feels toward the Church.

During the retreat he began to realize that what he was taught and took so much to heart is not necessarily what he needs to continue believing. He feels he was robbed of his childhood related to some of the teachings he internalized. Now he has heard from a priest that God is all-loving and that this loving is unconditional. He has heard that before, but now he believes it.

I don't know that he will ever return to an organized religion. I do know that he is a good and kind man who has been imprisoned by negative feelings for most of his adult life. But I want you to know that since the parish retreat the process of setting him free has begun.

A letter from a retreatant in 2000.

THE OPERATIVE WORD IS "WE"!

*Easter means life, new life, resurrection,
hope, the best of good news!*

I quote from the previous chapter: *We all look for answers; we look for some sign that we can and will emerge from the crisis faced by the church purified, strengthened, wiser, more virtuous than we were before.*

And we will; I have no doubt about that. The way it will come about is suggested often in the scriptures, perhaps nowhere more emphatically than in John's gospel (14:15-21), where Jesus assures his disciples that he will ask the Father to send them the Holy Spirit, who will help them and remain with them always, guiding them/us in the ways of wisdom and love. But like any gift, this one will not and cannot be forced on the recipients – we get it and possess it and benefit by it only if we want it and make ourselves open to it.

In order to dispose ourselves to a new vision and a new future, we must acknowledge that in many ways our thinking about the church, its priorities, its mission, its very structure with regard to the role of leadership and of membership, has in some ways been incorrect, off the mark, not in line with what Jesus and the early church founders had in mind. And because of our skewed ideas and their increasing momentum over many generations, we have rendered ourselves largely incapable of perceiving and following the direction of the ever-present Spirit of Wisdom and Love.

I recall a summit meeting in my home diocese several years ago for the sole purpose of discussing the topic of abortion. The vast majority of the invited participants were priests, I among them — and there was *not one woman invited or included*. Would you think that possible? I guess the answer is yes.

Well, this is a time for us all to be as open as we can be to an infusion of truth from the Holy Spirit and the sharing of our personal gifts with no regard to rank or position. Our very ideas about God, the way we perceive or imagine the Creator, have to change and give way to sounder concepts (not rooted in ancient superstitions) which foster a healthier, more realistic relationship with God and with the world.

The make-up of the church and who we are as its members have to be explored and understood much better. The function of leadership in the church must be seen in a different way, so that we no longer view the hierarchy as the privileged princes who get directly from God what they pass on to us, but rather as good and humble servants who keep their eye on the community of believers to see where and in whom the Spirit of God is acting, and then call forth that revelation and make it available to the whole community.

That's the way it was in the beginning and the way it should have stayed. The church was a revolutionary democracy in which the divine Spirit moved and constantly created. That Spirit is no less alive and powerful and loving than she has ever been; it is we who got terribly distracted along the way. We've got to continue recovering and rebuilding!

Consider the following passage from the Acts of the Apostles, chapter 6, verses 1-7, which I'm taking from Eugene Peterson's *THE MESSAGE, the Bible in Contemporary Language.*

During this time, as the disciples were increasing in numbers by leaps and bounds, hard feelings developed among the Greek-speaking believers — "Hellenists" — toward the Hebrew-speaking believers because their widows were being discriminated against in the daily food lines. So the Twelve called a meeting of the disciples. They said, "It wouldn't be right for us to abandon our responsibilities for preaching and teaching the Word of God to help with the care of the poor. So, friends, choose seven men from among you whom everyone trusts, men full of the Holy Spirit and good sense, and we'll assign them this task. Meanwhile, we'll stick to our assigned tasks of prayer and speaking God's Word.

The congregation thought this was a great idea. They went ahead and chose Stephen, a man full of faith and the Holy Spirit, Philip, Procorus, Nicanor, Timon, Parmenas, and Nicolas, a convert from Antioch. Then they presented them to the apostles. Praying, the apostles laid on hands and commissioned them for their task. The Word of God prospered. The number of disciples in Jerusalem increased dramatically. Not least, a great many priests submitted themselves to the faith.[22]

Father Roger Karban enjoys a growing reputation for Scripture interpretation, for his clear teaching and practical, contemporary applications. His take on the foregoing passage from the Acts of the Apostles

202

is interesting and helpful. He calls our attention to the fact that Greek-speaking widows, who were the minority group in the early Christian communities, were complaining about being cheated in the daily distribution of food.

Instead of resorting to official authority and issuing a command to eliminate the disturbance, the leaders convoke an assembly of the entire community and challenge the people to resolve the problem. What they do is to choose supervisors for the task of food distribution, seven of them, deacons – and all of them Greek![23]

St. Luke, author of the passage, knew full well, from his experience of the Roman Empire, how efficient it can be to solve problems by appeal to the throne, to the "head office," but instead he highlights this communitarian approach probably because he so appreciated the logic that a decision made by community is more fully owned and more vigorously facilitated by it.

But as 21st century Catholic Christians, we are conditioned by the principle that "father knows best." We have been trained to submit and obey, and in the process we surrender our adulthood, our maturity, our dignity and become dependent juveniles; we deprive the whole church of the wisdom and energy that could have come only from us had we not sold out to a bad idea.

Today we face a far greater problem than the doling out of food to a small community, a problem now known to virtually the whole world: sexual abuse by a small percentage of priests. We ask the same questions: how shall it be solved, and by whom? Who will address it? It cannot be that we leave it to a small group of church officials, no matter how exalted their positions.

Every time an ordinary, non-ordained member of the church is interviewed on radio, TV, or the press concerning a matter of Catholic teaching or practice, we are witnessing an example of the exercise of what is called the *sensus fidelium*,[24] the "mind" of the people of faith, their innate perception of what is right and true, conclusions drawn from their Spirit-led lives. Infallible? No. Always right? No. But an authentic voice that deserves a hearing and is vital to the health and integrity of the church. To disregard or to silence that voice of the people is to disregard or silence the Spirit of Truth, who speaks to and through all persons in the particular setting of their own lives and work.

The official church must be open to that voice and call it forth always with respect and eager anticipation for the benefit of all.

It is not only those who are chosen to teach, lead, direct, and command who exercise authority in the church. Rather, every member, by virtue of Baptism, Confirmation, and Eucharist, by virtue of the grace of his or her particular state of life, has a share in the decision-making processes that affect the entire church.

It becomes increasingly obvious to a growing number of loyal Catholics that many aspects of the structure of the church need badly to be examined, critiqued, and modified, if not discarded and replaced. The church has always acknowledged this by speaking of itself as the "ecclesia semper reformanda," Latin for "a church always in need of change."

Against the background of what we've learned from the Acts of the Apostles about how important decisions were made in the earliest days of the church, consider this small sampling of questions very much at issue for us 21st century Catholics especially at this time of crisis –

- Would an end to mandatory celibacy be helpful toward a more stable priesthood and better service to all the people?

- Should currently married priests, now barred from priestly ministry, be welcomed back to active priestly work?

- Should women who feel called to priesthood be allowed to prepare for it and to be ordained?

Even if the appropriate reforms these questions suggest may be seen in the wisdom of the people to be necessary and highly advantageous to the overall mission of the church, surely we would not expect them to materialize immediately, but all of us must work now toward the day when they can become a reality.

It's healthy, right, necessary for us to talk about these things at our home tables and in gatherings everywhere, and when a coalescence of wisdom and insights has developed and finally matured, we shall have made progress toward greater truth and a church far more effective in being the compassionate Jesus to a hurting, needy world.

THE "BODY AND BLOOD" OF JESUS

I believe I am correct in saying that the priest who leads the Eucharistic liturgy is not properly called the "celebrant," because he is but one of the many celebrants present and participating, including, above all, the faithful laity. His correct title is "presider."

We celebrate the institution — the beginning or the establishment — of the Eucharist on Holy Thursday, making that day not one for sugary sentimentality, not primarily an occasion for worship, but for personal commitment. On the night before his inexpressible suffering and cruel death, Jesus asked if his followers would be willing to carry on in the real world of human beings according to his teachings, his understanding of God, his love for the people. Would we pledge ourselves to be him to a wounded, waiting world? The reception of Communion is a statement of intention made normally along with many other persons of the same faith. But Jesus added the encouraging promise that we would never be without him: he would be with us, he said, until the end of time. His intention was to strengthen us, not for places and positions of honor, but for compassionate action on behalf of all our brothers and sisters, especially the poorest, the littlest, the most oppressed and the least respected.

At least on a par with the transformation of bread and wine into the personal presence of Jesus in Eucharist is the washing of feet at the Last Supper as a symbol of our expected service to all who are in need. The ultimate transformation that Jesus hopes and looks for is not that of bread and wine into himself, but that of *us into acting as he did*.

The Last Supper was not the bestowal of divine power on a few chosen men, but the beginning of a ritual involving all of us, a ritual so intimate, so filled with history and promise, so connected with and expressive of the life, death, and resurrection of Jesus, that it is true to say, again, that we are never more fully the church than when we are engaged in the act of Eucharist.

In the Mass of the Chaldean Church, the Assyrian Church of the East (which is in union with the Roman Catholic Church and the pope), there do not appear the words of Consecration that we of the Latin Church are so familiar with and that we have been taught to regard as the very essence of the Mass — "This is my body...This is the cup of my blood..." This approved absence of something that we of the Latin Rite church hold to be indispensable suggests the question, "Is Jesus, then, really present in the Assyrian Mass?" And Rome answers that the Mass of the Assyrians is valid even though it does not contain the words of Consecration.

Hard for us to understand such a judgment, because we "good Catholics" have grown up in the "Magic Moment" mentality, which might be aptly characterized by the simple word, ZAP! Picture a crowded church. Halfway through the Mass, a hush descends, inviting bowing, kneeling, striking breasts, silence, etc. Why? Because the powerful formula is about to be enunciated by the presiding priest, at which time everyone is imagining Jesus "coming down" onto the altar! My own earliest education in my inherited Catholic religion and the instruction I got in seminary included strong emphasis on the glory of the priesthood as seen in this awesome power the priest possesses to turn bread and wine into the total person of Jesus. The "Real Presence," we thought, was absolutely dependent upon the utterance of those few sacred words.

But now the Vatican says that a Mass celebrated without the words of Consecration (as in the Assyrian ritual just mentioned above) also effects the Real Presence of Jesus! Yes, Jesus becomes sacramentally present without the words of Consecration! What does this tell us about the Eucharist that we did not know before — or that we somehow forgot over the passage of time? It tells us that it is the entire action of the Mass, performed by the assembly of the faithful under the leadership, the presidency, of the ordained priest. We have the grace to believe that that action of inspired faith brings about a unique and exquisitely intimate presence of the Risen Jesus for us and in us.

What is that "entire action?" Let's review its parts, as presented a few pages back:

- Our gathering around the table in response to Jesus' invitation.

- Our proclaiming and receiving the word of God in scripture — proclaimed to all of us as one people (which is why we are not to read individually, but rather to listen together).

- Our prayers of praise, thanksgiving, repentance, and petition, spoken and sung.

- Our remembering the suffering, death, and resurrection of Jesus.

- Our eating the sacred meal of fellowship with Jesus and with each other, and with those who have gone before us from life to Life. The Communion ritual places us at the Last Supper, whose table spread is extended through time and space in order to include us.

- Our anticipation of the "heavenly banquet" symbolized by this earthly meal.

* Our resolving to assist each other in living as he did —
in generous service, in faith, in unyielding hope, and in
peace.

It is in all of that, that entire fluid action, that the actual presence of
the risen Jesus is realized.

As he holds and uplifts the consecrated bread and wine before the
assembled faithful, the priest could be saying:

> *The gift of faith enables us to believe what our senses can-*
> *not perceive: that this is the real, sacramental presence of*
> *Jesus, in whose life, death and resurrection, there is life for*
> *everyone. Come, let us eat and drink in peace!*

UNION, FOOD FOR THE JOURNEY, COMMITMENT

I t's taken me this many years — I am an octogenarian — to recognize what I now see as a logical development in our Catholic understanding and practice of the Sacrament of Eucharist. The stages of that development have been marked mostly by the various emphases we placed on the sacrament at different times in our history. Let me explain –

As a child, and long after my childhood, I was taught that "receiving Communion" was a great privilege granted to us young Christians as we were gradually moving from infancy toward adulthood. Born some 2000 years after Jesus was born, we were taught that we were being welcomed into a privileged friendship with him. Therefore, **spiritual togetherness with the crucified and risen Jesus** was the essence of this wonderful sacrament.

We were carefully schooled in how to participate in the awesome act. We learned about the Communion fast from food and drink, freedom from serious sin (or the sacrament of Penance to absolve us from that impediment). We rehearsed the attitudes and the bodily gestures of profound reverence. And so forth.

I knew a priest back in the early 60s who preached emphatically on the occasion of children's First Communion that the boy or girl who had received Communion carried the sacramental Jesus in every part and every cell of his or her little body ("right into his/her fingers and toes," he used to say) for at least 20 minutes, while the sacred host dissolved and was digested.

I used to react with an unspoken "Nonsense!"

But the fact of the matter is that the emphasis in those days was on this mysterious union of a person and Jesus, who had somehow taken the place of the bread and wine while leaving the perceptible characteristics of the bread and wine unchanged.

In my reckoning, that was stage one.

Next came a new insight: The Eucharist — Communion — was also regarded as **food for the journey of life**. When kneeling to receive the sacrament, the prescribed requirement at the time, was replaced by standing not too many years ago, the explanation given — a very good one, I thought and still do think — was that we don't go to Mass to linger at a shrine or to worship. No, we were to regard ourselves as pilgrims, a people on the go, on our feet and ready to move on. The church building, or whatever was the setting in which we celebrated the Eucharist, was essentially a stopping-off place where we'd find rest and healing and nourishment for the journey ahead.

I liked that analysis, that theology, and it still appeals to me strongly. I have always relied on that benefit of the sacrament as I struggle with the challenges of my life, and I know that I have been helped by the Eucharistic Jesus more than I will ever fully appreciate.

That was stage — or phase — two.

Not too long after that step, a third followed, a different insight into what Eucharist means and what our part in it should be. For me, that revelation came mainly in the form of a one-page article in the Jesuit magazine, *America,* published in March of 2000 and written by a now deceased diocesan priest from Detroit by the name of Monsignor Gerald Martin. I knew at once that it was the most important thing I had ever read on the topic.

Father Martin, in that brilliant piece, shifted the emphasis of Jesus' words "Do this in memory of me" from changing bread and wine into himself to **our being changed into the likeness of him**! He wrote, "'Do this in memory of me' means you should imitate my self-giving, which is represented in these symbols of bread broken and wine poured out. When you take and eat and drink, you enter into this action and commit yourself to imitate my self-giving in your own life."[25] That makes perfect sense to me.

If I never learn anything more about the Eucharist, I will be content with the understanding we have achieved thus far.

So then

- I believe that Eucharist is a special bonding between us and Jesus.

- I believe it is powerful, energizing and healing food and drink for the faith journey of life.

- I believe that each time we receive the Eucharist we are pledging to imitate Jesus in every aspect of our individual lives.

"Corpus Christi"…the consecrated bread and wine…the consecrated people of God.

THE PEOPLE OF GOD

Scripture commentator Father Roger Karban wrote very recently, "As members of a highly structured church, we adhere to a pattern of strict rules and regulations which guarantee us salvation. Unlike our sacred (biblical) authors, we believe Jesus set up this structure and passed on these laws because he wanted us to get into heaven."[26]

Yes, we've been educated to think that way, but that is not the Judeo-Christian tradition from which we originally came. Our earliest ancestors in the faith were eager for the Spirit of God to be shared with them. That's what they thought was the reason they had been called into the faith community: so that the Spirit would be poured into them.

For my parents' funeral liturgies (my dad's in 1969, my mother's in 1997), I chose for the second reading a passage from the 7th chapter of the Book of Wisdom. The first verses speak of the commonality of our conception and birth, whether we are beggar or king, and are followed by, "And so I prayed, and understanding was given me; I entreated, and the spirit of wisdom came to me. I esteemed her more than scepters and thrones; compared with her, I held riches as nothing."

The section I selected ended with, "May God grant me to speak as God would wish and express thoughts worthy of God's gifts, since God is the guide of wisdom, since God directs the sages. We are indeed in God's hand, we ourselves and our words, with all our understanding, too, and technical knowledge."

That was the passion of our spiritual forebears: to be filled with the Spirit of God, so as to think and judge and act in union with the Divine Presence!

During the weeks of Advent each year, we hear the prophet Isaiah say that it happened to him: "The Spirit of God is upon me," he announced, not as an accolade, but as an empowerment for a mission of justice and peace, hope and love among the neediest and most oppressed of God's creatures. He would do that by passing on the Spirit to others, enabling them to enter into life-giving relationships with God and with each other — something that all the laws and regulations in the world could not accomplish.

In those same weeks of Advent, we hear John (Jesus' cousin?) minimize his own ministry and exalt that of Jesus because what John was offering, he said, was merely the sacramental gesture involving water, while Jesus, he said, would give the Spirit.

On a larger scale, the Catholic Church is wrestling with the same conflict today. Forces even at the highest levels of its hierarchy are trying to increase the institutional aspect of the church by tight control over theological teaching and writing, by censure of those who speculate on new horizons, by promulgation of restrictive laws in liturgy and worship, by narrow interpretation of morality, and so forth. In such a climate, there can be little room for a Spirit that moves how and where she will. We can only regret that church authority too often does not acknowledge the unpredictable activity of the Spirit among the people, honor it, call it forth, process and develop it, and then share it for the benefit of the entire Christian community.

The Second Vatican Council declared emphatically that the church is not primarily an institution; rather, it is the People of God. All of us, without exception, are the church. The church is not an establishment that provides certain goods and services to those who seek and accept them. No, those very persons who seek and accept — and who also in turn offer and provide — are themselves the church!

214

This most important rediscovery about the nature of the church contains a major implication: the church must be a listener. Its leaders must listen to the people, to each other, and to the scholars and theologians; the people must listen to their leaders and to the other branches of the church; the whole church must listen to the world of which it is a part – listen and constantly learn.

A kind of euphoria came upon us Catholics as we realized back in the 60s and 70s that our notions of what was right and true had value and would be heard and considered by our leaders. But soon after came the disappointment of another clampdown on creative thinking and loyal opposition and with that the restoration of the church as a unilateral, top-down, authoritative institution was underway. No longer could there be dialog on such issues as mandatory celibacy for priests and responsible birth control for the married and priestly ordination of women, and so on. Rules and laws and curtailing regulations once again were easing out the Spirit of Truth and Love.

What we must do now as 21st century Catholic Christians is to clarify in our own minds, and hold onto, the principle that we are not required to repeat and preserve *everything* that has been said and done in ages past. Rather, we must imitate those who went before us by being open to the Spirit of God, as they were in their day, and, with the new sciences available to us, take our turn at being instruments of that Spirit in and for our world.

LAW AND ORDERS: CHURCH AS COMMUNITY, NOT DICTATORSHIP

T he *Canonical Doctrine of Reception*, by the eminent canon lawyer, scholar/author, Fr. James A. Coriden, sets forth these principles:

For a law or rule to be an effective guide for the believing community, it must be accepted by the community... the obligatory force of church law is affected by its reception by the community. When a law is not accepted, it is an indication that the lawgiver has acted irrationally and the law need not be obeyed. Thus the community has a share in its own care, in its own direction toward the common good. One way in which it plays that part is by accepting or rejecting the laws promulgated for its use. A prominent example of non-received papal legislation... is...Veterum Sapientia (ed: the "Apostolic Constitution," similar to an encyclical, of Pope St. John XXIII, which would require seminarians to take a thorough course in the Latin language before beginning their ecclesiastical courses) ...widely disregarded because it was viewed as completely impractical.[27]

The function of authority in the church is not only to safeguard the tradition of the authentic Christian message from generation to generation, but also to call forth from the people their experience of the Spirit working in their lives, processing and refining it, and ultimately distributing that revelation for the good of the entire community.

The church is essentially tri-partite (looking like the old Ballantine Beer three-ring sign!) – 1) the hierarchy, 2) the scholars and theologians, 3) the members. These are interlocked, interdependent. When they are functioning with mutual respect and expectation, the church is at its best.

Kenny Moore is a former priest-monk who became the Human Resources Director at KeySpan Corporation in New York City. He is a survivor of what was termed "incurable" cancer and heart surgery. In his article, *"Everything I Know about Business I Learned in the Monastery,"* he wrote, "Much of my work continues to remain priestly: building community, repairing trust, offering hope, and trying to heal an inherently flawed human system."[28] Mr. Moore explained the process he had in mind:

- Building community. Leaving the appropriate selfishness of infancy behind us and growing daily in relationship with all its demands, promises, and rewards as we move into adulthood.

- Repairing trust. We disappoint one another and always need to be forgiven, to be given another chance to be our better, truer selves. "Do not judge," Jesus said. "Forgive one another as the Father forgives you." Trusting others is always risky business, but it is what Jesus requires of us, even though the trust he dared place in us led to his terrible execution.

- Offering hope. The troubles and worries of life can blind us to the light at the end of the tunnel, and we all need to be surrounded by others who can reassure us and inspire new confidence in the good things that lie just ahead.

* Healing the system. Everything human is flawed. Name the institution or the organization or the group and you will have to judge it imperfect, sometimes even corrupt. It is clear that the church is no exception. But each of us who are pledged to Jesus, each of us who have accepted the invitation to be his body in the world, has the obligation and the privilege to heal, as best we can, the societal wounds that are within our reach. No one of us can do it all, and not all of us together can do it quickly or completely, but continue trying we must. It is a cellular process that we are involved in, one member connecting with another with renewed and more vigorous life. Like a good germ, that life works its way gradually through the entire corporate body, infecting every part with new health.

Seems like good advice indeed!

A CHURCH OF EQUALS

T he scandal of clergy sex abuse has put the leadership of the Catholic Church in the spotlight as never before in its history. I was present to hear at least one bishop say to a group of priests, "Don't lose your confidence or your self-respect. The problem that we are facing is not with you, but with us bishops. We've made some terrible mistakes in our handling of the crimes of that very small minority of priests who have acted in such a shameful way."

I think that bishop expressed the sentiments of most Catholics, who are almost incredibly willing to forgive but who also have the right and the need to know the whole story of what we are still faced with. That is why organizations like Voice of the Faithful, of which I am a long-time member, have been established at this time of unprecedented crisis. Their goal and their hope is to clarify the issue at hand and to work in close union with church leaders at every level to bring an end to this ugly period and to reestablish the church in integrity and goodness.

One prominent and beloved archbishop expressed the opinion only a few years ago that the troubles of the church will be solved only when lay men and women are granted their rightful participation in decision-making along with the clergy and the hierarchy. I applaud that statement because I feel strongly that it is absolutely true. No, the church is not a democracy, per se, but neither is it a monarchy or a dictatorship or an oligarchy. It is a worldwide communion that began as a simple movement of reform and, in order to make progress in the world of human beings, it borrows from all forms of government and social organization.

The fact that the church believes and teaches that the Spirit of God resides in the people, its ordinary members, and creates the phenomenon called the *sensus fidelium* (that is to say, the understanding or the wisdom of faithful people) demands that there be a democratic component in the Catholic Church. It is not an exclusively top-down organization. I use a much over-worked slogan to express the point differently: the role of the people is not merely to pray, pay, and obey. Those days are gone forever and should never have existed in the first place.

Against this background of a church of equals, the only kind that Jesus and his first followers would have recognized and endorsed, how are we to understand a theme such as "Christ the King" celebrated on the last Sunday of the liturgical year? Doesn't the very term suggest a monarchy on which the present and future church must be modeled? The answer is a resounding No. Kings, in our historical experience, do not wash others' feet; that is the work of slaves and servants. No earthly king says that he has come to serve and not to be served. Jesus presented himself always as the servant of others and invited his followers — expected them — to do the same.

It is we who have elevated the Carpenter from Nazareth to royal status and then used what we had made of him to justify our own grandiose role-playing as little kings. One can think of Puck's lament, in *A Midsummer's Night's Dream*, "What fools these mortals be!"

In Rilke's *Book of Hours: Love Poems to God*,[29] we read this compelling lament:

We must not portray you in king's robes,

you, drifting mist that brought forth the morning.

Once again from the old paint boxes

we take the same gold for scepter and crown

that has disguised you through the ages.

Piously we produce our images of you

till they stand around you like a thousand walls.

And when our hearts would simply open,

our fervent hands hide you.

However off the mark the designation "King" may be for Jesus, it does say something true about us: that our primary and overriding allegiance belongs to him. It is in him that we see the model and the pattern of genuine and uncompromising humanness. While every aspect of every good life deserves our respect and imitation, none quite gets to the heart of what it means to be human as do the person and the life of Jesus. By the title "King" or by any other name that we may give him, that is what we are proclaiming. No human potentate need fear him or feel threatened by him. His kingdom competes with no other as a material institution. Rather, it appeals to and is found only in the hearts of human beings who want to become as fully human as they can be and who want to live in love that will last, knowing that his kingdom is not confined to this world.

PRIMACY OF CONSCIENCE

A s mature Christian adults we should not have to be informed or reminded that the ultimate standard by which we are to make moral decisions is our conscience. But we are so imbued with the notion of subservience, of obedience to authority, of surrendering personal responsibility in making personal decisions that indeed it does come as a surprising revelation, a shock, that not only is that an inherent right of every human being but that our Catholic Church, from which we have, largely, acquired our exaggerated notion of acquiescence to authority, itself endorses at its highest level of authority that very principle. Just in case there are some who have never heard the liberating, emancipating, empowering words, I share with you the following precious paragraph from one of the 16 documents produced by the Second Vatican Council, *The Church in the Modern World*. The church at its highest levels emphasizes the primacy of conscience.[30]

The Church in the Modern World declares,

> *Deep within their consciences men and women discover a law which they have not laid upon themselves and which they must obey. Its voice, ever calling them to love and to do what is good and to avoid evil, tells them inwardly at the right moment: do this, shun that... Their dignity rests in observing this law, and by it they will be judged... For God willed that men and women should 'be left free to make their own decisions'... Their dignity therefore requires them to act out of conscious and free choice, as moved and drawn in a personal way from within, and not by their own blind impulses or by external constraint.*[31]

The best-read human being that I have ever met, a preeminent scholar and stratospheric intellectual, Henry Beck, formerly "Monsignor Beck," was my teacher, confessor and confidant on the most fundamental level of personal Christian faith. In the final decision he made concerning his vocation and state in life, a decision he arrived at and executed so quietly, Henry inevitably demonstrated to all of us a cardinal but surprisingly little known principle of Catholic moral theology: the absolute primacy of human conscience. This faithful servant of Jesus I suspect emboldened many priests to pursue bravely the dictates of their own well-formed consciences because of his sterling example. His influence continues to affect us in so many ways.

I think of the humbleness of his post-resignation ministry among the elderly, the poor, the sick, and the dying. I think of his faithful, respectful love for his companion, his wife Mildred. (Just before Christmas, 1998, he wrote to me, "I try to live with the recognition that it is in my sisters and brothers that I find my Lord. For me, that means caring for Millie more than I care for myself.") I think of the personal sacrifice of his obedience to legitimate ecclesiastical authority when his own Spirit-molded concept of church was evolving into a new paradigm. I think of his wholehearted participation in ecumenical conversation and action, his expansive, inclusive image of the Kingdom of God on earth. I think of the lightness of heart, the gracefulness with which he dialoged with all comers without ever a trace of disrespect or condemnation.

Henry Beck lived in awe of his fellow human beings, not only those who had achieved notable success in intellectual and scientific pursuits, but all of them — all of us. He was quoted in his local press as confessing his constant amazement at what he called the "wonders of humankind." He continued: "I find something to admire and something to be impressed with in even the most simple of human beings."

223

I asked him once how he would define a true intellectual. His response surprised and pleased me. A genuine intellectual, he said, is not necessarily or by definition one whose knowledge is deep or broad; it is, rather, one who is ever open to new ideas, new possibilities, one who is always moving toward the horizon and not constrained by present boundaries.

The record shows without doubt that in virtually all those moral issues so contentiously debated to this day, as well as disciplinary matters within the church, his thinking touched the horizon, if indeed it did not go beyond it. He trusted the *sensus fidelium*,[32] convinced that the Spirit of Wisdom and Love spoke through the ordinary experience of good-willed people every bit as authentically as through the church's chosen leaders.

SPEAKING TRUTH TO POWER

I once read the testimony of a priest, a man highly regarded and respected by both peers and people in general, in which he said that the deep psychological problems for which he was being treated were rooted mainly in the bullying he endured many years ago in his young boyhood. He recalls, with pain, the mocking and the jeering he got from schoolmates, based apparently on their perception of him as "different" from them — in what way, he did not say. The merciless daily attacks wounded his innocent spirit, and he was left, full of fear, to struggle through it all without relief or hope.

Remember that great song in the musical "South Pacific" which insists that prejudice has to be systematically taught, that it doesn't come naturally to anyone? We can be taught, subtly and sometimes boldly, to reduce the person who is "different" from us to an almost sub-human level, assuring us that we will thereby stand all the taller by comparison.

In the ancient Hebrew Book of Wisdom (2:12-20) we read of a classic case of violent bullying. Switched to common parlance of today, it says, "Let's get after that guy! Who is he to make us look bad? And if he's such a saint, let's threaten to kill him and then see if the God he claims to know so well will save him!"

In the gospel according to Mark (9:30-37) Jesus refers to his future violent death – Jesus, the ultimate "different" person rejected by the powers that be. The Roman government and the religious leaders of his time were uncomfortably challenged by the person and the message of this revolutionary Jesus, and they knew that they'd have to silence him if their rapacious business was to go on unhindered.

225

Jesus was killed, certainly not as a sacrificial offering demanded by God, and not primarily for anything he was said to have done, but primarily because he was a threat to persons and institutions that were petrified at the prospect of being exposed by him and of being forced either to go into exile or to change. They were increasingly aware that Jesus was speaking truth to power and that truth would be their undoing.

I find it to be ironic that the very church that preaches Jesus' message and knows that it is his mystical body on earth, might itself from time to time be silencing him as it uncritically perpetuates its own traditional interpretation of how things are and ought to be. Maliciously? No. With all good intention, I am sure.

But we are called today to take the risk of examining, with as many opponents and proponents who want to join in, those teachings and laws of the church that have long been questioned by large numbers of good-willed persons who see the need for new interpretations based on new evidence, new circumstances, and a fuller understanding of the mind and heart of Jesus.

It isn't right to snuff out the voices of loyal opponents, whether within or outside the church. It's only when human intelligence is allowed to go at the search for truth, a process of layered discoveries, that the Spirit of Wisdom has something to work with, to hone and refine and bring to completion.

Jesus didn't fit into the established religion of his day, as much as he loved it and lived it. He was an enigma, sometimes an annoyance, an embarrassment to his family and friends. He was rejected by authority because his version of God's word was different from theirs and very unsettling. What a crime it would be if that same Jesus were to continue

226

being unheard by the church that is charged with proclaiming his word, a church that would prefer simply to leave things as they long have been instead of working toward a better understanding and a stronger unity fashioned from diversity.

A SECOND LOOK

We are now a thrice-wounded church – self-wounded, sad to say. One: We are to this day suffering from the clergy sex abuse crisis, nowhere near resolution even after so many years of public exposure. Two: We have still not succeeded in becoming a truly people's church instead of the dominantly hierarchical church that we seem to prefer or at least to have made peace with. Three: We are dealing with an ever-increasing unavailability of Eucharistic liturgy because of our rapidly shrinking priesthood and the unwillingness of our leaders to ordain other than single, celibate males. These three major wounds sap our energy and keep us from being the vibrant, productive church that was the intention of its founders.

We must not lay the blame for our present compromised condition solely on arrogance or incompetence on the part of any of our leaders, nor can we charge errant priests alone with taking us to where we find ourselves today. And the vast body of the faithful, that largest segment of the church, while not singularly to be blamed, cannot disclaim all culpability for what has happened. But all of us together must work at healing our wounded church. How?

I suggest the following plan. First, we need to rethink the meaning and the function of authority in the church. It can't any longer be "power over" in any sense, in any circumstances. Rather, it has to be understood and exercised always and only as "service to." And the function of that authority must from here on be, not only to guarantee the safe passage of authentic Catholic tradition from generation to generation, but also to welcome all voices, to discern where and in whom the Spirit of God is speaking today, to honor that revelation, to collect and reverently process it, and to distribute it ultimately for the benefit of all. Reader, you will notice several variations of that critical statement throughout this modest book because of my deep conviction that it is a central question and principle of this time in the evolution of the Catholic Church.

Second, we need to develop the courage to speak up frankly in all matters of church life and discipline in which we have knowledge and experience to share. This is the duty and privilege of every member of the church, no matter his or her rank or station. No one simply belongs to the church; we are the church!

We are so fortunate to live in a time when to think and say such things as I am saying to you now are increasingly acceptable, even regarded more and more as a sacred and solemn obligation. Unlike the brave prophets of former ages who were cruelly killed for their integrity, we have nothing of that sort to fear. So let us move on with determination, with unyielding hope, and with charity for all.

I once heard a psychologist say that the word "respect" really means "to look again" – "re-spect." "Spect": to see, to look. (I wear *spect*acles as I am writing.) "Re": again. Respect: to take another look. For what purpose? To pierce the obvious, visible surface of this other person and penetrate closer to his/her core. To see not merely what presents itself exteriorly, but, as far as is possible, also what lies deep within.

This is a very strained and contentious time for our Catholic Church. We are plagued by sharp divisions in our thinking about many matters of church practice and teaching. I once participated in an interstate convocation of *Voice of the Faithful* in New York City. It is made up of mainly older Catholics whose concerns include a completely just resolution of the clergy abuse crisis, the manner in which bishops are chosen, the welcoming back of married priests into at least part-time ministry, the broadening of authority and decision-making in the church, and so on. The members of the organization are seasoned Catholics whose love for the church has been long-since proven by years of faithful service. Yet it is not welcomed to meet on any church property and is not recognized by church leadership.

This is a sad situation that should not exist and must be brought to a peaceful and mutually satisfying resolution as soon as possible.

But how shall we approach such a hoped-for reconciliation in this particular instance and in so many others like it? First of all, with the expectation that there are goodwill and virtue on both sides of the unfortunate divide. A wall exists between us that certainly no one has intended to build and that no one ever wanted to be there. How shall we regard those who stand, for the time being, on the other side? Are we determined to make the effort to look more deeply into their innermost thoughts and feelings and intentions? And then to begin a new dialog in mutual respect, hopeful expectation and, above all, charity?

GENUINE PRAYER

In my hometown in north Jersey the Sisters in one of its Catholic Schools had the children pray together every day for the safe return of a former graduate, a military officer serving in combat in Afghanistan. They said to the children, "If we pray very hard, God will protect him so that he will come home safe and uninjured."

What if, after all their earnest praying, the young man had been killed? What would the Sisters, so sincere and well-meaning, have said to those disillusioned students? Would they have said something about how God often chooses the best to die early, or how God needed this young man as an "angel," or how God often does strange and hurtful things through a vision and a wisdom far superior to our own that we cannot understand and must not question?

Isn't it time that we put such notions of God to rest once and for all—a God who micromanages the universe, pulling strings like a puppeteer? A God who acts capriciously, testing the faith of professed believers? A God with whom prayer sometimes "works" and sometimes doesn't "work"— a God who answers prayers with an unexplained "No"?

When will we teach our children, instead, that prayer is *always* answered, if prayer is simply, as the catechism taught us, "lifting the mind and heart to God"? The answer to that kind of prayer is infallible: it is the assurance of the abiding presence of a loving, caring, forgiving God. It is not the granting of a particular request.

We can advance our own adult spirituality by acknowledging first that life is full of random, often colliding forces and that all living creatures, including us humans, get hurt badly, even die, when they happen

231

to be where those forces strike. Planes fall out of the sky, cancer invades an organ, babies die at birth, bullets and bombs kill soldiers and civilians.

None of this is orchestrated (or some would say "permitted") by a God-in-the-sky; and none of it is prevented in answer to prayer. It simply happens because that's the way the universe is. Those who suffer are not chosen by God for their fate any more than those who escape a potential tragedy are divinely destined for their good fortune. It just happens, period.

> *Prayer doesn't change anything outside ourselves. Prayer changes us.*

Prayer doesn't change anything outside ourselves. Prayer changes us. We should learn for ourselves and teach our children that through it all God is lovingly present to us. Teach them that faith is not a belief in God so strong that through it we can control anything we want to, or feel we need to. No, that's a pagan notion.

Faith, rather, is a confident awareness of the presence of God that is so unshakable that, even when the uncontrollable calamity threatens or attacks, we are not dehumanized, we are not destroyed, we are not deprived of our ultimate destiny in God. In such times we sense a power that is far greater than our own, enabling us to carry the inevitable cross in the direction of new life, temporal or eternal.

My view is that truly spiritual Christian persons are not those who pray ardently and believe that they will get specific favors from God in return. Truly spiritual persons are those who pray to be more closely united with the divine presence within them and then accept life's joys with greater gratitude and life's hurts with greater strength.

232

AUTHENTIC RELIGION

"Put your money where your mouth is! What you're saying sounds true and noble, but it's all just words. You're not living in line with your pious pronouncements. You're acting like a phony!"

In colloquial terms, that's the root meaning of the prophet Isaiah's message. He could be a fiery preacher – very determined, convinced that what he was saying was the authentic word of the unseen God. A particular passage (Isaiah 58:7-10) from the long work that appears under his name was written at a time in history when the scattered Jews had returned to their beloved Jerusalem and were rebuilding the violated temple. All the while they were grumbling because it seemed that the God they so trusted was ignoring their pleas for help. Things were going painfully slowly: the horn blast that would call them to worship still had not sounded. They were home, but not completely; they were still feeling the pain of their long and lonely exile.

The man of God, Isaiah, tells them that the reason God will not hear and respond to them is that they are still not listening to God. They do all the right religious rituals and say the prescribed prayers; but what the sacred actions and words signify they are not yet determined to fulfill. For example, they fast from food and drink and solemnize their pious deeds with the traditional ceremonies. But at the same time they don't realize that the fasting God wants is not merely giving up food, drink and pleasure. No, what God wants, the prophet insists, is that they give to those who do not have enough of what is even minimally necessary for a basically human life. The giving up, he says, in whatever form it

233

may take, is truthful and pleasing to God only if it represents and is matched by generous charity on behalf of persons in desperate need.

By the way, let's remind ourselves here how important it is to teach our children that fundamental truth in the hope that it will stay with them all the days of their lives. Teach them, for example, that their decision to give up candy or TV or whatever for Lent is made all the more meaningful when it is deliberately joined to something else. That "something else" is a greater effort to locate and to help others – perhaps children of their own age – who are suffering because of the greed and violence of persons who care only about themselves or by the occasional cruelty of nature.

We'd do well to fix in our minds something Jesus said: Religion is authentic only when it is expressed in works of loving concern on behalf of the oppressed, the weak, the vulnerable, the helpless, the disenfranchised. It is only when we are reaching out to them that we have the right to go to the altar. The "stuff" that is transformed in Eucharist and returned to us in Communion as the sacramental presence of Jesus is simply the good acts we do for others and the offering of ourselves as instruments through whom Jesus can touch and help them.

> *Religion is authentic only when it is expressed in works of loving concern on behalf of the oppressed, the weak, the vulnerable, the helpless, the disenfranchised.*

Jesus called us the salt of the earth, hoping that we, his followers, would be conscious agents of change in a world so infected with the seeds of self-destruction. He says we are a light, lifted up, meant to be conspicuous without calling attention to ourselves. Rather, we are to shed light for others to find their way to fuller life.

234

How many years do you think you have left on Planet Earth? I'm sure the thought occurs to you occasionally. It certainly does to me. Shouldn't we commit ourselves now to a more radical, practical Christian life? Let's pray for one another, that we may accept the help to do just that.

Every time I proclaim a Gospel passage that contains one of Jesus' scathing references to tax collectors, lumping them, as he does, with public sinners, I scan the congregation in fear of finding someone who is employed by the municipal tax office or by the IRS, and I wonder how he or she must be feeling. I wish I could get to them all right now and explain that Jesus lived and labored in an occupied country, where taxation by the Roman government was another detestable sign of the Jews' lack of freedom. In that situation, the tax collectors – often enough, Jews themselves – were consorting with the government, strong-arming their fellow Jews to pay up and getting a commission for their work. So, in the moral judgment of the people, it wasn't the collection of taxes that was *per se* and necessarily shameful: it was the collaboration with the oppressor for personal gain that was regarded as condemnable.

Well, that said, let's shift gears and consider what makes a good Eucharistic celebration, a "good Mass." One can respond, of course, within a variety of frameworks: on the one hand, a good liturgy can mean a beautiful setting, compelling communication of the Scripture passages, inspiring music, a meaningful homily, the devout service of many ministers, the reverent participation of an enthusiastic congregation, and so on.

On the other hand, a good liturgy may be said to have taken place when the hungry are fed, the sick and imprisoned are visited, the naked are clothed, the homeless are housed.

Perhaps the correct answer to the question includes both; but, if we had to make a choice between the two, I believe it would have to be the latter. A really good liturgy is one that goes beyond words and sends all the participants, all the yes-sayers, into effective action among the needy and the poor — including (perhaps beginning with) those in our own families, neighborhoods, and circles of friends.

Re-visit Jesus' famous story about the two sons (Matthew 21:28-32) and note the very recognizable dynamics that evolve. Their father approaches one of them, ordering him to go out to the vineyard and put in a day's work. "Yes, Dad, I'll be glad to." But the YES doesn't get translated into action. The second son, for whatever reason, says the wrong words in quick response to his father's command but then thinks the matter over and decides to comply. The danger we constantly run is not so much that we'll at first react poorly to an inspirational call to a good action, but that we'll be satisfied with having responded perfectly in word – and leave it at that.

However, neither should we make the mistake of running from church and trying to implement every idealistic concept we've there expressed or assented to. The late, brilliant, contemporary theologian, Monica Hellwig (a beloved and much respected teacher of mine) used to caution us that while we can be radical in all our thinking it is simply not possible for any of us to be radical in all our actions. Noble words and sentiments inevitably outnumber the deeds possible for us to do. But it is absolutely essential that we do *something* with and after every liturgy that gives flesh and blood reality to our firm statements of faith and our bold pledges of charity. If this is not generally the case, we have reason to question how sincere and truthful our praying and our worshiping have been.

In this connection, I remember a very touching story – fictional or factual, I cannot recall. It goes like this: at a party, a famous actor was asked by an elderly gentleman to recite the 23rd Psalm for all the guests.

236

The actor agreed, but only on condition that the old man would follow him with the same recitation. The actor began, "The Lord is my shepherd; I shall not want" and continued in such an awesome fashion that at the end of the piece the people rose to their feet in thunderous applause.

"Now it's your turn," the actor said, as he bid the old man to speak. In a creaky voice and with none of the orator's skills, he said the Psalm. When he was finished, there was not a sound in the room, only stillness and tears. The actor broke the silence as he said, "I know the Psalm – this man knows the shepherd."

CHAPTER SIX

Why Stay In The Church At All?

WE ARE THE CHURCH!

I n a discussion about religion I once participated in, one of the persons that made up the group said simply and passionately, "I believe in God, but I don't believe in the church. It doesn't speak to me, and I don't buy its magic anymore." Another person, pointing to him, said, "This man is one of the most Christ-like persons I've ever known" and went on to support that assessment by recounting the good acts and the good attitudes he recognized in his friend. I knew him just well enough to be impressed by those very qualities that shone through his somewhat rough exterior, an image he seemed to enjoy cultivating, despite his high intelligence.

The other two persons in the group took the opportunity to announce that they, too, were finding that more and more of what they experience in church worship is irrelevant to them. It's boring and repetitive, they said, and they feel as though they are performing a mostly mindless ritual, a habit instilled in them since their earliest days, which they are very reluctant to abandon, but which they see as less and less valuable or worth their time.

It seems to me that anyone who would bristle at these comments and tell the complainers that they are malcontents who need to work on themselves instead of criticizing the 2000-year-old church has his or her head in the sand. There are valid reasons that so many intelligent, well-educated men and women are leaving the church of their birth and upbringing. Their number includes former priests and religious, something we all know only too well.

The church had the humility and the wisdom to own up to this fact of life a half century ago, when Pope St. John XXIII stunned the church by announcing that a great, worldwide council would be held, the purpose of which would be to let in much-needed fresh air and to evaluate and reform where necessary the ancient practices of the Catholic Church.

That process of reform reached an all-time high in the late 1960s and the 70s. Those were exciting, promising years, when dreams that so many of us had long cherished began to take on flesh and blood and become real! Of course it wasn't all perfection; trial and error never can be that. And while some persons welcomed the changes and breathed in the fresh air with gratitude and soaring spirits, others mourned the passing of the old ways that were so much a part of their lives. We became a much divided church, a brand new experience for most of us. The divisiveness goes on to this very day, aided and abetted by a strong backlash against the reforms of Vatican II from some members of the hierarchy as well as ordinary people in the pews who still resist change and want instead the church of their childhood to be restored.

I realize that it is not possible for us to find a one-size-fits-all solution to this vexing problem we are encountering; there's no way we can all suddenly be satisfied and at peace – we can't make things right for everybody. But surely there is something that each of us can do toward an eventual resolution of the present malaise, and I hope you agree that we have to do at least that.

What we can do must start, I suggest, from a fundamental conviction that the Creator of this marvelous universe does communicate with us in a unique way through the church, in spite of the weaknesses of its human structure. That means we must be loyal to her in good times as well as in bad. It is our filial duty to protect and defend her, even while we are working toward her — our — rehabilitation, because she brings into our lives treasures of wisdom and knowledge and beauty and goodness and hope and more. I think we scarcely appreciate what our lives would be like if the church and all its influences in our life were to be withdrawn from us.

And then, we must admit that we don't only belong to the church; we *are* the church. We may be tired of hearing that, but also it may be a truth we've not yet fully imbibed. Every time we hear the message of the scriptures, especially in the context of Eucharist, we should immediately apply it to ourselves, not to anyone or anything outside of ourselves. Take just the words of Jesus as quoted in the Gospel passage appointed for any Mass and be reminded that it is not only, or even necessarily, the things we do and say in formal worship that bring us into closer union with our Creator; it is, rather, every effort we make to pay attention to, and to understand and conform to, the underlying spirit of Jesus' instructions.

> *And then, we must admit that we don't only belong to the church; we are the church.*

241

In our weekly Mass we do a lot of calling out to God in voice and in gesture; but it's what we deliberately take with us and put into practice in the days beyond Sunday that makes us more faithful friends and followers of Jesus. We may fail in many important ways as human beings and as Christians; our church as an institution will go on failing in some pretty disgraceful ways because it's made up of persons like us. But if, at the table of Eucharist, we can hear the voice of Jesus in the church's age-old mix of strength and weakness, where else ought we to be?

A Trappist monk friend of mine, with over 50 faithful years in the monastery, once said to me, "Dick, do you believe, as I do, that the church is wrong in some of its teachings?" Answering yes to that question, as indeed I did, in no way indicated that my faith was weak or shaken, because I was so certain, as I am today, of the presence of Jesus and the Holy Spirit among us. But the arrogance of our "one true church" mentality is going to die slowly, and she will not easily acknowledge that she has been in error on many issues. It's been noted that when Pope Paul VI rejected the conclusion arrived at by the very committee he had appointed to study the morality of artificial birth control, his decision, contrary to the committee's recommendation, that there be no change in the church's longstanding teaching on the matter, was based on keeping the church from being seen as having been in error.

It's at first almost amusing that St. Paul, who tells us that there must be no dissension among followers of the Risen Jesus, is the same Paul who had to disassociate himself from his missionary partner Barnabas on one of their journeys because of arguments and irreconcilable differences regarding what they thought were the message and the meaning of Jesus. I believe that the two never did get back together again – two great saints, two apostles, two martyrs who couldn't work peacefully together! Is this a case of do-as-I-say-not-as-I-do? Or are we missing something?

In fairness we have to acknowledge that Paul insisted that in one thing at least we must remain undivided, and that is the centrality of Jesus in our lives. On that there can be no question: Jesus is Messiah, Lord, the Word of God dwelling in and among us.

Almost in the same breath, Paul speaks of the one aspect of Jesus that will continue to be a stumbling block, a cause of confusion, and this factor will turn many away from Jesus because it seems to be an inherent contradiction. He is referring to the crucifixion: what sense does crucifixion make in the story of a savior? He claimed to be saving us from oppression and death – and he himself experiences both. What kind of a savior can he be? We are reminded of the observer at his execution who, we are told, said, "If he is really the Son of God, then let him come down from that cross and save himself. If he can't save himself, then how can he save others?" A reasonable and legitimate question. Had you or I been there, it is quite possible that we would have had similar thoughts.

The lack of unity that Paul found among the Christians in the city of Corinth was expressed in the claims they were making concerning how they got their knowledge of Jesus and the personal faith that grew out of it. They were competing with each other, some saying that they had a purer, more enlightened, faith because it came to them through the preaching and instruction of Apollos. Others boasted that they got it straight from Peter himself, the appointed chief of the Apostles. Still others believed their faith to be superior on the grounds that Paul had been their teacher, sharing with them the depth and richness of his personal, spiritual experience of the post-resurrection Jesus. And so on…

Paul decreed: This has to stop immediately! It doesn't matter how any of us came to the knowledge and love of Jesus, or what particular bent or flavor our personal faith has. These factors will always differ from person to person. What is essential is that we hold on to our one conviction that it is in him that we most clearly encounter the profound mystery that we call God: to know him is to know God. To know him is to know how to live a basically and essentially human life. To know him is to know the way to our eternal home and perfect union with our Creator – a way, however, that will necessarily and inevitably involve the cross of suffering and death.

Who would deny that we are a considerably divided church today? Ordinary conversations as well as opinion polls show over and over again how we differ from each other especially with regard to what is perceived as right or wrong in the area of human behavior, particularly sexual. We argue; we criticize. Nonetheless, we call ourselves Christians — followers of Christ. We can show that rock-bottom unity by being tolerant and respectful of each other and of each other's point of view. Although at the moment we are divided in certain matters of belief or practice, we simply have to give each other the benefit of the doubt and assume that this person with whom I disagree is as sincere and convinced as I am. Where there is such trust and charity, such bigness of mind and heart, we can and will stay together as sisters and brothers, siblings of Jesus, confident that the Spirit of God that led him through his challenging life will also lead us to a more perfect unity and peace.

MEMBERSHIP HAS MEANING

How often have you heard someone say, "Why should I go to church on Sunday and be surrounded by hypocrites? They look so pious when they pray and receive Communion, and then they leave for another week of cheating on their bosses or on their spouses or some other violation of the Commandments."

"Hypocrite" may not be the correct word in most cases, but I should think it's true that few if any of us practice completely what we say we believe and commit ourselves to. That's just another way of saying that we are human, which means that we are weak and inconsistent, filled with contradictions.

In this connection I recall the film *The Last Temptation of Christ*. And, incidentally, I never did and still can't understand what all the fuss concerning that movie was about, especially since it begins with a clear disclaimer from the producer that it was not intended to be a life of Christ or a faithful presentation of the Gospels, but a kind of parable in itself through which the viewer might be led to a fuller, more personal image of Jesus. A priest friend of mine told me that the movie made him think of Jesus in such a different way that he had never felt closer to him in all his life. It left me with some deep impressions of the humanity of Jesus, in which he struggled mightily to grow in the awareness of his mission of generous, sacrificial love.

There's a place in St. Matthew's Gospel (Chapter 13) in which he reports three of Jesus' parables in a row, each of them about the phenomenon of growth. Through them Jesus teaches us that the church is destined to be small in comparison with other institutions and powers of the earth, but that it will have a disproportionately large effect on the lives of people and of nations — like the tiny quantity of yeast that makes the bread dough rise (one of the parables). It'll be strong and supportive just like the sturdy shrub that develops from the little mustard seed (another of the parables) and then provide a secure place for birds to make their nests. At the same time it will be made up of both good and bad elements, like wheat and weeds on the same farmland (the first of the three parables): heroic and saintly virtue will thrive side by side with deceit, insincerity, compromise and halfheartedness.

What's true of the Church as a community is also true of each of its members — you and me, for example. Even late in life we may be of small spiritual stature, but, as the old expression has it, God is not finished with us yet. Despite our weakness and woundedness, we are still able to be supportive of others. And we, too, are a combination, each of us, of good and evil.

> *Despite our weakness and woundedness, we are still able to be supportive of others.*

I mentioned before that the mother of a priest friend of mine said, "I have four children, three are married and one has a vocation." Said in innocence and ignorance, of course, but what a heresy such a statement expresses. Translated into my own life, it means that I am better, closer to God, and more important in the transforming work of Christ than my siblings are — simply because I am a priest. Absolutely not true. Are my brothers and sister not also called to a life of sacramental union and love? We tend to think and say such things because we still have not buried the notion that membership in a certain class or caste or organization is the measure of our worth. But no, not even membership in the church counts for anything in the final analysis unless we listen to the word of God, keep it with us always, and try to live it in every situation of our lives.

That's why we belong to church – with all those other imperfect people who are convinced that God will not fail, no matter how long it may take, to confirm us in goodness and in love.

LEAVEN IN THE LOAF

Y ou may be old enough to remember, dear reader, the late 1940s and the long-running case of Father Leonard Feeney, the priest who publicly declared that eternal salvation is not possible for anyone except a baptized, faithfully practicing Roman Catholic. The pope finally excommunicated him from the church, but he continued his energetic efforts to push his doctrine and win over thousands of sympathizers. I was a late teenager at the time and very much interested in this theological warfare that would help to define the church and its mission for at least the rest of the century.

The struggle goes on, although not quite at the same fever pitch. There remain those who believe that the goal of the church is the conversion of the world to Catholicism. While they are considerably more broadminded than the fanatics of the 40s, you can still hear them saying things like, "Thanks be to God that she was baptized and received into the church just hours before her death!" Or, "Do you know Father So and So? He has the greatest number of converts to his credit of all the priests in the diocese."

If we Catholics believe that belonging to the church is a good thing — and of course we do because it is — then it is natural that we should be eager to share it with others. I can give, as you can, many important reasons for membership in the church being among the greatest blessings of my life. But whether or not we should be concerned about getting everyone into the church is another matter; and whether salvation requires membership in the church is certainly a question that must be faced and answered in the light available today.

St. John says that "the Spirit of God blows where it will," and yet for centuries there has been a persistent voice among us Catholics insisting that eternal life is granted only to those who belong "in some way" to the Roman Catholic Church. Jesus spoke of his followers as the leaven in the loaf. From using my home bread machine, I have learned that the leaven, the yeast, although one of the smallest ingredients in the recipe, is the one that lifts all the others by a process of interaction.

Isn't that how we should see ourselves as church — maybe destined to be among the global population's smaller constituents, but also among the most influential? Why should we put any restrictions on that clear declaration we hear from the prophet Isaiah, speaking for God in his day: "Israel, I will make you a light to the nations so that my salvation may reach to the ends of the earth!"?

There is ample evidence in our own time that Pope Francis is radiating that light. However, each of us in his or her unique way is empowered and expected to do the same.

There is no need for us Catholics to claim everyone for Roman Catholicism and no need for anyone to claim the world for Christianity. We need only claim everyone for God and leave the rest to the Spirit. We do that mainly by living the Gospel of Jesus within the circumstances of our own individual lives: taking stands for justice, acting mercifully, living in reconciliation and forgiveness, sharing generously, making righteous decisions in all things, carrying our crosses with confidence in the love of God; hoping, expecting, celebrating in good times and in bad. That's enough, because that is the Christ-life that sheds light on the way for all.

ON A PERSONAL NOTE

When I announced to my family in 1952 that I had decided to study for the priesthood, the reactions of my parents were surprising. This time it was my father who said much more than Mother did. I don't remember her exact words, only that she knew that this was the right thing for the eldest of her four children to do. She said she was proud and grateful and that she wished me well.

About my father: it was immediately clear that the idea of my entering a seminary and going on to priesthood bothered him. His Catholic faith was not as deeply ingrained as Mother's was. He practiced his faith mainly because his wife expected that of him. So his approach was unambiguous. He said, "Son, you're only 22. You've had little experience in the world outside of home and school; you've lived a rather sheltered life, never having had to work to support yourself or anyone else. Why not take a year or so to think more about your future and to work at maturing? How about some long trips to see the world? I'll be only too glad to make that possible. And after that, if you're still inclined to become a priest, you'll have my total support." And I recall answering, "Thanks, Dad. What you've said makes a lot of sense, but I've been thinking this over for a long time, and I'm certain that this is what I should be doing." He backed down and never addressed the subject again.

After a year of classical languages at Seton Hall University and another year of the same in a special school in Massachusetts, I entered Immaculate Conception Seminary in Darlington, New Jersey, and from that time on never had the slightest doubt that that was where I belonged and that diocesan priesthood was indeed my authentic vocation.

As I tell my story, I recall that brief conversation between Jesus and the young man whom he called to follow him. The man did not say no to the invitation; he merely said that the time was not right for him to make such a change in his life. Those who understand the scriptures far better than I do advise us that he was not actually on the way to his father's funeral and that almost certainly his father was very much alive. What he was saying was, "This is a huge commitment you're asking of me, Jesus, and you know how it is in families, especially between a father and a son. My father is bound to object to my following you and taking up your lifestyle. Without doubt he would consider that a waste of my life and of my heritage. But someday, when he is no longer living, I'll be free to do as I please. And, yes, I think I'd be inclined to join you and your group then."

It seems to me that it would be hard to find fault with his reasoning — or with my father's. Family bonds are always to be highly respected. Jesus knew that, and it's more than likely that he admired this considerate son.

But the lesson in Christian living that we get from this gospel excerpt is that sometimes we find ourselves in situations in which what we are convinced is the "will of God" trumps all other considerations and possibilities and requires us to follow its direction even if that means disappointing or hurting those we love.

Trust me, if you've not experienced it yourself, although I doubt there is any mature person who has not: it is extremely difficult to distinguish what divine providence would have us do from what our reasoning and emotions are urging. That can be a major struggle because the case looks so convincing on both sides. I don't know of any formula or process that can resolve it except prayer, interpersonal dialog, patient waiting, and finally a possibly risky leap.

Dag Hammarskjöld, Secretary General of the fledgling United Nations from 1953 to 1961, was a deeply spiritual man and very prayerful. He described his famous book, *Markings*, as the record of his negotiations with himself and with God. In that post-World War II period, he so appreciated the significance of what the United Nations was established to accomplish that he prayed constantly to be open to divine wisdom, divine direction, knowing how limited are human intelligence and human love, beginning with his own.

Well, we are all cut from the same cloth, filled with astonishing potential and also burdened with enormous weaknesses. Optimum good comes into our lives, enriching us and others, in the same way for all – with the surrendering words, "God, my Creator, what would you have me do?"

And the answer comes, not normally in personal apparitions, but through the usually painful ordeal of honest, patient, charitable, expectant dialog.

THE DIVINE PRESENCE

The chief engineer of the Sunday Radio Mass at which I have presided for nearly 50 years needed major surgery. The day after the operation, while he was in the Intensive Care Unit, a critical part on the rolling table over his bed went bad, making it impossible to move the table. Nurses, doctors and technicians tried to fix it, but to no avail. They all finally left the room in search of a maintenance man. When they got back, the problem had been solved – by the patient himself, who, his wife told me, got out of bed and, despite her strenuous protests, did what was necessary! She told me that she was expecting him to be rather uncooperative when he'd be home recuperating under her care. I wished her luck!

Inspired by his courageous and charitable foolishness, my next emailed message to him contained this line: "I think your active nature, your optimism, and your sense of humor have a lot to do with the progress you are making — to say nothing about those two most important factors in your life: your faith in God and the love you share with your wonderful wife."

How many times I have heard — as you have, I'm certain — the testimony of men and women who are convinced that their belief in the constant, loving presence of God has been the number one reason for their recovery from illness or their endurance in a time of crushing pressure of one kind or another. How many service men and women there are who have seen combat and later on told us what their awareness of that divine presence meant to them in their darkest, most terrifying hours.

Atheists may accuse us of self-deception; they may be convinced that we have fabricated the God we claim to have known, the God who has been compassionately active in many of the most stressful situations we have ever endured. We cannot prove them wrong or prove us right. We can only honor their sincerity, their good will, and the basic goodness of their humanity. We can only be grateful that we happened to have made conscious connection with the Creative Spirit that we call God and that this bonding has brought us immense peace and joy.

The writers of Scripture have given voice to God in the adventure of their response to God's activity in their lives. That divine presence was real, we can be absolutely sure, even though the conversations they report are made to sound as if they are between two humans in order that we might understand what they had understood in their contemplation, their meditation, and their listening to God within them.

Think of Isaiah (Chapter 56), the sacred "playwright," who put words in the mouth of God (as if God had a mouth!) that assure us that there is plenty of room for all in God's house. (Reminds me of Pope Francis' statement that the Church is a very big tent with room for all who wish to enter.)

And how about St. Paul in his letter to the Christian converts in Rome (Romans, chapter 11), with more of his logical gymnastics designed to convince the Gentiles – the non-Jews – that, though they may have been in God's disfavor previously, the door to favorable status is now wide open to them? It's almost as if he is saying that God plans it that way: everyone being given a turn at being in God's disfavor only that they may experience the joy of coming back home to God's extravagant generosity. I think I'm safe in saying that scripture scholars, except for the most conservative among them, do not interpret that last scenario literally (that God puts anyone in disfavor only to increase their joy at being pardoned); nevertheless, it does add an appropriate layer to the concept of a wildly loving God who rejects no one.

And then in Matthew's version of the Gospel (chapter 15, verses 21-28), such a poignant vignette: Jesus' encounter with the persistent woman who is asking that he make her daughter well. Masterful teacher that he was, he humored her at first, pretending that he has no concern for her appeal and that she is not worthy of his time anyway – all the while just testing her and exhibiting to others her deep, unshakable faith.

> *There is no reason for anyone to live in fear of God.*

I think it's pretty hard to miss the point here: There is no reason for anyone to live in fear of God, for God is love that waits patiently for even the greatest of sinners to return home to its comforting embrace. A 2013 translation of the bible understands Paul to say, "God's gifts and God's call are under full warranty – never cancelled, never rescinded" (The Message/Catholic Ecumenical Edition, by Eugene H. Peterson).

So, what more do you need to know? Be at peace!

FORWARD OR BACKWARD: A PAINFUL DIVIDE

I t's hardly news to anyone, I'm sure, that some members of the church want it to remain unchanged, although unchanged from what is not always clear. They want the church even to reverse some of the changes it has made over the past few decades and to get back to what they imagine the original church was like. They felt more secure under the leadership of Pope Benedict XVI, who had indicated for many years his dedication to strict orthodoxy. But then, with his surprising resignation and the entrance of the more liberal Pope Francis, it was the progressive wing of the church that rejoiced.

These "progressive" or "liberal" Catholics (Is there a better, more fitting term for them?) are eager for the church to move ahead, not abandoning its past, but continuing the development that has been going on since its very beginning. They do not see change as shameful compromise but instead as the highest fidelity to what and who had come before them. They would be happy with a pope who makes it clear that Catholic theology and practice are constantly evolving and adapting under the direction of the Spirit of God, and they look with renewed hope for promising indications of how Francis, who is pope as I write these words, will guide the church toward a more Gospel-oriented future.

The week after Pope Benedict's election, I received a passionate, angry letter from a lifelong Catholic who announced his decision to leave the church and, as he put it, "to begin a new effort to get serious about Christ outside the Catholic Church."

An extreme reaction, for sure, and I'm certain that what I wrote back to him did not persuade him to abandon the path he was taking. I

256

recognized at once that his is an all-too-common story today. It is happening in disturbing numbers in families that can claim generations of unbroken Catholicity.

I do not judge the sincerity or integrity of anyone who comes to such a conclusion, and I would urge you not to do that either. I think this is one of those special times for us all to discover each other anew. It is not a time for condemnation or argumentation or even attempts to persuade. It is rather an opportunity to find Jesus in each other, very likely in ways we have not sufficiently appreciated before. With our separating friends and relatives, our children and grandchildren, many of us are not enjoying that precious bond of unity in religious practice to which we had grown so accustomed. We may not be at Sunday Mass together or receiving the same Jesus in the Sacrament of Eucharist. We will live with concern about the children involved and we will be heartbroken about their departure from a church that we love so much, despite its terrible human failings.

Did Jesus anticipate conditions like these in the community he was forming? I believe that he did. Such thoughts must have been in the back of his mind with almost everything he taught, especially when he urged his followers to keep him at the center of their lives. He is the way, the truth, the life, he said; we would be united with each other to the extent that we are united with him.

Changes will certainly continue coming to the church, maybe some very desirable ones inspired by the contemporary spirit Pope Francis espouses, making it more attractive and meaningful to the people of our time, particularly to those who are estranged or who have rejected her for whatever reason. In the meantime, we must be patient and faithful and hopeful. The more we discover the goodness and love of Jesus in the goodness and love of each other, the more we will have to celebrate when once again we are united around his table.

A young friend of mine, married mother of two children, told me a while ago that she has given up hope of finding Catholic worship that nourishes her and meets her spiritual and moral needs and those of her family. She has experimented with Christian churches other than Catholic, but with time she has judged them to be similarly shallow. She ended her confession by saying, "I'm never again going to allow other people, no matter their rank or authority in the church, to tell me how to relate to my God. I know what it means to be a responsible human being, and I live in constant gratitude to God for the gifts of life and love. I don't think I need outside help anymore."

(I thought it was very telling that she should refer to church leaders as "other people" and "outside help." No awareness there that she herself embodies the church; she does not merely belong to the church — she *is* church.)

Lest you get the impression that she's an arrogant fool, let me assure you that she is not. She has tried hard to remain within the Catholic Church of her birth and education, but time and again she has been disappointed by the soulless character of the liturgies her parishes have provided, the lack of relevance and substance in the homilies and sermons she has painfully sat through, and the aloofness of pastors and priests who gave the impression that they were divinely appointed schoolmasters disciplining small children rather than brothers in service to their equal siblings.

I understood her completely, and I felt for her deeply. By no means was this the first such story I had heard from once devout Catholics. I wish I had an answer that could help them to resolve the matter, help them to find their way back to the church, but I don't. As trite as it may sound, what springs to my lips immediately in such encounters is my sincere comment that I feel their pain and wish I could make it go away.

And then I tell them that I too have lived with the considerable human failings of the Catholic Church and have contributed a few of those failings myself, but that I voluntarily remain a Catholic and still want to do my part toward purifying and healing the church. I remind them that the church started out with a small number of very human, very imperfect, even sinful, persons who sometimes succeeded and sometimes failed in their professed following of Jesus. I then suggest that in a way things haven't changed very much: we're still weak and selfish and shabbily human, a long way from the ideals we aspire to. We're not a fallen race; we are a developing race, and we have a long way to go. All the more, then, do we need each other's good example and inspiration, each other's forgiveness and acceptance. We can, and we will, do a lot better, I try to assure them.

At this writing, our beloved Catholic Church is experiencing very difficult times. One factor alone is enough to disturb and worry us: that our membership is rapidly decreasing. Recent polls show that for every person received into the church, four are leaving. Some strongly conservative Catholics believe that this is "God's way" of pruning the church, purifying and sanctifying it. The reasons for departures from the church appear to be many and have to do mostly with the disappointment people are experiencing in what they are hearing within its walls. Alarmingly many of the "good Catholic families" that I know are telling the same story about their children and grandchildren who are no longer going to church but profess to be believers in God and followers of Jesus. These parents and grandparents almost invariably describe their offspring as charitable, just, caring, and generous – but not Catholic anymore in the sense that we have known and lived the faith.

The curious Pharisees and Sadducees went out to take a look at John the Baptist and decide whether or not he was a threat to them, tied as they were to the temple and its hold on the people. He accused them of being religious in word only — empty, hypocritical words at that. He tells them that, if they really were allowing God's word to penetrate their hearts and minds, their actions would be marked by humility and forgiveness and loving concern for others. But, no, instead they are bloodsuckers, taking life from the people, not giving life.

And then John warns them not to hide behind their lineage as religious men who can claim Abraham as their father and founder. That will get you nowhere, he shouts, because, I tell you, God cannot be constrained by any human institution; God doesn't need family descent or temple tradition or religious faith or any such thing to live and love and work within a willing human being. God can fashion faithful children of Abraham out of those stones at your feet if God wants to!

It's true:

God doesn't need our religion — but we do! We do because it is the vehicle that has carried into our lives the long tradition of the human race's interaction with the unseen God. We need

> *God doesn't need our religion — but we do!*

it because it provides the helpful setting and sacramental instruments for our celebration of life and God's presence with us always. We need the church because through Eucharist and public prayer, and by keeping before us the example of the faithful persons who preceded us, it enables us to expand and deepen our individual lives. And we need our Catholic religion because it constantly gives us reason to hope, when otherwise we would be discouraged or in despair.

I wish that those who have left or are contemplating leaving the church would give her another chance. I wish also that the officials of the church – all of us who have chosen the profession of serving the people from the storehouse of the church's great tradition — would carry out their appointed tasks with the love and humility of Jesus. If that's what the people were always experiencing, who would ever want to leave?

BUILDINGS AND FOUNDATIONS

There's an ancient piece of fiction about two brothers who were secretly doing kind and generous things for each other – neither one knowing who his mysterious benefactor was. One night, as each of them was going to his brother's home to carry out another good deed, they bumped into each other and instantly realized what had been happening for so long. They embraced, they cried and laughed, and one of them said, "Let's build a church on this spot!"

That fictional, improbable tale suggests very effectively the real meaning of the word, the concept, "church." Church is a gathering of persons who are already building bonds of unity by acts of love and who come together to celebrate their oneness, to thank God for the gift of shared life, and to ask for the grace of continuing reconciliation. Whenever church becomes a purely private enterprise — a "Jesus and me" affair — it is something very different from the definition and etymology of its name.

The history of our world is one of alienation, hostility, disintegration. The Hebrew Book of Genesis, the first book of the bible, confirms that and makes it clear that in the evolutionary development of the human species into intelligence and self-reflection we deliberately chose to reject one another in a selective way designed to serve our own selfish purposes. So deeply ingrained is this evil tendency that the bible tells of the murder of a man by his own brother for the sake of personal, material profit: the Cain and Abel myth.

So universal is this tendency that the Tower of Babel is put forth as its symbol: human beings, all creatures of the one and only God, therefore conceived in love, are unable to work together because they will not communicate with one another. Mind does not reach mind; heart does not reach heart. The condition has continued down the centuries even to our own day, taking different forms from age to age, but remaining the same in essence.

It's the momentum that Jesus was dedicated to breaking and reversing. Jesus is God's saving presence in the world: he gathers us into one community, one church, as a sign of the unity he has sworn to restore and as a source of power for all who are willing to love and labor with him.

We splash a stroke of white and gold across the calendar once a year as we celebrate the feast of the Church of St. John Lateran. That church is the cathedral of the Bishop of Rome, who is also the pope of the world-wide church. It is the head church, the mother church of all Christendom. It represents every Christian church in the entire world, of all centuries past, present and to come.

The name Lateran is that of a prominent Roman family that provided administrative assistance to a succession of emperors; and the name John refers to both John the Baptist and John, the author of one of the four gospels.

Over the centuries of its existence, the basilica underwent one calamity after another: at least three very destructive fires, a major earthquake, total vandalism, and deliberate demolition. It contains the tombs of six popes, it has been home to the stairs that were popularly thought to have been used by Jesus on his way to his crucifixion and has been a model of church design and architecture and liturgical worship for well over a thousand years.

The honor we give the building or the place is not the core of our celebration, which is much deeper than just that. Ezekiel's prophecy speaks of God residing with God's people and God's presence filling the place of worship. St. Paul teaches the Corinthians that they are the temple built on the foundation of Jesus. It is they, each of them, all of them; it is we, each of us, all of us, in whom God resides.

And so, Catholics might be saying, why is this something for us to be celebrating? Well, with help from others whom I have consulted, I can offer an answer to the question.

One of them is Father Roger Karban. He approaches the topic with his typical good humor by saying, "the person who first referred to church as a building is going to spend lots of extra time in purgatory!" He points out that the earliest Christians had no separate buildings in which to celebrate the Eucharist; they simply met in each other's homes, having learned from Jesus that there is no distinction between the sacred and the secular.[33] As my theologian friend Michael Morwood so well puts it, "God is not present in some persons and some places and absent in others."[34]

Again, Father Karban speaks about the radical change that Jesus made: "Everything, every place, every time and every person could now be sacred. Jesus had torn down the veil which separated the two opposing elements. One's home had become just as sacred as the holiest temple on earth." And then he quotes St. Paul: "You are God's building… The temple of God, which you are, is holy."

"I have chosen and sanctified this house," says the Lord, "that my name may remain in it for all time."

We have a long and persistent tradition of attempting to "clean up our act," so to speak, by going faithfully to church once a week to be

264

purified of our careless, selfish, sinful behavior. In itself, that's not entirely a bad idea. But the problem is that it can suggest that we live most of our days cooperating with a sinful, godless world and then run to church to be sanitized, when the truth is that God is no less present to us those other six days, wherever we are, whatever we are doing, whomever we are with.

Annually we celebrate the mother church of the Christian faith, the Basilica of St. John Lateran. But it would be a mistake to let it be merely something outside of us, remote from us, disconnected from us. Instead we have the opportunity of allowing it to deepen our awareness that, as spectacular as that building is, it ranks below the temple of the Spirit of God that you and I actually are.

Jesus referred to his own body as the temple that will be sacrificially destroyed and then triumphantly rebuilt so that all may dwell happily and securely in him forever!

What are you building? A family? A business? A treasury of knowledge? A battery of skills? A bank of memories? All building, this unusual feast day reminds us, is in vain, useless, doomed unless it is somehow related to the Mystery of Mysteries called God.

We now turn from buildings to builders. The Christian Church honors its original heroes. We can call them the founders of Christianity, especially since we have come to realize that it was not Jesus' intention to establish a new church but rather to reform his beloved Judaism and to start a movement of faithful Jews that would spread out into the known world, attracting to it every nation and every race.

We remember with gratitude two giant contributors to the foundation of the church that we inherited 2000 years later. They are, of course, Saints Peter and Paul.

265

Father Karban points out that in the generation that separated the deaths of Peter and Paul from the writings of the New Testament, there was time to reflect much more deeply and comprehensively on the impact these two men had on the early Church, an impact that they themselves could not have appreciated during their lifetimes. Among the treasures they have bequeathed to us is their invincible conviction that Jesus actually did experience resurrection after death.[35] I am among those believers who hold that his resurrection need not necessarily be understood as bodily, but instead as his moving on to new and transformed life after his inevitable death – into the very life of God that is not possible here on earth.

His followers spoke of him, after his crucifixion, as "in glory," a term whose meaning and full implications inevitably escape us. That "glory" could have meant only complete union with the Creator God that not even the most devout believer can achieve in this mortal life.

Peter and Paul comprehended what happened, at least as far as human beings are capable of comprehending, and nothing, not even the threat of torture and cruel death, could dampen their enthusiasm and their burning desire to share with all human beings this most welcome of all good news. The fact that you and I can speak of our beloved dead as not dead but gloriously alive in the presence of God we owe largely to Peter and Paul. Our looking forward to that same transformed life when our earthly journeys have ended is our expression of the faith that was passed on to us by these two very human saints.

However, Jesus' main concern for his followers was not the attainment of heaven, which he seems to have left in the hands of the One he called Father. It was, rather, that they live in peace and love and joy here on earth. His chief command to them – to us – had nothing to do with the formalities of church-going; it was that we love one another as he has loved us.

Yet, this basic faith in life after death that our ancestors have passed on to us affects everything we now experience. We know that the troubles of our life — chronic, nagging, unyielding — will not survive death, but that our hopes and joys and fondest desires will be totally satisfied and more. It's that faith that ultimately keeps us going as it enabled Peter and Paul and the other founders of our religion even to welcome martyrdom on its behalf.

George Washington gave us a country for which we are grateful beyond words; Peter and Paul gave us an interpretation of Jesus according to which we build our entire lives and on which we pin our longest-ranging hopes.

MANY REFORMATIONS

For most of my life I believed that Martin Luther, the Roman Catholic Augustinian monk of the early 16th century, was the founder of the Lutheran Religion. Actually, he was not. Had he been asked just before his death to state his religion, he would have answered, "Roman Catholic."

Father Luther's intention was to stimulate major reform in a church he recognized to be corrupt: false teachings, immorality among the clergy and religious, questionable and sacrilegious practices like the granting of indulgences for payment, etc. But the church was not humble enough to consider the demanded reforms and instead condemned the "whistle-blower." His followers, after his death, chose not to remain in the unrepentant Roman Church but rather to break off as a protesting branch. Hence, the Lutheran Church of the 16th century and of today.

Similarly, neither was Jesus the founder of what we call Christianity, an appellation we too facilely ascribe to him. Jesus was a reformer, a revolutionary. He challenged the corrupt Jewish religion of his day, thus making himself a *persona non grata* with its authorities. He was not attempting to establish a new religion but to purify his beloved Judaism. Had his followers, among them Peter and Paul, been questioned about their religious affiliation before their deaths, they would have said that they were Jews, because that's what they were and knew themselves to be. Like Lutheranism centuries later, Christianity itself began as an offshoot from the Jewish religion of Jesus' day and was called at first "The Way."

All reformers have much in common, including their looking back to the origin of the institution which they are hoping to bring to honest reflection and radical renewal. They try to exhibit the strength and truth and goodness and beauty of its birth and early life and then they compare these to the shabby, eroded, distorted state of its present existence. Pope St. John XXIII did exactly that when he called the Second Vatican Council. He said that, when he looked at the church of Apostolic times, in those first decades after the death and resurrection of Jesus, and placed it side by side with the church of the mid-20th century, the distressing discrepancies were undeniable. Work must be done, he said, to restore the church to its original wholeness and simplicity. An aggiornamento was in order; the windows must be opened to let in fresh air. The accretions of the centuries were not all worth keeping; some were destructive to the life and mission of the church.

In the familiar gospel account of Jesus' meeting with the woman caught in adultery, we recognize him as the reformer that he was. To appreciate this, we have to see that he was led into a no-win situation. His enemies had him, they thought, in an inescapable corner. They reminded him of the Mosaic Law that covered incidents like the one at hand: a woman discovered in the act of adultery was to be stoned to death. They asked him what his judgment would be concerning this woman: should she be executed or not? The corner they thought they had him in was that either a yes or a no would condemn him as a law-breaker: If he said no, he was violating the Jewish law and setting himself above it. If he said yes, he was transgressing the Roman law, which forbade a Jew from killing anyone. And Jesus masters the challenge with his brilliant dare that the one who is without any sin should throw the first stone.

Note what he is doing in the judgment he renders: Reformer that he is, he reaches back over more than a thousand years of Jewish law and tradition and consults instead a law that the founders of Judaism had known, the law of God's love and mercy. It is by that overriding, underlying law that he resolves the case of the sinning woman, not by the narrow legalism of sinful religious leaders.

So many moral issues beset our church today. You know them well. Among them are birth control, marriage after divorce without benefit of a church annulment, celibacy in the priesthood and the possibility of a married clergy, the movement for women's ordination, the participation of sexually active gay and lesbian Catholics in church worship and ministry. These are but a few; there are so many more. How shall we solve such thorny problems unless we follow the example of Jesus and reach back to the best of our Christian tradition at whatever time in history it existed and call forth its principles and its examples of love and compassion? Applying them to contemporary issues will assure us that we are meeting and resolving the troubling issues of our day according to the mind and the way of Jesus.

Benedict XVI, shortly after becoming pope, said, "Why should faith and reason be afraid of each other, if they can express themselves better by meeting and engaging one another?" We'd do well to follow that counsel with courage and eager anticipation.

Fifty-three years ago, Dominican Father Yves Congar (one of the most influential voices at the Second Vatican Council) wrote that a main reason for the Protestant Reformation was that educated lay persons and ordinary parish priests did not strongly enough protest against the abuses that they were seeing in the teachings and the practices of the church at the time.[36] Power at the highest levels of church leadership had gone almost completely out of control; simple people – not stupid, just poorly educated – were browbeaten into believing that their eternal salvation depended on strict obedience to every dictate that came from church authority. They were taught to purchase indulgences so as to relieve themselves and their beloved dead from a certain amount of punishment in purgatory, indulgences that could be purchased in advance as a kind of credit against their future sinning! Heretical tripe and abominable corruption are terms too mild to express the enormity of the moral morass into which the church had sunk.

A reform from within, a self-purification, would have been the best approach, but instead it turned out that reformers had to leave the church and establish Christian denominations of their own in their attempts to return to the purity of the Scriptures and the Christian tradition. It is that very divided Christianity that we are only too familiar with today. Among our "what-ifs" is the one suggested by Father Congar: What if intelligent, thinking men and women and the humble priests who ministered faithfully to them had dared to speak out, creating a chorus of voices that had to impress their leaders if only because of its sheer magnitude? And might, therefore, the disintegration of Christendom into a thousand pieces have been avoided in favor of a gradual recovery and renewal from within?

The Catholic Church is at a similar juncture today, although not for precisely the same reasons. There are many serious, unresolved issues on the outcome of which millions of concerned Catholics believe the future of the church depends. The dire shortage of ordained priests threatens the church as a Eucharistic community. The statistics in this regard are alarming. I once visited a parish in central New Jersey in which there were no weekend Masses because no priest was available. The lay people held five Scripture/Eucharistic services on Saturday evening and Sunday morning, as they had done a few times before, but no Mass, of course. (Who shall be permitted henceforth to be priests, and what will be asked of them?)

The whole area of human sexuality, including marriage and divorce, homosexuality, and birth control, needs to be rethought in a changed and ever-changing world. How many persons are excluded, or made to feel excluded, because of some aspect of their sexual lives in which what their consciences tell them is right and good runs contrary to the church's official teaching — the same official church that tells them that their moral decisions must be based finally, not on any church law, but on the judgment of their own sincere, well-formed consciences?

The role of lay people in the decision-making processes and structures of the church is another issue that sharply divides us today. For almost all the years of my formal education, I was taught that the church is an exclusively top-down organization, through which the laws and the teachings of God were communicated by the chain of command put in place by legitimate authority and that the response of the membership was simply to listen carefully and to obey without compromise. But now many of us understand better that the Spirit of God is as present and as active among the people, both individually and collectively, as among our leaders.

These are only a few of the many matters that are presently at the forefront of our Catholic life. They will not go away — but many more Catholics will go away, they will leave the church, unless these issues are addressed with open minds and mutual respect.

The dialog must go on, no longer as a debate in which we are determined to prove how right we are, but as an honest search for the truth, no matter where or in whom it may most fully reside.

I read recently the full text of a sermon given by a Protestant minister in which, pulling no punches, he indicted the Catholic Church —

the roots of his own tradition after all — for its sins and crimes during that period when the Protestant Reformation took place. Despite my imperfect knowledge of history, I found the sermon to be truthful and factual. I wish that we Catholics would react humbly and remorsefully when presented with the more shameful aspects of our past, admitting that, like all things human, our beloved church has also sinned and erred. From a plateau of such sincerity and candor we can then join hands with those of other denominations and other faiths and move on together in an unbiased, unending quest for truth.

If a hundred Catholics were asked if they believed that Jesus founded their religion, I would not be surprised if upwards of 95 of them answered, "Yes, of course." Some years ago, I would have made the same response, so unquestioning was our acceptance of everything taught to us by well-meaning representatives of the church, who were full of sincere faith but woefully ignorant of the history of the church.

Jesus lived and died a Jew. He loved his Jewish tradition and religion passionately and knew that the Spirit of God, present everywhere and in everyone, regardless of religion, had been heard by his ancestors in a way that no others had heard since the beginning of human history. There was no doubt in Jesus' mind that the truth and the wisdom of God had been perceived by the Jewish prophets with uncommonly receptive minds; but he was also painfully aware of corruption and compromise in both Jewish teaching and Jewish practice, as he experienced it in his own time and place.

Unlike Christians of some 1500 years later, who did not speak up against the abuses they observed in their leaders and teachers, Jesus did speak up, always at great danger to himself and ultimately at the cost of his life. His goal was not to begin a new religion; he believed totally in

Judaism as the primary voice of God on earth. He was determined to do all that he could to purge that religion of everything that was unseemly and restore it to the simple beauty that it once was perceived to possess. But authority in any human institution does not respond well to efforts at reform; it resists them tooth and nail in the frantic resolve to preserve its own status. Jesus felt the full brunt of that resistance and died at its hands, agonizing over his failure to accomplish the objective of reform but confident nonetheless that out of his sacrifice the victory would eventually be won.

His followers for a long time thought of themselves as faithful Jews and became known first as members of "The Way" and much later as Christians. It's interesting to note that 2000 years later the church calls itself *Ecclesia Semper Reformanda*, which is translated "Church Always in Need of Reform."

But when we speak of reform, what are we really talking about? The way we "do" Mass on Sunday? Yes, that's an important concern. Who our priests shall be and what shall be required of them? What the laws and requirements of membership in the church must be? How we relate to other religions? How we collaborate with the world around us? Certainly these and many other aspects of church doctrine and practice have to be kept under constant scrutiny and refined or changed to meet the needs of the times. And yet, important as they are, they must take second place to that overriding concern that Jesus was constantly expressing, and that is simply how we relate to each other as human beings.

There can be no true religion, no worthy worship of God, unless they come from persons who are doing their best to relate to each other in positive, affirming, charitable, and forgiving ways.

Pick any one of Jesus' instructions and stories, and you will see how homely and down-to-earth his themes were. The reform for which he labored and gave his life had nothing to do with grand institutions or with style; it was about the everyday behavior of men and women – whether it was loving and generous, or hateful and selfish. The change that he envisioned included compromise and sacrifice that individual persons make for the sake of peace, lifestyles that make room for sharing with others in need. True religion, the Gospel writers had come to understand from him, is shown by the care of orphans and widows.

> *There can be no true religion, no worthy worship of God, unless they come from persons who are doing their best to relate to each other in positive, affirming, charitable, and forgiving ways.*

The disappointment that so many of us rightly feel with the quality of leadership in our church today may incline us to think that is where the primary focus of reform should be placed, but to conclude that is to deceive ourselves and miss the message of Jesus and maybe even to choose a convenient scapegoat in order to avoid our own personal responsibility. The reform for which all of us are responsible must be in our daily, personal lives. No change anywhere in the church outranks that.

> *A holy church is simply a community of people who try to live as Jesus did.*

A LIVING TESTAMENT

T he Hebrew Bible tells us that there is but one Father God. By contrast, in St. Paul's Letter to the Thessalonians, he reminds us that those who minister in God's name must do so with the gentleness of a nursing mother caressing her child. (I wonder how many men are big enough, secure enough, to accept that and to work toward it.)

It's really too bad that the traditional formula that expresses the mystery of the Holy Trinity does not include obvious reference to femininity in God. It was a patriarchal, male-dominated society that considered it enough to label God "Father, Son, and Spirit." Who knows what future generations will do to modify that basic statement of faith and make it truly inclusive?

In the meantime, we can be grateful for such beautiful images as the one cited above from St. Paul and others from Jesus, like the one in which he described himself as a mother hen eagerly enfolding her young under her wings. "Enfolding" is itself a characteristically feminine concept, expressed most fundamentally by the womb itself. I hope there are fewer people today who prefer to picture God only as an old man with a long beard, because breasts and embracing arms are also useful and truthful elements in the ultimately impossible task of imaging the invisible, infinite God.

A dear friend of mine, a first-time grandmother, told me about the difficult and dangerous last days of her daughter's pregnancy. But the baby arrived safely and the mother was soon on her way to restored health. Then came this email: "I always knew that God could not be confined to the limitations of human imagination. And I hated the idea of being 'tested' by God, as if God plays games with us to see if we can make the grade, so to speak. No, God is in my lovely daughter and her young husband, in their doctors and nurses, in each and every member of our family and friends – and now in this beautiful baby, my grandson!"

And that's the truth, which we cannot say too often or too emphatically: that we all reveal God to one another. Everything good and true and beautiful seen in any person has to be a unique reflection of the Creative Spirit, God. Where else or whom else could it ultimately have come from?

That's the kind of religion we need more of — sensing and responding to the signs of God, the loving presence of God, we are daily encountering. No one can limit the infinite God to a single definition, when all the religions and cultures of the world could not begin to contain God, to "put God in a box," as we are fond of saying. The very question "Is God male or female?" should tell us how off the mark our thinking can be, how narrow our perspective.

> *You, dear reader, are the "scripture" that many persons are reading!*

You, dear reader, are the "scripture" that many persons are reading!

Pope St. John Paul II said that people pay more attention to personal witness than they do to formal teaching. How true that is. In their own often perverse way, some television idols are far more influential in the lives of us humans than are the teachings of Jesus as they come to us in the church. Male or female, married or single, heterosexual or homosexual, young or old, etc., we are all creatures of God. Like specks of diamond dust, we inevitably and necessarily show in our visible being the marks of the invisible Creator.

ADDENDA

A CHRISTIAN'S PERSONAL CREED

In his reference to the new patch on an old garment and the new wine in old wineskins, Jesus was obviously saying that the receptacle has to be suitable in order for the addition of new content to be successful. If it is not rightly disposed, the end result will be disastrous: in the metaphor he uses, the whole garment will shrink with the patch's first exposure to water and the wine pouches will burst as the fermentation of the fresh wine continues.

He was acknowledging that he was speaking to the people differently about the nature of God and their relationship with God and with each other, and he was lamenting the obvious fact that they were not accepting the beautiful things he was telling them because his teachings did not fit into their old mindset. *The God you think you know could never approve of what you are hearing from me. You need a new idea of God, different from the ones you so righteously and stubbornly cling to.* Were not these his thoughts and the essence of his message to that crowd?

Jesus was always redefining God, mainly through his parables, in order to help his hearers create a new concept, a new mindset, on which to develop a healthier, more life-giving relationship with God and with each other.

Beyond the precise words he is said to have spoken, what can we derive from his teachings and from the whole of his life? The following belief statements suggest how this Christian understands God through the mind of Jesus:

* God and we are never apart: God is not "up there" and we are not "down below." God is *in* us, the way two persons are in one another in a union of love, but far more intimately.

* God is the deepest foundation of all that exists – from the tiniest particles of matter to the largest stars, from amoebas to humans, and all that is spiritual. God is the ground of all being; if God were not the sustaining power of anything that exists, it would not exist. God is the energy of the Big Bang, the birth of the universe billions of years ago. God is the power that sustains the process of evolution that produces us humans and all things living and inanimate.

* God is love, and when we love in any way we are living actively in God.

* God and we create and struggle together; God neither observes nor manages from some distant place, but

280

instead is the empowering energy of everything we think and say and do.

- God's "kingdom" is within us; we can choose to make the decisions of our life in harmony with the principles of that benign rule or not, yet its power is always accessible to us.

- God creates us simply to be good human beings, caring for others as we care for ourselves, trying to overcome our selfishness, forgiving generously, moving on in hope in even the worst of times. Good human beings, nothing more, nothing less.

- We cannot control God, never did, never will, no matter what prayers we say or rituals we perform. Nor does God ever control us: we are always left free to act as we choose.

- The prayers and sacred rituals don't save; they don't protect us or win us special favors. Rather, they celebrate the relationship between God and us, between us and all other creatures; they remind us of God's loving presence to us at every moment of our lives; they encourage us to look forward eagerly and peacefully to that perfect life Jesus says awaits us after our biological death; they call us back when we have wandered from his way.

I have come, he said, that you may have life and have it to the full.

PRIMACY OF CONSCIENCE

A s the Catholic Church is well into the 3rd Christian millennium, let's hope there will be a resounding emphasis on the sanctity, the primacy, and the inviolability of human conscience. We must be done with coercion and intimidation, with blind, unquestioning obedience, and acknowledge that each member has the right, the need, and the obligation to be Spirit-directed – not in a separatist or ruthlessly individualistic fashion, but within the nurturing, supportive, sometimes corrective atmosphere of the Christian community. Lockstep conformity is for totalitarian states; intelligent, resourceful, considerate decision-making is for the Christian community.

One of those "best kept secrets" that continue to astound first-time hearers is found among the documents of the Second Vatican Council. It is taken from the one entitled, *The Church in the Modern World*:

> *Deep within their consciences men and women discover a law which they have not laid upon themselves and which they must obey. Its voice, ever calling them to love and to do what is good and to avoid evil, tells them inwardly at the right moment: do this, shun that...Their dignity rests in observing this law, and by it they will be judged...For God willed that men and women should "be left free to make their own decisions"...Their dignity therefore requires them to act out of conscious and free choice, as moved and drawn in a personal way from within, and not by their own blind impulses or by external constraint. (Chapter 1, #16,17)*

In its *"Declaration on Christian Education,"* the same Council teaches that –

Children and young people have the right to be stimulated to make sound moral judgments based on a well-formed conscience and to put them into practice with a sense of personal commitment...(Section #1)

Beyond the Council, voices expressing its spirit have also been heard in the intervening years. The late Archbishop William Borders, of Baltimore, not very long after the Council issued a pastoral letter in which he wrote that our life in Christ *"cannot be satisfied by a mere recitation of answers that are composed by somebody else for our benefit...we have an obligation to act with an informed conscience."*

Living our Catholic lives according to personal conscience will make certain demands on us. The first and most essential will be the never-ending task of forming a good conscience, a conscience that is not only worthy of being followed but, as the Council emphasized, *must* be followed. That often means the hard work of agonizing and objective thinking, periods of self-doubt, informative reading, peer consultation, counseling, prayer, and patient waiting. The church assures us that we will know, by the urging of an inner voice, when the time to act has come and what form that action must take.

CORPUS NATIONAL CONVENTION, JUNE 24, 2006

C ORPUS *is one of the oldest reform groups in the Catholic Church, and is active in reform movements both in the U.S. and abroad. It is committed to working for a renewed priesthood of married and single men and women dedicated to serving God through the Community of Believers. CORPUS is a faith community affirming an inclusive priesthood rooted in a reformed and renewed church. I was privileged to say to the members:*

Had anyone ever asked me how many priests in my modest-size Diocese of Paterson have left the active ministry, I would have said maybe 30 or so. I was astounded to be informed shortly before being invited to give this talk that there have been 116! Project that statistic across the country to appreciate better the dimensions of the exodus and to wonder again why the church does not respond more proactively to a situation that cries for attention.

I regard our beloved church as seriously thrice wounded and, sadder to say, self-wounded. I consider you, and all that you represent vis-à-vis the total mission of the church, as a sign and a very important part of the recovery of health and vigor that we are all so eager to experience. In fact, in each of the three wounds I think you have a key role to play as healers.

The first wound, from which we bleed daily, is our lingering failure to become what Jesus obviously had in mind: truly a people's church.

I had the treasured privilege a few years ago of presiding at the joint funeral of two beloved, elderly sisters – siblings and also long-time and much loved members of the same religious community. Jayne and Eileen were full of life and love; their very presence lighted up whatever space they occupied. Their deaths in a car accident brought grief and sadness to countless persons whose lives they had brightened.

Jayne had asked me long ago to preside and preach at her funeral, and she sent me from time to time personal writings that she hoped would enable me to reveal her true mind and heart to the mourners at her funeral. In one of those jottings, she wrote –

> *Jesus began his message with friendship, not only because it is powerful, but also because it is hopeful. It is the key, the only key that can unlock the door to a worthwhile future in love. Jesus saw the truth of that 20 centuries ago. Instead of organizing institutions, he started a movement based on friendship, on love. That is the only solution to the problems of the human heart. People can live together under almost any conditions if they are friends, if they are in love.*

For whatever historical reasons, that I certainly am not qualified to delineate, in general we seem to show a preference for a pyramidal, hierarchical church, in which the normative modus operandi is still vertical: God, pope, hierarchy, clergy, religious, laity, in descending order. Commands and teachings from above, compliance and assent from below.

The eminent theologian Elisabeth Schüssler Fiorenza said once that the church is run more like the Roman Empire than the *ekklesia* of Christ. Asked, then, why she stays in the church and still calls herself a Catholic theologian, she answered that such questions are wrong-headed because they presuppose that the hierarchy is the church rather than that we, the people of God, are the church, that the hierarchy is called to serve.

Symbols are helpful, and I share with you one that I got from a teaching theologian, himself a resigned, married priest. Think of the church, he said, as three interconnected circles (the old Ballantine Beer sign!), each representing a major segment of the church. One is the hierarchy, the magisterium, the chief teaching and governing authority of the church. Another is the scholars and theologians, who carefully examine our past and look outward with discerning eyes at what the horizon seems to promise. And the third is you and I, the ordinary members of the church, possessors of the *sensus fidelium*.

When the hierarchy is not written off as irrelevant, when theologians are not silenced, and when the members are not denied their legitimate collaboration, the church is functioning at its best and we can be certain that the work of the Spirit is being optimally facilitated. But when these three are out of sync, when there are distrust and contention among them, the church is crippled and unable to function as it should.

A beloved member of the hierarchy, of blessedly advanced age, told me not so long ago that he is convinced that the problems of the church will never be resolved until it honors fully the rightful role of all its members in the process of decision-making.

I appeal to you, my brothers and sisters: do not deny the church your input regarding matters in which you know you have something true and valuable to contribute. Do this, not so much from book learning, but from the authentic experience of your Spirit-filled lives.

The second self-inflicted wound is the clergy sex abuse crisis. Is there anything new or different or particularly revealing to be said about it? I think not; however, we might well point out that it is related to a much larger and more pervasive problem within the church, namely, its unenlightened view of human sexuality that has been too long with us. The dis-

286

connect between the official teaching of the church in that area and what the vast majority of the people are believing and practicing is just one sign that something is radically wrong with the church's approach to human sexuality. Another is the obvious fact that bishops themselves here in our own country and around the world admirably placed compassion and clear thinking above sheer conformity with Rome when many of them counseled us priests, after the promulgation of the encyclical *Humanae Vitae*, not to probe the sexual decisions of the faithful, but to leave those matters to their own well-formed consciences.

My own training in human sexuality was nothing short of tragic both at home and in Catholic schools, and especially in seminary, leaving me with a sexuality that was out of touch with human nature and virtually identified with sin, for almost never was sex discussed except in the context of sin. I am still trying to expunge from my deepest self those jaundiced, joyless, cautionary, and frightening views of the precious gift of human sexuality.

The sex abuse crisis of today can be a wake-up call. Only one among many sexual issues, it demands of us attention not just to itself but also to the much broader context of which it is a part.

Again I appeal to you, my brothers, and you wives, to realize that you have a critical role to play. We must not turn principally to men who represent a thousand-year tradition of celibacy for insight into our stewardship as sexual beings. No, you who have experience in marriage and parenthood must be among our chief teachers of the present and the future. I urge you to speak up in every way you can, you with your Spirit-led instinct for the truth, you who have made such difficult conscience decisions in the management of your lives, you with your respect for the bearers of truth, whoever they may be.

Twice already in this talk I have addressed you on the basis of your life in the Spirit. My understanding is that a spiritual person is one who lives his or her life always conscious of that divine presence, constantly trying to incorporate its power and direction in the decision-making that life demands.

I am convinced that we have interpreted much too narrowly the relationship between the Spirit of God and us Christians. Consider just these three factors among many others: 1) the Feast of Pentecost, which is recounted in the bible with so much rich symbolism; 2) our traditional devotion to the Holy Spirit; and 3) our one-time reception of the sacrament of Confirmation. These alone certainly can imply that we Christians have been given by God an exclusive privilege denied to 90 % of the people of the world. That cannot be so. We humans are all creatures of the same loving God, whose Spirit acts in all who invite her to. From religion to religion we name that God differently, but, as the Scriptures emphasize, it is the same Spirit in each and all of us.

The third serious and self-inflicted wound I see in the church today is the increasing unavailability of Eucharistic action in our parish churches. By that I don't mean Eucharistic presence in the tabernacle-reserved sacrament; I mean the whole fluid, dynamic action in which what the people have brought to the liturgy, namely themselves intentionally placed in the bread and wine, is returned to them with the most special and exquisite sacramental presence of Jesus. Receiving Communion from a pyx or a tabernacle, no matter what prayers and rituals may surround the act, is in a category different from participation in the entire Eucharistic action. But fewer and fewer persons have full access to that central act of Catholic Christian worship because of the increasing shortage of ordained priests. I have read that one quarter of our American parishes do not have a resident priest.

The first time I felt keenly the import of this situation was when I was invited to give a half-day of recollection at a parish in south central New Jersey, not far from where I live. As I pulled into the parking lot a bit after noon on that Sunday, I noticed large numbers of people pouring out of the church and assumed that the last Mass of the day had just ended. But, entering the church, I learned otherwise: there had been no Masses for the entire weekend. The concerned parishioners had sent their hard-working, exhausted priest off on a two-week vacation and, not being able to find a priest they considered suitable for their particular needs, they asked their deacons to lead them in a Eucharistic service, which they did four times on those two days. Of course, I had long heard of this phenomenon occurring in remote areas of our country and beyond, but here it was in my own backyard.

How I wish that we could turn to you men who are willing, perhaps eager, to return for at least a weekend service. I would anticipate that your experience of marriage and child-rearing and your earning a living in the marketplace would make your homilies uniquely relevant. I should think that your respectful, loving relationship with that one chosen person of the opposite sex would signal to all women that you honor them as true equals. And I say these things not unmindful that there are occasional failures among the marriages of priests. In what category of relational commitment will that not always and inevitably be the case?

In the earliest days of my priesthood, at the invitation of a fellow priest of my diocese, I made a two day retreat with 11 Episcopal priests in western New Jersey on the banks of the Delaware River. It was conducted by an Anglican bishop who had resigned his episcopacy and had become a Franciscan friar in the Anglican tradition. I remember getting the impression that he was revered among those men the way Archbishop Fulton Sheen was revered among Catholics. They considered it an honor to sit at his feet and receive the pearls of spiritual wisdom he had come to share.

During those two days, there was time for us Roman Catholics to engage in many conversations with our Episcopal counterparts. My selective memory has stored but one part of only one personal dialog among the several I must have had. It was with a 42-year-old priest, a husband and father, who said to me, "You know, Dick, you Roman Catholics and we Episcopalians have so much in common. We can count on the fingers of one hand the really important differences between us. But certainly one of those is our respective outlooks on the matter of marriage and celibacy in priesthood. Let me put it this way: "My dear wife is such an intimate part of everything I do as a man and as a priest that, if you took her out of the equation, I would not know how to be a priest."

I do not know how many married priests of whatever religion or rite would make the same statement. I am not aware of what percentage of wives share actively in the ministry of their priest husbands, nor am I at all sure that there must be such sharing. I suspect, instead, that there are as many arrangements between priest husband and wife as there are priestly marriages. And there is, of course, a mortality rate among the marriages of priests.

Nonetheless, I look at you men, my brother priests — and you, their wives, my sisters — as foretelling in these present times a dispensation restored after a thousand-year hiatus. Surely it has to come: a married priesthood and optional celibacy. An increasing number of bishops, theologians, and persons in the trenches like you and me are hoping, believing, and praying that it will.

It seems to me that it is precisely for the Sunday Eucharistic gathering that we need you most of all, and I very much regret the unwillingness of Rome to dispense with a discipline that now works as much against the church as for it. Your return to priestly leadership in liturgy would not, of course, resolve the problem far into the future; after all, you cannot be too many years younger than I am. But it would be immensely helpful in the short term and also the most influential factor in establishing among the people a climate of receptivity to a married priesthood.

A word about the Eucharist, so central to our Catholic life and worship:

We don't get theological technicalities and complexities from Jesus; he speaks plainly, commonly, most often in simple stories. From that consistent style of his, we can be sure that he had no obscure theology in mind on the night before he died when with bread and wine he made a parting gesture of love, his graphic way of saying, "Remember me. Don't ever forget that I am with you always, because I love you."

The essence of that gesture, which has become our Eucharist, is undoubtedly *presence*, Jesus' desire, his intention, to be with us in a unique way — and the fact of his actually being with us.

Friends and lovers can be present to each other in ways other than the physical, bodily, tactile presence that two persons experience as they stand face to face and converse or as they are locked in an embrace of love. But even when there is no such contact or visibility, when for example they are thousands of miles apart, persons can still be present to each other in many ways. The sound of a melody dear to both can make one present to the other. The recollection of a shared experience, a card or letter taken from a drawer, a photograph, a familiar place, even an idea that came from one and is treasured by the other – all these are examples of how human beings can be present to each other even though they are physically apart.

We Catholics maintain that that there is an intensely personal presence of the Risen Jesus in the mysterious sacrament of Eucharist.

It seems to me that it is no more useful to dissect and analyze this mystery than to analyze any act of genuine love. Some things are so sacred, so precious, so profoundly personal, that to subject them to microscopic examination is to fail to appreciate them. The words "Body and Blood" are, of course, anatomical in their primary, conventional definition. But in the context of the Eucharist I understand them to mean real – real not in the sense of physicality but real in the sense of sacrament.

When we do this sacred action together week after week, this fluid action called Eucharist, Jesus is uniquely present. Unseen, yes, but as intentionally and really present to us as he was to his original disciples and apostles, minus only the physical, or bodily, elements.

We must content ourselves with that alone and not be distracted by the scrutinizing that goes on in theological laboratories, which can only do further violence to the uncomplicated plan of Jesus to remain with us, not merely in memory, but in here and now sacramental presence.

Jesus does not ask to be adored, but only to be welcomed and loved in return for his own unconditional love of us. He invites us to follow him with trust and to accept the priceless gifts he offers.

The popular bumper sticker urges us in another context, "Keep It Simple." We would do well to apply that advice here as we contemplate and honor Jesus in Eucharist.

Theologians are speaking more and more these days about a paradigm shift that is taking place in contemporary Catholic thought and practice. In essence, it focuses on a radically different imaging of the ultimate mystery we call God. For an ever-increasing number of us believers, God is no longer that humanoid, male, Supreme Being who resides far above the clouds; for us God is not anymore the feudal lord who ruled over a relatively modest empire — the God of Abraham and Isaac and Jacob. We know now, through that form of revelation called science, that the universe, in every particle of which the Creative Spirit dwells, is immense beyond our comprehension. The author of the 8th psalm contemplated the tiny world known in his day and declared it awesome; what can, what should, be our response to the wonders we are privileged to know more fully with each passing day?

Who is the priest in that context, that "new story," as it is called? What is the function of the priest in such a radically different setting? He — and I am among those who hope that we can say "she" someday — will not speak about what my theologian/author friend Michael Morwood calls the "elsewhere God." The priest of the near future will not think of his ministry as one of mediating between a distant God and a suppliant people; he will not boast of powers bestowed on him for the purpose of making God present. Rather, he will do what Jesus did: he will reveal, he will point out, he will herald the presence of God already in everyone and in everything! He will say what Jesus said: that the Kingdom of God is here, the Spirit is here, as they have always been, in the hearts of all people.

He will speak mostly of love, love that alone opens our eyes to the universal divine presence.

Resigned and married priest that he is, Michael keeps reminding me that priesthood is primarily about affirming God's unfailing presence with us. Eucharist, he says, asks the question, will we live committed to being the presence of God in our world?

I trust that this is the priesthood you are living now; I hope it is the priesthood in which we can be reunited more fully someday soon.

Please know that, in the meantime, I admire and am thankful for the graceful way in which you accommodate to what I suspect must be at times an awkward state of affairs. Know for sure that to more and more of us your lives speak of the future and give us hope. And, therefore, a third time I encourage you to continue communicating to the church and its leaders your well-considered thoughts about what the church must do so as to recover from its present malaise and move resolutely into a robust future.

I am grateful to CORPUS member and my good friend, Joe Cece, for a quotation that seemed well suited to close this presentation today. On the website of the Paterson Diocese, which he produces, Joe recently included words from the late Carlo Carretto. I should think that some of you have read his books. He was a mid-20th century spiritual guide, author, and mystic. More than 50 years ago, he addressed the following message to the church. It is blunt, yet tender. It may well express some of your own sentiments. Listen carefully, please.

How much I criticize you, my church, and yet how much I love you!

You have made me suffer more than anyone,

and yet I owe more to you than to anyone.

I should like to see you destroyed, and yet I need your presence.

You have given me much scandal,

and yet you alone have made me understand holiness.

Never in this world have I seen anything more compromised,
more false,

And yet never have I touched anything more pure, more generous or
more beautiful.

Countless times I have felt like slamming the door of my soul
in your face

And yet, every night, I have prayed that I might die in your sure arms.

No, I cannot be free of you, for I am one with you,
even if not completely you.

Then, too - where would I go? To build another church?

But I could not build one without the same defects,
for they are my defects.

And again, if I were to build another church, it would be my church,
not Christ's church.

No, I am old enough. I know better.

PROPHECY OF THE FAITHFUL, THE DUTY AND PRIVILEGE OF SPEAKING OUT IN SERVICE TO JESUS AND HIS CHURCH

he Bernardin Lecture Series was a program of talks for the priests of the Archdiocese of New York. I was invited to make one of those presentations in March of 2010, the contents of which follow here.

This talk, "Prophecy of the Faithful," is subtitled, "The Duty and Privilege of Speaking Out in Service to Christ and His Church." It has to do with the rightness and the propriety and the necessity of such action, especially when the views expressed could be not in perfect harmony with the official teachings or positions of the church. More and more of us are sensing a special urgency about pursuing the topic because such "speaking out" is regarded in some major circles of Catholic leadership and membership as sinful disloyalty, as disobedience to rightful authority.

Those who hold that view would have us believe that committing ourselves to being Catholic Christians demands that we suppress our opinions and convictions in these matters and yield without question to the authority of the official church as if they did not in fact exist at all.

I strongly believe that we also must keep in mind that among our Catholic sisters and brothers there are without doubt many who need both encouragement and empowerment to lend their voices to the Spirit within, ourselves included.

So that's the first hurdle we have to clear: do the members of the church have the right to be so expressive? I have chosen two parallel avenues to approach the question: the primacy of human conscience, and the naturalness of collaboration by the membership of the church in the discernment of truth.

296

As mature Christians, we adults should not have to be informed or reminded that the ultimate standard by which we are to make moral decisions is our well-formed conscience. But we are so imbued with the notion of obedience to external authority, of surrendering personal responsibility in making such decisions, that indeed it can come as a surprising revelation, something of a shock, that not only is that an inherent right to be claimed and cherished by every human being, but that our Catholic Church endorses and proclaims it at its highest level of authority.

I invite you to consider the following liberating, empowering words found in one of the 16 documents produced by the Second Vatican Council, *The Church in the Modern World*:

> *Deep within their consciences men and women discover a law which they have not laid upon themselves and which they must obey. Its voice, ever calling them to love and to do what is good and to avoid evil, tells them inwardly at the right moment: do this, shun that...Their dignity rests in observing this law, and by it they will be judged...For God willed that men and women should "be left free to make their own decisions"...Their dignity therefore requires them to act out of conscious and free choice, as moved and drawn in a personal way from within, and not by their own blind impulses or by external constraint.* (Chapter 1, #16, 17) [37]

It would seem, then, from this remarkably reasonable statement that the behavior of every Catholic Christian is to be guided by the church's clear teachings and refined for practical, personal application by the judgment of individual conscience. Is not that the way that Jesus lived and made his decisions and moved resolutely into action?

As the church has long since entered the 3rd Christian millennium, let us hope that there will be a resounding emphasis on the sanctity, the primacy, and the inviolability of human conscience. We must be done with coercion and intimidation, with blind, unquestioning obedience, and acknowledge that each member has the right and the need to be Spirit-directed – not in a separatist or ruthlessly individualistic fashion, but within the nurturing, supportive, sometimes corrective atmosphere of the Eucharistic community. Lockstep conformity is for totalitarian states; intelligent, resourceful, considerate decision-making is for the Christian community and each of its members.

Living our Catholic lives according to personal conscience will make certain demands on us. The first and most essential will be the never-ending task of forming a good conscience, a conscience that not only is worthy of being followed but, as the Council emphasized, also *must* be followed. That often means the hard work of agonizing, objective thinking, periods of painful self-doubt, informative reading, peer consultation, counseling, prayer, and patient waiting. The church assures us that we will know, by the urging of an inner voice, when the time to act has come and what form that action must take.

Among those actions surely there will be from time to time the call to speak truth to power, to speak truth to the body of the church even when authority or officialdom is thereby being confronted or challenged or called to accountability.

In an article printed in 2009 in the *Tablet* in London, Father Daniel O'Leary wrote, "Since the Vatican Council announced by Pope St. John XXIII 50 years ago, people are still waiting for signs of a more human, repentant, spiritual, and ecumenical church. They long for a church that is more open and less certain. Above all, a church that creates a new vision for tomorrow from the fragment of yesterday's triumphs."[38]

Father O'Leary called the laity, not helpers, but "true and powerful leaders at all levels." He went on to emphasize that, "The gift of prophecy is alive in the priesthood of the baptized. The Holy Spirit in their hearts and minds is ready with undreamed of possibility. People have not given up on God, or in the spiritual reality of their own lives. What people are giving up on is going to church. It is in the institution, not God, that they are losing their faith."

If Father O'Leary has written the pure and unvarnished truth when he refers to the gift of prophecy that is alive in the priesthood of the baptized, then by what rule of logic, by what standard of exception, can anyone conclude that the act of a Christian's speaking up is treasonous or immoral or even just improper? By its very definition, prophecy is not prophecy unless it is articulated, unless it is broadcast clearly and loudly for all to hear.

Conscience: that inner voice of discernment that convinces us that we have distinguished the truth among its rivals and that we therefore have the privilege and obligation to speak it out in service to all.

But there is another cardinal concept that, I submit, resoundingly supports the legitimacy and the necessity of a church membership that exercises the function of free and responsible expression, and that is the naturalness, as I have chosen to term it, of the laity's collaboration in the discernment of truth. The laity's inclusion derives from the very structure of the church, which is (the venerable pyramid symbol notwithstanding) an intertwining of three fundamental organs, as it were, three essential components that make up the one church body.

I am grateful to my friend Professor Kieran Scott, of Fordham University, for this helpful analysis: Those three components, he says, are — in no particular or intended order: 1) the hierarchy: the leaders, beginning with the pope and including all those officeholders who surround him throughout the world and serve the church in many positions and at many different levels of authority; 2) the scholars and theologians: those countless frontline workers, male and increasingly female, who read our past and discern, as best they can, the church's way into the future; and 3) the ordinary membership, ungracefully called the laity, who are committed to being Christ in the contemporary world through a host of ministries.[39]

Please notice that I have labeled the word laity as "ungraceful." I want to make a big point of that, having been alerted to the concept first by Doctor Elisabeth Schüssler Fiorenza in the course of a talk she gave several years ago.[40] It is central to the very issue we are treating this evening. By that I mean this: Have you ever said to your physician, "Well, doctor, I'll tell you what I think is wrong with me; however, what would I know? After all, I'm only a layman in this field." Our baptized but not ordained sisters and brothers have been named lay people vis-à-vis the church, signifying precisely that. Carried to its logical terminus, the message could be, "Silence! What do you know about ecclesiastical or theological matters? You are a layperson. Stick to what you know and do best. Leave these higher things to us who are trained and deputed to handle them." In an ideal world, in a perfect church, structures for the intercommunication among these three segments of the Body of Christ on earth would be in place and operating smoothly. But that is not the case. Such infrastructure is still in very short supply, and what does exist is often enough poorly developed, frequently never having gone beyond the stage of tokenism, however well intended in most instances they may originally have been. I give you an example: Several years before my retirement in 1998, 35 persons, including me, representing a variety of ministries and departments of my diocese, were called together to discuss the critical issue of abortion and to attempt a new start at strategizing toward effective and appropriate response from the local church. No sooner had the session begun when I felt an irresistible urge to intervene. I addressed my bishop and fellow members of the assembly, calling their attention to the glaringly evident fact that there was not even one woman invited to this think tank. Just imagine: the topic was abortion, and excluded from what was hoped to be a sensitive, probing conversation were women!

Our topic here and now is not sexism in the church, and I must take care not to digress; however, does not that example suggest tellingly that there are some fundamental flaws in our church's discharge of the obligation to honor the presence of the Spirit in all its members in the ever-evolving search for truth?

In the absence of an adequate network for church intra-communication, the urgency of well-considered and well-placed intervention by the members increases.

When those three constitutive segments of the church are at odds with one another: when the hierarchy does not welcome others into a joint enterprise of Christian mission; when scholars and theologians are silenced because their findings and their speculations seem more to conflict with tradition than to grow out of and beyond it; when the laity write off the hierarchy as irrelevant – the church is crippled and dysfunctional. But when the three are living and laboring in mutual respect and expectation, the church is optimally the effective instrument of the Spirit of God it is meant to be.

The well-defined structures of the church that we are only too familiar with today were virtually unknown to Jesus' first followers, of course. At the funeral a few years ago of a dear friend of mine, an elderly nun, I read a penetrating little piece she had written on the dynamics of the founding of the church. She said that, starting with Jesus' own bonding with companions and recruited co-workers, it was built on love and friendship and a commitment to him and the values he held. In the in-your-face confrontation with Peter by Paul and Barnabas, we see human beings acting quite spontaneously out of deep conviction and very passionate emotion. With a bit of intervention by the divine presence, we are told, the thorny issue was resolved and put to rest.

It is our duty and our privilege to speak up! But structures can be intimidating; therefore, we must summon the courage not to be silenced or paralyzed by them. Our prophecy is to be exercised on the structures of integrity and charity.

About the oft-used word "authority:" we are accustomed to thinking of it and employing it in the sense of power over others. As children, we regarded our parents under that heading; as Catholics, we acknowledged our priests and bishops and of course the pope in Rome as those special persons who were charged with directing our lives in conformity with the rules of membership in the church. For all practical purposes, conscience became a fifth wheel, since all decisions of any import were handed to us tailor made; we had only to sign on the dotted line. If this were not the case, why would priests still to this day be hearing in the Sacrament of Reconciliation, "Bless me, Father, for I have sinned. Since my last confession a month ago, I missed Mass twice because I was ill and in the hospital. I know that's no excuse, Father, because the church teaches us that to miss Mass on Sunday is a mortal sin."

In fairness to the Magisterium, we have to say that these misguided Catholics must have paid scant attention to its clearly stated qualification about "without sufficient cause." But, no matter, in the struggle

302

between blind obedience to church law and following the dictates of individual conscience, the clearly observable truth is that authority as power-over triumphed to the extent that for most Catholics reliance on conscience as the ultimate norm of Christian behavior never did mature to an even minimally adult stature.

How, then, are we to regard authority in the church? I suggest that we see it as essentially two-pronged: On the one hand, it is that time-honored dynamic by which the authentic tradition of the church is safeguarded and nurtured and passed on from generation to generation. The roles of the hierarchy and the theologians and scholars are at once recognized as central to this function. The Church would never have survived beyond a generation or two or three had it not possessed this organizing principle, this skeletal strength.

On the other hand, authority is also charged with the responsibility of remaining alert to those ever-occurring "surprises of the Holy Spirit," in which further nuanced truth is expressed in the words and the lives of ordinary members of the church and, after careful scrutiny, is promulgated throughout the community for the good of all. It is in this second aspect of authority that well-considered speaking-out is seen to be of immense value to the church. Why? Because, if it is withheld or if it is suppressed, church authority is thereby denied the raw material, so to speak, out of which life-giving revelation suited to the times can uniquely come. We have only to recall the bold, brave, almost wordless statement of a Rosa Parks to be reminded that a national movement for human rights resulted from just one such unpolished speaking-up.

Several years ago, the great Jesuit theologian, Father Ladislaus Orsy, wrote that the church must move —

- from empire to communion;

- from confessional conflict to ecumenical understanding;

- from defensive isolation to expansive presence;

- from a static world view to dynamic perception.[41]

These are major shifts, requiring every ounce of energy and every spark of wisdom the church can summon. It simply cannot be that so great a project is reserved to the smallest minority of the Catholic commonwealth. No, it is a mammoth job that desperately needs and eagerly calls all of us.

And who would not feel compassion for the person who confesses a lack of confidence in self at the prospect of speaking up? "Who, me?" are the telling words that quickly come to mind and tongue at the mere suggestion of speaking up. (They were the very words I thought, if I did not indeed voice them, when I was asked to give this talk.)

Sister Jeannine Gramick, in a wonderful film about her conflicts with the Vatican concerning her ministry to gay and lesbian Catholics, suggests that we envision ourselves as pieces of cloth of different kinds – cotton, wool, silk, synthetic, etc. – each of which is made to endure a certain degree of heat without burning. A handy and helpful analogy, assuring us that we are not all made to do the same things in the same way. But we are all expected and invited to be vessels of expression for the Spirit of God present in and among us all. Prayer and consultation will make sufficiently clear to us how much heat we are capable of taking and will accordingly send us to the task.

By the way, the name of the film, a DVD, is *In Good Conscience*.[42]

It was directed by the Peabody and Emmy Award winner, Barbara Rick. I highly recommend it to you. You will at once love Sister Jeannine as a very good woman; you will admire her simplicity, her unassuming self-confidence, her unyielding commitment to principle, her unfailing charity. You'll never forget the gentle look on her lovely face or her soft and cheerful voice.

In a letter included in the film box, Sister Jeannine recounts her serendipitous experience of sitting next to the former Cardinal Joseph Ratzinger on a plane ride from Rome to Munich. That happened just two years before she was prohibited, via a Vatican decree, from continuing her pastoral work involving homosexual persons.

She writes about it now: "His gracious manner put me at ease as I talked with him, but I was later more struck by his spirituality. He was praying his breviary when I first spotted him. His parting words to me were, 'Pray for me and I will pray for you.' And at least three times during our chance encounter the future pope whispered, 'Providence, providence...' He saw God's hand in that meeting. And so did I."

"It helped me put a human face on the institution of the church. Cardinal Joseph Ratzinger (who became Pope Benedict XVI) and I have had our differences. But this meeting taught me that our differences are less significant than our common journey of faith to follow God's call in good conscience."

If we need to learn, not only that we must speak up, but how to speak up, I cannot imagine a more complete model than Sister Jeannine.

The relatively minor sufferings that I have endured over my years of speaking up seem to me as nothing when compared with the punishment that the real heroes among us have undergone as they have courageously exercised the responsibility of speaking up, in truth and in charity, for the ultimate good of the church and the world. I know for sure that the fabric I am made of would not survive the heat they have been subjected to.

I thank you for your kind attention, and I hope that something I have said will be of help to you on this journey we share.

END NOTES

1   http://goo.gl/7Yfift
2   Giles Fraser, *The Guardian* (December 24, 2004)
    http://goo.gl/nQhPLJ
3   http://goo.gl/15mPyC
4   http://goo.gl/8XQgOR
5   https://goo.gl/WJu5tr
6   Fr. Denis Edwards, *The God of Evolution: A Trinitarian Theology*,
    (Paulist Press, 2009) 27-28
7   Michael Morwood, *Tomorrow's Catholic*, (Twenty-Third
    Publications,1997)   74-113
8   Max Warren, introduction to *The Primal Vision: Christian Presence
    Amid African Religion* by John V. Taylor, (Fortress Press, 1963)
9   Ronald Arbuthnott Knox, *Lightning Meditations*, (Sheed and Ward,
    1959)
10 Richard P. McBrien, *National Catholic Reporter*, May 23, 2011
    http://goo.gl/O31b8S
11 Ronald Arbuthnott Knox, *Lightning Meditations*, (Sheed and
    Ward, 1959) 12 Father Roger Karban, *FOSIL, the Faithful of
    Southern Illinois,* November 28, 2010 http://goo.gl/BA8SCH
13 William Sloane Coffin, "Alex's Death" from *The Courage to
    Love*, (Harper & Rowe, 1982)
14 Karl Rahner, "Experiences of a Catholic Theologian" (paper presented
    at Freiburg, Germany, February 12, 1984, cited in *America* magazine,
    June 16, 1984)
15 http://goo.gl/a5ks8y
16 http://goo.gl/bEy90t
17 Daniel Dombrowski and Robert Deltete, *A Brief, Liberal, Catholic
    Defense of Abortion*, (University of Illinois Press, 2000, 2007) 32-50
18 See also To the Members of CORPUS in Addenda
19 http://goo.gl/Hv7bnX
20 https://goo.gl/cCxQ4T
21 See also To the Members of CORPUS in Addenda
22 (NavPress Publishing, 2003) 1948
23 "Sunday Sermons by Rev. Roger Karban" http://goo.gl/ZLXdZi

24 See also To the Members of *CORPUS* in Addenda

25 Msgr. F. Gerald Martin, "Changing Elements or People?" *America* magazine, March 4, 2000 http://goo.gl/sihsSQ

26 http://goo.gl/vGCUi6

27 Rev. James A. Coriden, "The Canonical Doctrine of Reception" (prepared for the Association for the Rights of Catholics in the Church (ARCC), Washington, DC, 1991) http://www.arcc-catholic-rights.net/doctrine_of_reception.htm28

29 Maria Rilke Rainer, *Book of Hours*, (Riverhead Trade, 1997)

30 See also Primacy of Conscience in Addenda

31 http://goo.gl/TKvxBG

32 See also To the Members of Corpus in Addenda

33 Karban, Roger, Celebrations, Oct. 2007, http://goo.gl/6a6cZs

34 Morwood, Michael, http://goo.gl/7Stpav

35 Karban, Roger, The Evangelist, Newspaper of the Diocese of Albany, June 6, 2003, http://goo.gl/NOcCu5

36 Congar, Ives, La Foi et la Théologie, Tournai, (1962), https://goo.gl/YkMTil

38 O'Leary, Daniel, Defining moments The Tablet January 24, 2009

39 Scott, Kieran, *The Local Church as an Ecology of Human Development*, St. Bonaventure University, NY 14778, Religious Education: The official journal of the Religious Education Association Volume 76, Issue 2, 1981

40 Schüssler Fiorenza, Elisabeth, "Equality: A Radical Democratic Ecclesial Vision," Keynote address at the CTA National Conference Oct. 31, 1998 in Milwaukee

41 Orsy, Ladislaus *The Church: Learning and Teaching : Magisterium, Assent, Dissent, Academic Freedom*, Michael Glazier Publisher (December 1987)

42 *In Good Conscience*: Sister Jeannine Gramick's Journey of Faith directed by, Barbara Rick, Out of The Blue Films, Inc. 77 E 12th Street #7A New York, NY 1003

REFERENCES

A "STARTER" READING LIST *(in no particular order)* Assembled by Fr. Richard Rento for faithful but questioning people of faith (and interested others)

Good Goats - Healing Our Image Of God
> Dennis, Sheila, and Matthew Linn - Paulist Press (1994)
> A MUST for everyone!

A Merry Memoir Of Death Sex And Religion
> Dan Maguire - Caritas Communications (2013)
> Great, great book, with a hearty laugh on every other page!!

Jesus Before Christianity
> Albert Nolan, OP - Orbis Books – Revised (1992)
> A genuine classic with a pregnant title.

Stupid Ways, Smart Ways To Think About God
> Michael Shevack and Jack Bemporad – Triumph Books (1993)
> Two wise & witty Jews reinforce the imperative of examining critically our inherited concepts of God. Their list of 10 "stupids" is undeniably real!

Responses To 101 Questions On The Bible
> Raymond E. Brown - Paulist Press (1990)
> Contemporary theology may be reaching new horizons not envisioned in this book, but the scriptural insights of the masterful Fr. Brown are enduring and valuable.

Practicing Catholic:
The Search for a Livable Catholicism
> Penelope J. Ryan, Ph.D. - Henry Holt (1998)
> An unusually balanced presentation of where and what the Church is today.

Priesthood Imperiled
> Bernard Haring, CSSR - Triumph Books (1996)
> The late, saintly, courageous Fr. Haring was the Church's preemi-
> nent moral theologian, whose knowledge of tradition was matched
> by his vision of the future.

Reconstructing Catholicism For A New Generation
> Robert A. Ludwig - Wipf and Stock Publishing (2000)
> Professor Ludwig powerfully and clearly suggests new approaches
> to Christianity that may speak more convincingly
> to modern generations.

Why You Can Disagree And Remain A Faithful Catholic
> Philip S. Kaufman, OSB - Crossroad (1995)
> Fr. Kaufman simply and compellingly addresses the important issue
> of making moral decisions ultimately according to a well-formed
> personal conscience. An easy read.

Dare We Hope "That All Men (Sic) Be Saved"?
> Hans Urs Von Balthasar - Ignatius Press (1988)
> The answer proposed by this venerable priest-scholar is an
> encouragement to those who find the concept of an
> everlasting hell unacceptable.

All of Michael's books are recommended reads:

Tomorrow's Catholic:
Understanding God and Jesus in a New Millennium
> Michael Morwood - Twenty-Third Publications (1997)
> This short paperback offers a radically new and different theology in
> harmony with today's new and different knowledge of the universe.

Is Jesus God? Finding Our Faith - The Crossroad
Publishing Company (2001)

God Is Near: Trusting Our Faith - The Crossroad
Publishing Company (2002)

Praying a New Story - Orbis Books (2004)

From Sand to Solid Ground: Questions of Faith for Modern Catholics
– The Crossroad Publishing Company (2008)

Faith, Hope, and a Bird Called George: A Spiritual Fable
- Twenty-Third Publications   (2011)

It's Time: Challenges to the Doctrine of the Faith
- Kelmor Publishing (2013)

*Children Praying a New Story: A Resource for Parents, Grandparents
and Teachers* - Kelmor Publishing (2014)

In Memory of Jesus - CreateSpace Independent Publishing
Platform (2014)

Reluctant Dissenter, An Autobiography
James Patrick Shannon - The Crossroad Publishing Company
(1998) "The moving, first-person account of the first Roman
Catholic bishop in the United States to resign from his office over a
matter of conscience."

Liberating The Gospels -
Reading The Bible With Jewish Eyes

John Shelby Spong – Harper San Francisco (1991)
Although Episcopal Bishop Spong is criticized by some theologians and bishops in both the Episcopal and the Catholic
communions, I like what he writes and have had the good
experience of hearing him lecture.

The Changing Faces Of Jesus

Geza Vermes - Viking Adult Publisher (2001)
The author was born a Jew, converted to Catholicism and
was ordained a priest; after WWII he returned to the practice
of his Jewish faith. An eminent scholar and prolific author, he
traces the evolutionary development of the idea that Jesus is
God. Challenging!

The Coming Catholic Church

David Gibson - Harper San Francisco (2003)
A convert to Catholicism, religion reporter for major news
media, Gibson writes a no-holds-barred account of the
very human Catholic Church that somehow leaves the reader
in awe of its rich tradition and sacramental vitality. A true gem!

Broken Promises: Whatever Happened To Vatican Council Ii?

Finbarr Corr - Trafford Publishing (2012)
Corr, a resigned priest, describes the hierarchy's failure to follow
through on the dictates of Vatican Council II.

INDEX

abortion, 147–151

    discussion by priests excluded women, 201

Abraham and Isaac, 103, 158–159

Abrahamic religions, 13

absolutism, 24–25

Acts 6:1-7, 202–203

Acts of the Apostles 10:34, 35, 39

Adam and Eve story, 42, 84–86, 91, 187

Advent season, 214

afterlife, 117, 144–145, 267

Alcoholics Anonymous slogan, 109

alcoholism, 100, 156

"alteri Christi," 80

Always Our Children, 135

America (magazine), 211–212

American Indian Museum, 184

analogies, 76

annulment, 132–133

answers or action, 83

anthropomorphic imagery, 41–42

apologia, 93–97

Apostles' Creed, 55

"Apostolic Constitution," 216

ascension, 75

Assumption of Mary, 98

Assyrian Church of the East, 207–208

atheism, 158

    public signs about, 4–5

atonement, 61

author

    decision for priesthood, 250–252

    early education of, 55

    personal note from, 250–252

    talks given by, 279–306

authority, responsibility of, 163–165

Made in the USA
San Bernardino, CA
07 November 2016